Student Worlds
Student Words

Student Worlds
Student Words

Teaching Writing
Through Folklore

Elizabeth Radin Simons

BOYNTON/COOK
HEINEMANN
PORTSMOUTH, NH

Boynton/Cook Publishers, Inc.
A Subsidiary of Reed Publishing (USA) Inc.
361 Hanover Street
Portsmouth, NH 03801-3912
Offices and agents throughout the world

The author would like to thank the following for permission
to reprint copyrighted material in this book:

Excerpts from *Children of Strangers* by Kathryn Morgan. Copyright © 1980 by
Temple University. Reprinted by permission of Temple University Press.

Every effort has been made to contact those whose words and illustrations
appear in this book. We regret any oversights that may have occurred
and would be happy to rectify them in future printings.

Library of Congress Cataloging-in-Publication Data
Simons, Elizabeth Radin.
    Student worlds, student words : teaching writing through folklore / Elizabeth Radin
Simons ; with a foreword by Alan Dundes.
        p.   cm.
    Includes bibliographical references.
    ISBN 0-86709-256-4
    1. English language—Composition and exercises—Study and
teaching. 2. Folklore and education. 3. Students—Folklore.
I. Title
PE1404.S55   1990
808'.042'07—dc20   89-71286
                                                                    CIP

Designed by Hunter Graphics
Printed in the United States of America
93 94 9 8 7 6 5 4 3 2

Contents

Foreword

Folklore is one of the oldest forms of human creativity for which we have a written record. There is no people on the face of the earth that does not tell traditional tales and sing traditional songs. Just as soon as a people develops a written language, we find that one of the first things to be set down in that language is that people's folklore. That is why we have books called *Sumerian Mythology*.

Yet folklore itself rarely exists in written form, for it tends to be transmitted by *oral* means or by example (in the case of gestures or folk dance). Most folklore involves oral performance—one need only think of the difference between *hearing* a joke well told and *reading* a joke in a book. Left out of the written record may be the dialect, the vocal shadings, the audience response, the accompanying eye and body movements, etc. In short, written records of folklore consist of fragmentary and incomplete reports of what was once a live oral performance. That is why one cannot learn about folklore by simply reading such echoes of performances in books; one must encounter folklore in the flesh, so to speak, by listening to scary legends at a slumber party or a dirty joke in the locker room. One of the principal challenges to folklorists over the past two centuries has been precisely how to translate the vital oral force of folklore into a faithful and authentic written form.

Most professional folklorists tend to be concerned with the pure oral folklore that exists, and they regard the often inadequate records of that oral tradition with some disdain. Even the Grimm brothers censored their folktales, changing the wicked mother of the oral version of Hansel and Gretel into a stepmother in the eventual written version. They did not think it was seemly for a natural mother to be so cruel. The censorship is also evident from the fact that the famous Grimm collection of German folktales includes not a single bawdy element. Yet we know for a fact that bawdy tales were told in Germany in the early nineteenth century. The Grimm brothers were imbued with nationalistic fervor and wanted to present a sampling of their Teutonic heritage. So we can understand why they chose to leave out anything that they felt might damage the image they sought to construct. But the censorship problem remains. Oral folklore tends to be independent of normal censorship standards and this holds true for children's folklore as well. Most discussions of folklore simply avoid the whole issue by failing to include any risqué examples.

The use of folklore in primary and secondary school settings is minimal. Most elementary and secondary school teachers have not been exposed to formal academic training in folklore, and, except for occasional coverage in children's literature courses, the field of folkloristics, the serious study of folklore, is virtually unknown to these teachers. Strangely enough, some selected bits of folklore are conventionally used in schools, but this folklore is typically of *other* people, e.g., ancient Greeks and Romans. The study of Greek and Roman mythology or Aesopic fables has been used for centuries in both elementary and secondary school curricula, but children often have difficulty in seeing much connection between their own lives and what appears to them as rather esoteric stories of a bygone age.

One reason why folkloristics is so little known among teachers is that professional folklorists have failed to make the results of their various researches available to this group. Teachers who first encounter the field of folklore may become terribly excited by the material, but they invariably ask, "How can I use these materials in my classroom?" Professional folklorists have as a group refused to answer this fundamental question, and, as a result, professional educators have had difficulty in translating folklore theory and method into a meaningful curriculum.

It should have been obvious that the only way to answer the question of how to use folklore effectively in a classroom setting in middle and secondary schools was to have an individual who was both a professional folklorist *and* a professional educator tackle it. Fortunately, Elizabeth Simons possesses the necessary expertise, and she has spent the past decade working out a curriculum designed to help children learn to write using folklore materials from their own backgrounds. The results of this practical application of folklore data for the development of critical writing skills are contained in this unique book intended for teachers of writing.

The outlines for many an exciting classroom period are contained in this book. A teacher who is willing to take a bit of an intellectual risk will find the risk well worth taking. Not only will there be many delightful and insightful class discussions of individual exemplars of folklore, but the teacher will learn a great deal too from this encounter with folklore. Teachers of writing may want to adapt the strategies suggested by Elizabeth Simons, depending upon their own interests and more importantly, the backgrounds and interests of their students.

Even a teacher who may never have previously considered using folklore in his or her classroom in any rigorous way will find enough detail in this book to institute a fascinating folklore unit. As a folklorist, I can almost guarantee that any teacher who gives this subject matter a chance will become hooked and will offer the unit again and again, especially when that teacher sees firsthand how challenging and pleasurable the material is for students. Even those students who normally are not motivated to participate in more conventional classroom activities will become inspired by the use of folklore. One must keep in mind that students bring their own family, ethnic, religious, occupational, national, and peer-group folklore with them into the classroom. It is more a matter, then, of tapping an already-existing resource than of introducing a foreign subject matter. Classes with great ethnic diversity are particularly advantageous in the teaching of writing through folklore as each new bit of ethnic folklore can be explored and enjoyed by all the members of the class.

Elizabeth Simons is ideally qualified to bridge the gap between folkloristics and the needs of education. After receiving her B. A. in history from Bryn Mawr College in 1957, she earned an M. A. in social studies and history from Teachers College at Columbia University in 1962. She taught history at George Washington High School in New York City from 1960 to 1962 and social studies at Newton South High School in Newton, Massachusetts from 1962 to 1965.

Then, after some years to raise her family, she returned to school to earn an M. A. in folklore at the University of California, Berkeley in 1980. From that time on, her principal intellectual goal has been to bring folklore into the classroom, with special emphasis upon its great potential for the teaching of writing. She has given in-service workshops in folklore and writing in dozens and dozens of schools both in the United States and abroad, e.g., in Ecuador, Finland, Brazil, Italy, and Sweden. Her enthusiasm for her subject matter is contagious and has inspired many teachers who have become vitally interested in using folklore materials in a new and creative way. The present book is the result of her years of teaching in Bay Area schools and her extensive in-service workshops on folklore and writing.

There have been countless books written about folklore and there are many, many collections of folktales and folksongs, but this is the only book I know that is designed to encourage teachers of middle and secondary school students to learn how to write using their own folklore—with the help of a personalized, detailed set of curricular chapters.

Alan Dundes
Berkeley, California

Acknowledgments

I didn't know what folklore was until I was almost forty. I listened to a tape recording of a talk given by Alan Dundes, a professor of anthropology and folklore at the University of California, Berkeley. When the tape ended, I called Alan Dundes and asked if I could audit his introductory course; he told me to come and take it. What I learned about folklore from Professor Dundes forms the core of the content of this book. "Folklore," Dundes writes, "always tells it like it is or at least tells it as some people think it is or as they would like it to be. Folklore is a kind of popular pulse, ever indicating what is on a people's mind and in a people's heart. . . . (1973, 2)." Folklore, I realized, could be powerful in the classroom.

What exactly I should do with folklore came into focus four years later in 1980 when Mary K. Healy and Jim Gray invited me to participate in the Bay Area Writing Project (BAWP). With their guidance I made the connection between the educational potential of folklore, especially modern folklore, and the teaching of writing. Like hundreds of teachers in the Bay Area, I am indebted to Jim Gray for founding and sustaining the Bay Area Writing Project. Mary K. Healy taught me about workshops for teachers, and through BAWP I have given many of them. The enthusiasm of the teachers attending these workshops and their subsequent correspondence and telephone calls have helped shape this book.

Jillian Steiner Sandrock of The L. J. Skaggs and Mary C. Skaggs Foundation was an early supporter. Skaggs provided the funding for three complete tryouts of the folklore units. Jillian also steered me toward the first school where I taught the course, the predominantly black Far West High School in Oakland, California. The following year Jane Juska welcomed me into her classes at Ygnacio Valley High School in Concord, California. Bethel Bodine graciously loaned me one of her classes for several months and then arranged a semester for me with Latino students at Harry Ells High School in Richmond, California.

In the summer of 1982 I returned to BAWP. At that Summer Institute I met Anne Barrows, Sheila Jordan, and Tina Staller, who have been my writing group ever since. They have been my staunchest supporters, patiently listening and honestly critiquing the many versions of this book.

Marcy Williams, an anthropologist, folklorist, and a thorough and relentless researcher, has kept me on track and abreast of new developments in the discipline. She has also read and responded to several of my drafts.

Along the way other friends were important. Verda Delp tried out many of the ideas in her classroom, expanding and finding new directions for them. Pat McGrath and Andrée Abecassis, longtime friends, have discovered folklore themselves and helpfully spotted new folklore as they cheered me on. Mijo Horwich has followed the progress of the book as we run around the track each morning.

When I was teaching and writing about folklore, my children, Rachel and Daniel, were in high school. Having grown up with a mother who is a folklorist, they are able collectors who brought home many an item found in this book.

My husband, Herb, who brought me that original tape of Alan Dundes's talk, has known that I was made for folklore and has believed in this project.

Peter Stillman, my editor, has an eye for folklore and appreciated the value of this project. He is also a canny and witty editor. He has made many helpful suggestions often cast in memorable language, such as this reaction to my enthusiasm for folklore in an early draft: "What isn't folklore, for heaven's sake?" It was a good question.

I thank all these people, and most importantly I am grateful to the students whose words and writing supply the lifeline of the book.

Introduction

Knowing Our Insides
and Our Outsides

While studying folklore, Lupe, a Mexican-American student, wisely observed in her learning log[1] that folklore helps us " . . . to know each other better in our inside and our outside."

What is folklore[2] that it can, in fact, teach students to know themselves and others better? Roger Abrahams, a leading American folklorist, writes that "All groups inherit and develop ways of entertaining and instructing each other, ways that can be described as folklore" (1980, 370). Folklore encompasses all the traditional cultural forms (and there are between three hundred and four hundred different forms or genres) that entertain, instruct, and serve other diverse functions such as the releasing of cultural tensions and the bonding of groups. The forms of folklore include traditional genres such as riddles, proverbs, myths, and fairy tales, as well as modern genres such as children's games, legends, and graffiti.

Seven Reasons for Teaching Modern Folklore

To know our folklore—the folklore of our country, our ethnicity, our family, our childhood, our age group, and our ethnic group—is to learn to know ourselves in new ways. In the folklore of an individual or of a group, one finds "a human involvement and genuineness . . . that is not found in public expressions of national life" (Bronner 1986, 124). Viewing ourselves through our folklore is akin to looking at our lives through another lens, which focuses on aspects of life often overlooked or undervalued.

1

The personal benefit for students (or anyone, for that matter) from the study of folklore is not only greater self-knowledge but a better understanding of people different from themselves. This was Lupe's realization in her log: studying and writing about folklore, she was getting to know herself and others better from within and without.

Two disciplines are combined in this book: folklore and writing. While the students study folklore, they use writing to support and enhance their learning (initially in their logs), and they develop their writing skills when they work on their papers. The combination of disciplines is powerful; it helps students achieve full personal involvement and intellectual understanding of the discipline, and at the same time it improves their writing skills.

By the time they reach junior high or middle school, many students have developed dated notions of folklore. Lynn, a suburban high school junior, is fairly typical when she writes in her log, "I always thought of folklore as being just 'old mountain tales,' you know, Pecos Bill and Paul Bunyan and that sort of boring stuff." Contemporary folklore is a surprise to these students.

Once young people learn what modern folklore is, they typically take to it quickly. This can be seen in a log entry, written at the end of a semester of studying folklore. Susan, a junior, writes:

> Well to begin with it was really interesting. All my English classes have been pretty much the same until this one. I learned something I hadn't given much thought to—that people learn folklore from their friends. . . . We have studied children's games and heroes all of which were really fascinating topics. And I know I've learned something new about myself in studying it. I wish it didn't have to end.

Susan has touched on the first two reasons for teaching modern folklore: students like it, and they acquire new perspectives about themselves and their culture.

A third reason: when students study their own folklore, they come into the class as experts, for they know better than anyone about the games they played as children, their family rituals, their ethnic celebrations. Students, especially those with poor academic skills, otherwise rarely get to be acknowledged experts in anything. Being an expert is motivating; it builds self-confidence.

Fourth, the study of folklore is a positive and supportive way of bringing ethnic heritage into the curriculum. One way to honor ethnicity is through discrete units on, for example, Black or Latino folklore. But an equally effective approach is to have ethnicity as a theme or *leitmotif* while studying folklore. Cultural diversity is inherent in folklore; it comes up naturally in each topic.

In a multicultural class studying family folklore, for example, Mexican-American students told their legend of *La Llorona*, the crying woman, who murdered her own children and now roams streets and alleys after dark killing little children who are out alone. Mothers and grandmothers use the legend to frighten children into staying close to home, especially after dark.

Most students are not aware that *La Llorona* is a folk legend that has been studied by folklore scholars. Its origins are obscure, but it seems to date from the Spanish Conquest. Some versions of the legend tell of a beautiful Mexican-Indian woman who became the mistress of a Spanish nobleman. They were deeply in love and had beautiful children but never married. The nobleman's family didn't accept the woman. With time he succumbed to family pressure, abandoned her, and married one of his own kind, a Spanish aristocrat. In her grief, *La Llorona* murdered her children. She was executed for her crime. After her death, she came back as a revenant, prowling the streets at night for two kinds of prey: lost children and men. She takes the children to replace her own and kills the men for revenge. When seen from behind, she appears to be a beautiful woman, her head covered with a white veil. But when men approach, she turns and uncovers her skeletal face. To see it is to go mad.[3]

A glimpse into the history of *La Llorona* reveals a bit of Mexican history and uncovers another dimension of *La Llorona* as a victim of colonialism and inequality.

When the folklore of different groups is brought into the classroom, everyone benefits. For example, in this class the Mexican-American students entertained the rest of the class with their versions of *La Llorona*. They also described and drew their Dracula-like visions of what she looked like. Furthermore, in this positive, relatively value-free atmosphere, students learned about the diversity of American experience. After hearing of *La Llorona*, other students recollected ways in which their families kept them at home nights. Some had been warned about characters like the bogeyman. Others remembered family sayings repeated so often they become family lore, such as, "I don't care what they do in John's family, in our family we do it this way."

Sharing family folklore, students see both similarity and diversity across family and ethnic groups. The similarity here is that families use folklore to teach and enforce rules and codes of behavior, but the lore varies from family to family. Through the study of their folklore, students in multicultural classes can come to appreciate the richness of living in a country of many cultures. On the other hand, a culturally homogeneous class will be more a celebration of one ethnic group—not a bad result, just different from what happens in more ethnically diverse classrooms. Also, a class that looks homogeneous from the front of the room can be deceptive. Once students start studying their folklore, a surprising degree of diversity surfaces within an apparently single cultural group.

While one important reason to study folklore is to bring the worlds of minority students into the classroom, mainstream students need not feel—as they sometimes do—that their lives aren't as colorful as those belonging to any other ethnic group. There is as much WASP or middle-American folklore as there is of any other group, and it is just as rich and varied. Any group of children growing up in a neighborhood playing together has folk traditions. Any family, by virtue of being a family, has folklore. Any student who has friends has traditions.

When students study folklore, they are introduced to an intriguing new discipline, a fifth reason to teach modern folklore. The content of this discipline is aspects of our culture that are often overlooked. Richard Dorson, a major American folklorist, describes folklore as "the hidden submerged culture lying behind the shadow of official civilization" (1968, 37). We don't see our folklore partially because it is so proximate as to be largely invisible, and even if we do notice it, we often dismiss it as unworthy of our attention. But as a subject, folklore transforms the traditional aspects of daily life into a study of contemporary social and cultural relations.

The study of childhood games is an example. At first students are puzzled; why study their childhood play? But as they look into, for example, "Red Light, Green Light," they begin to appreciate its role in their education. Playing it, they were being socialized. They were learning, for example, to obey authority. At the same time they were absorbing an American cultural value, for the purpose of the game is to win, to become the authority. Yet what some teenagers remember most vividly about "Red Light" is cheating, testing the rules, seeing what they could get away with. A closer look at the play and games of childhood can offer insights into contemporary American culture and how it is absorbed by children growing up in America.

As students look at their childhood folklore, they begin to appreciate the ubiquitous nature and role of oral tradition in society. They gradually realize that since birth they have learned much of who they are, what they value and believe, and how to behave through their folklore. No child's education is limited to the classroom. Outside of it they continue to receive their folk education, an education that continues throughout life. Yet, students have little sense that they are learners outside of class. Susan, quoted above, noticed this only when she wrote, "I learned something I hadn't given much thought to—that people *learn* folklore from their friends. . . . "

For students who don't excel in school it often comes as welcome information that there are areas in their lives where they are proficient learners. They realize this as they contemplate how quickly they became expert at jacks or intricate handclapping games or how well they learned, by playing sandlot and pickup ball, to become basketball, baseball, or soccer players. Outside of school they are successful learners. In a class in folklore their success in other settings can become part of the curriculum. They can take pride in it. This change in self-image can rub off favorably in their schoolwork.

A sixth reason to use folklore is that through its study students can often see the connection between their own lives and history, between the personal and seemingly impersonal multi-dimensional world beyond them. Children's lore, for example, frequently includes political jokes like this one told by a third grader:

> There were three men in a boat—Carter, Reagan, and Kissinger. The boat turned over and the men were drowned. Who was saved? The American people.[4]

Students can ponder how this joke got into the repertoire of elementary school children and what is taking place when children tell and laugh at it. This third grader happened to have learned the joke from his older brother, but no matter where it comes from the children are being exposed to and perhaps internalizing political attitudes.

History often comes up when students write about how they got their names. George, a junior who disliked his name, interviewed his parents and learned:

> My father named me after my great grandfather.[5] My great grandfather died in the Crimean War . . . in the famous battle of the Charge of the Light Brigade. Before I found that out I didn't like my name. . . .

George explained that his great-grandfather, a patriot, went into the battle knowing he would die. George was struck by his great-grandfather's bravery and, after learning the history of his name, decided he liked it. Researching his name, George not only changed his opinion of his name, but he also made a personal connection to a moment in history and learned firsthand that history is made by common folk like his great-grandfather, as well as by the famous.

The study of their folklore also connects the lives of students to contemporary issues. For example, in a class studying school and teenage folklore (see chapter 10), a student writing about lunch-period rituals described student groupings (which are folk groups)[6] as racially segregated. Her observation caught the interest of the class. Some agreed, some disagreed. They wanted to look more deeply into the issue. Studying themselves and their peers, the students saw in the folklore of their lives a reflection of two major American problems—discrimination and segregation.

There is nothing new in a classroom study of this sort; what is unusual is that the impetus and the topic came from a student paper, not from the teacher, and the students, not the teacher, decided that it was something worth pursuing. The study of folklore, then, offers a chance for students to study cultural concerns important in their lives.

At first some students are suspicious of folklore. It doesn't sound like a legitimate course to study. As Shawn, a junior from the suburbs, wrote in his end-of-the-term evaluation:

> Before you came to our class I never knew anyone ever seriously studied folklore especially not at Berkeley!

The majority of students are intrigued by folklore and immediately comfortable with it, but to allay others' doubts, it's important to establish early on that folklore is a serious academic discipline. Chapters 1, 3, and 4 have sections devoted to folklore scholarship, and every chapter has references to it.

When students' lives become the core of the curriculum, the teacher conveys something powerful to them. By making them part of the curriculum, the teacher is saying that they are as important as any other subject—literature or math or science. This is the seventh and final reason for studying folklore and is particularly important for minority students whose lives are seldom included let alone given center stage in the curriculum.

By the time students have reached junior and senior high school, they have quite a bit of living behind them. When we study their folklore and mine, we get to know each other in new ways. The retelling of the folklore of their lives and their reflections on the significance of their experience gives me much to think about and praise in their writing. For example, Lupe's log, quoted above, was written in response to her observations on the discrimination against Latino students in her school. When school counselors see Latino names, Lupe wrote, they automatically put them in nonacademic classes. This is folklore that the Latino students believe to be true. I wrote back telling Lupe that I thought she had tapped an important vein of school folklore. Her response to me sums up the potential of the study of folklore:

Thank you for saying that my ideas are excellent. . . . I really enjoy what you are doing with us. You are helping us to know each other better in our inside and outside.

Using Folklore to Teach Writing

The hypothesis underlying this book is that the content of modern folklore lends itself perfectly to the teaching of writing. When students are learning to write or to become more fluent at it, they need plenty of material. Topics must honestly engage students, and students must be knowledgeable about them, must have plenty to say and write about. Contemporary folklore is a cornucopia of such topics. Furthermore, when students are improving their writing, the first skill they work on is fluency. To encourage fluency many teachers begin with personal writing. Every topic is this book begins with personal writing, a piece based on a memory, an experience, or an observation.

There is, of course, considerable variation in what individual students are willing or ready to share about themselves. Here again folklore is useful, for it allows each student to reveal as much or as little personal information as he or she chooses. Each topic can be approached from a closely personal point of view or observed detachedly, from a distance. The student mentioned earlier chose to study lunch-period rituals impersonally. She described the groups on campus, where they hung out, and how they spent their time. One group, for instance, played basketball; another sat on the hoods of their cars and flirted. A classmate chose a more intimate route to the topic, writing a narrative about his crowd, who called themselves the "groupies." (See chapter 10 on school and teenage folklore for a discussion of these papers.)

In general, students are less likely to write openly at or near the beginning of the year. Therefore, early in the term I begin with the units that are the least personal—children's folklore or modern urban legends. When students are more at ease, we move to the units that tend to be much more personal, such as family and teenage folklore. Once students have achieved some fluency, they branch out to more distanced forms of writing. Using the example of children's folklore again, students first write down a memory of childhood play, often a narrative. This can then become the source or inspiration for a piece of expository writing. Students might, for example, speculate about the skills and worldview they learned playing hide and seek. Or they might tackle the assumption of some folklorists that children's play is a microcosm of adult culture and argue for or against this proposition. Variations on this model (a personal connection leading to expository writing) are found in each chapter. The focus of this essentially non-narrative writing varies. In one case it is mainly argumentative; in another research-oriented; in another the stress is on comparing and contrasting.

Some Notes on the Plan of the Book

When folklore is taught in secondary schools, it usually appears as a unit in English class. Therefore, each of the chapters in this book is designed as a one- to three-week unit. The first two chapters are background for teachers. Chapter 1, "An Introduction to Modern Folklore," is what its title implies. The second chapter, "Teaching Writing While Teaching Folklore," describes ways to integrate teaching writing and teaching folklore. Each of the following ten chapters deals with a different folk genre. In writing this book, I've had in mind as an audience the busy classroom teacher who may not have time to read the whole book before starting a unit. Teachers may want to start with the classroom chapters (chapters 3–12) and then turn back later to chapters 1 and 2 for background on folklore and writing. Therefore, each chapter includes enough background information to allow a teacher to approach the topic right away. For each chapter to work as a discrete usable unit, I've had to resort to occasional redundancies, alas.

While the content of the units typically comes from oral tradition in the lives of students, reading is an active component of each topic. Readings include collections of folklore; analytical writing by folklorists; articles from the newspapers, magazines, and journals; and autobiography and fiction focused on folklore. Also, students often read one another's writing. Student writing is probably read more in these units than in literature-based courses since the content is the folk world of the students.

In the Selected Resources for Teachers and Students and the Works Cited both at the end of the book and in the Notes at the end of the chapters, there are suggested background and classroom readings and references for teachers and students.

Since 1980 I have been experimenting with folklore and writing in junior and senior high schools. The chapters in this book are set in three classrooms in three different schools: an inner-city school with a predominantly Black student body, a White middle-class suburban school, and a multi-racial city school where the class was predominantly Latino.

The chapters tend to be narratives, with dialogue transcriptions taken from audiotapes of the classes. Since the chapters are narratives, I've included at the end of chapters 4 through 12 an outline called "Unit in Brief." This is a reference for the teacher who wants a fast check on what happened from day to day in the unit. The chapters are written in narrative form to capture the atmosphere of a classroom studying folklore. I've tried, that is, to recreate the emotional highs for both the teacher and the students studying this subject. Folklore entertains. The class studying folklore is at once intellectually challenging and fun. Since the materials are unusual, showing what happens with them in the classroom may be the best introduction. Sometimes a chapter is a retelling of the unit as taught in a single class; sometimes it is a composite of more than one class. And student writing is presented uncorrected unless otherwise noted.

The book reflects my interests, teaching style, and the concerns and lives of my students. We all teach differently and have different kinds of students; our classrooms are shaped by our personalities and interests and those of the students. Teachers using the ideas presented in this book can reshape them to suit their classroom styles. The students, too, will exert a strong influence since the content comes directly from their lives—not from a classroom text.

Notes

1. Learning logs are a type of journal described in chapter 2.

2. See chapter 1 for a fuller discussion of the definition and meaning of folklore.

3. For printed versions of La Llorona, see "The Wailing Woman," in E. Adams Davis, Of the Night Wind's Telling (Norman: University of Oklahoma Press, 1946), pp. 109–16, and "La Llorona," in Hector Lee's Heroes, Villains and Ghosts: Folklore of Old California (Santa Barbara, California: Capra Press, 1984), pp. 121–26. For a discussion of La Llorona in the past and present, see John O. West, Mexican-American Folklore (Little Rock, Arkansas: August House, 1988), pp. 75–77.

4. This is an ever-serviceable joke. The 1988 version: Bush, Quayle, Dukakis, and Bentsen are in the boat.

5. Since George was born circa 1967, the ancestor who fought in the Crimean War was more likely his great-great-grandfather.

6. See chapter 1 for a definition of folk group.

Chapter One

An Introduction to Modern Folklore

"Folklore comes early and stays late in the lives of all of us," writes Barre Toelken in *The Dynamics of Folklore* (1979, 23). Some people know this, but many people think of folklore as part of the past and as belonging to others who are rural, quaint, and/or backward. In workshops on folklore and writing, I often start by asking teachers to write down what they think is going to happen. One participant wrote, only partially in jest:

> I thought you were going to be steeped in Nordic tradition, maybe you'd talk about the Kalevala, and maybe you'd wear a long flowing skirt and flat sandals. You'd be zealous on the subject; we'd all leave feeling very philistine.

This is a common notion about folklore: it comes from the past and embodies the wisdom of foreign peasants.

A few teachers come to the workshops with inklings that folklore is contemporary, as did this one:

> Maybe you'll talk about how each of us has a folklore and that we can dig deep for this in our writing. Maybe you'll say folklore is a personal, oral tradition that explains cultural differences better than history books. Maybe you'll say to know a people, to know their folklore will tell you their traditions and mores better than psychology and sociology books.

Both teachers are right. Their impressions are, in fact, compatible: folklore encompasses the Kalevala, the national epic of Finland, and our personal lore.

Explaining what the Kalevala and a family's Thanksgiving dinner have in common—which amounts to defining folklore—can lead
one into a quagmire, especially since folklorists themselves remain
divided over the nature and province of their discipline. A common
approach to explaining folklore is to sidestep the definition at first
and begin instead with a list of examples. Toelken continues his
opening discussion of the folklore process this way:

> In spite of the combined forces of technology, science, television,
> religion, urbanization, and creeping literacy, we prefer our close
> personal associations as the basis for learning about life and trans-
> mitting important observations and expressions. From the child-
> hood rhythms of "Patty Cake" to the joy of humorous graces, ("Good
> bread, good meat, good God, let's eat") to the imagined sophistica-
> tion of drinking games ("Cardinal Puff," "Fuzz-Buzz"); from court-
> ship protocol to showers to wedding customs ("But you *can't* wear
> a red dress, dear; it's not *right!*") to birth cigars; from birthday
> spanks to hacks; from tree house clubs to stag and hen parties; from
> the Tooth Fairy to the Birthday Girl to Santa Claus; from Black doz-
> ens to Native American "forty-nine" songs to *curanderismo*; from
> Valentine's candy to Easter eggs to firecrackers to pumpkins to
> turkey to fruitcake to Tom-and-Jerries; from riddles to barroom jokes
> to epitaphs, death, and burial customs to placing flowers on a grave;
> from wart cures to waiting twenty minutes for a full professor; from
> cement-filled Cadillacs and girls with spiders in their hair to mirac-
> ulous carburetors (kept off the market by the auto industry) and
> death cars for sale (cheap); from the pink and blue of the nursery
> through the white of the wedding to the black of the funeral, we con-
> tinue to wend our traditional way through life (23–24).

In this list Toelken follows the life cycle, giving examples from each
stage; he demonstrates what Americans have in common in their
national folklore. He also shows diversity, mentioning, for instance,
some ethnic folklore not as widely known, such as "the Black
dozens," verbal dueling done in rhymed couplets most often by
young black males, and *curanderismo*, Latino folk medicine. All of
Toelken's examples are taken from contemporary America.[1]

In his introduction to *The Study of Folklore* (1965), Alan Dundes
also begins with a list, this one organized by genre:

> Folklore includes myths, legends, folktales,[2] jokes, proverbs, rid-
> dles, chants, charms, blessings, curses, oaths, insults, retorts, taunts,
> teases, toasts, tongue-twisters, and greeting and leave-taking formu-
> las (e.g., See you later, alligator). It also includes folk custom, folk
> dance, folk drama (and mime), folk art, folk belief (or superstition),
> folk medicine, folk instrumental music (e.g., fiddle tunes), folk-
> songs (e.g., lullabies, ballads), folk speech (e.g., slang), folk similes
> (e.g., as blind as a bat), folk metaphors (e.g., to paint the town red),
> and names (e.g., nicknames and place names). Folk poetry ranges

from oral epics to autograph-book verse, epitaphs, latrinalia (writing on the walls of public bathrooms), limericks, ball-bouncing rhymes, jump-rope rhymes, finger and toe rhymes, dandling rhymes (to bounce children on the knee), counting-out rhymes (to determine who will be "it" in games), and nursery rhymes. The list of folklore forms also contains games; gestures; symbols; prayers (e.g., graces); practical jokes; folk etymologies; food recipes; quilt and embroidery designs; house, barn and fence types; street vendor's cries; and even traditional conventional sounds used to summon animals or to give them commands. There are such minor forms as mnemonic devices (e.g., the name Roy G. Biv to remember the colors of the spectrum in order), envelope sealers (e.g., SWAK-Sealed With A Kiss), and the traditional comments made after body emissions (e.g., after burps or sneezes). There are such major forms as festivals and special day (or holiday) customs (e.g., Christmas, Halloween, and birthday) (3).

Dundes cautions that this list is incomplete. There are between three hundred and four hundred genres of folklore.

Dundes does not trace the life cycle as Toelken did. Instead, he begins with the best-known forms of folklore: myth, legend, and folk tale and then lists other genres, irrespective of specific cultures or time. While Toelken wanted to show folklore in America, Dundes seems more interested in conveying that folklore is old as well as new and is cross-cultural (although his specific examples are American.) Both these lists are meant to be introductory, intended to give a feel for the subject.

Over the last century and a half, folklorists have puzzled over what folklore is, who the folk are, and what the best or proper way is to study it/them. In the nineteenth and early twentieth centuries, the focus was on the folk and the lore. During that time folklorists continually broadened the definition of folk and lore. Since the mid-twentieth century, many folklorists have further reconceptualized the field, rejecting past scholarship that tended to isolate the content of folklore (the genres) and the folk from the *process* of folklore. They still see folklore as encompassing the content and the folk, but their emphasis is on the *performance* of the folklore and the communication that takes place during this process. However the subject is approached, the central aspects of the discipline will always be the folk and the lore. Thus, we begin with them.

Who Are the Folk?

In 1846, an Englishman, William Thoms, unhappy with designations like "popular antiquities," coined a new word for his field—*folklore*. His understanding of the term was shaped by romantic and nationalistic movements, as it was for Wilhelm and Jacob Grimm, leaders of the German Romantic movement and two of the founders of the study of folklore. As young men, the brothers collected local folktales, from which they created a masterpiece, Nursery and Household Tales. This enormously popular work, since translated into sixty languages, inspired folklorists all over Europe to collect folk—or peasant—lore, seeking nostalgically for survivals of their heritage.

The Grimms were scholars who not only popularized folktales, but more importantly gave them status. Serious inquiry of folklore began with the Grimms. However, theirs was the classic nineteenth-century view. Folklore, they believed, had been created in the past by "the folk"—the peasant or lower classes. It was their mission to collect it quickly before it disappeared. Never did they consider themselves as a "folk" with a contemporary "lore" of their own.

The Grimms' nineteenth-century survival concept still has strong appeal. Most people, like the teacher quoted earlier, associate folklore with the past, with people close to the earth, wise in ways now lost to us. That imagery, with its Edenic overtones, continues to hold sway.

Sometime in the 1930s or 1940s, however, a redefinition began, which extended the folk to the city and eventually included everyone—city and country dwellers, rich and poor, peasant and patrician. An early formulation of this broad definition of group came from Dundes:

> The term "folk" can refer to any group of people whatsoever who share at least one common factor. It does not matter what the linking factor is—it could be a common occupation, language, or religion— but what is important is that a group formed for whatever reason will have some traditions which it calls its own (2).

More recently, folklorists have added an important qualification. The group must communicate. For example, those who read this book have something in common, but they are not a folk group if no communication about the book has taken place and if they have no sense of being a group. Therefore, Toelken defines a group as "any group of people who share informal communal contacts that become the basis for expressive, culture-based communications" (51). And Roger Abrahams describes a group as "a social unit which has some notion of its own groupness (1983, 345).

We are, however, all folk and belong to many folk groups. Dan Ben-Amos writes, "A [folk] group could be a family, a street-corner gang, a roomful of factory workers, a village, or even a tribe" (1971, 12). Probably the largest folk group we belong to is national. We have national stereotypes about ourselves and others. An easy place to spot them is in jokes. Here are two that play on national stereotypes:

> There is going to be an international congress on the study of the elephant. The major nations of the world are invited to give papers. So the Russians write about "The Elephant and the Five-Year Plan," the French about "*Les amours des elephants,*" the Germans do a twenty-volume introduction to the study of the elephant, and the Americans write on "How to Build a Bigger and Better Elephant" (adapted from Dundes 1975, 32–34).

> A survey is being made about a meat shortage and a Russian, a Pole, an American, and an Israeli are questioned. First, the interviewer asks the Russian: "Excuse me, what do you think about the meat shortage?" And the Russian, confused by the question, asks, "What is this word 'think'?" Next he asks the Pole, "Excuse me, what do you think about the meat shortage?" He responds, "What means 'meat'?" Next the American is asked, and he too is confused and asks, "What is this 'shortage'?" Finally the Israeli is asked, "Excuse me, what do you think of the meat shortage?" He is also confused: "What is this 'Excuse me'?"

Both of these jokes could be told by any nationality. In fact the second one I heard from an Israeli, who was proud of the feisty, rude stereotype the joke conveys. A joke like this is multifunctional, serving different purposes depending on the teller and the audience, but both teach and perpetuate stereotypes.

Young children learn national and ethnic stereotypes early. In elementary school, they say "Pardon my French," after they have said a "dirty" word. They sing rhymes like this one:

> All the girls in France do the hula, hula dance
> And the way they shake is enough to kill a snake

The stereotype of the French as sexy is learned in the primary grades.

Besides our national folk group, we belong to occupational folk groups. Employees in corporations, for example, are a folk. This is no surprise to folklorists, but it was to two nonfolklorists, Peters and Waterman, studying corporate culture. In their bestseller, *In Search of Excellence: Lessons from America's Best-Run Companies* (1982), they write:

> As we worked on research of our excellent companies, we were struck by the dominant use of story, slogan, and legend as people tried to explain the characters of their own great institutions. All the companies we interviewed, from Boeing to McDonald's, were quite simply rich tapestries of anecdote, myth, and fairy tale. And we do mean fairy tale. The vast majority of people who tell stories today

about T. J. Watson of IBM have never met the man or had direct experience of the original more mundane reality. Two HP engineers in their mid-twenties recently regaled us with an hour's worth of "Bill and Dave" (Hewlett and Packard) stories. We were subsequently astonished to find that neither had seen, let alone talked to, the founders. These days, people like Watson and A. P. Giannini at Bank of America take on roles of mythic proportions that the real persons would have been hard pressed to fill. Nevertheless, in an organizational sense, these stories, myths, and legends appear to be very important, because they convey the organization's shared values, or culture (75).

Peters and Waterman are not folklorists, and they use the words myth and fairy tale in the popular sense,[3] but they clearly make the point that even large corporations are folk groups with their own folklore.

Teachers are another such group, as are students. All English teachers have, for example, endured the folkloric response to their profession, "Oh, you're an English teacher. I'd better watch my grammar." Students have an extensive folklore about school that starts early when, for example, children chant:

> Row, row, row your boat,
> Gently down the stream,
> Throw your teacher overboard,
> And listen to her scream.

(Chapter 10, "All Right! We've Got a Substitute!" is the study of folklore of high school students.)

We also belong to regional folk groups. A student, Glenda Fay, shortened her name to Glenda when she moved from Mississippi to Northern California. At home Glenda Fay sounded right, but not in the West. There are regional naming patterns: double names are common in the South but unusual elsewhere.

Within the folk group of American children, there are smaller groups determined by, for example, sex. Female children are more likely than males to play with Barbie dolls; boys more often play war games with GI Joe. Age figures too. This is a funny joke to a first grader:

> Look up, look down,
> Look all around,
> Look at my thumb,
> Gee you're dumb.

An age-specific joke, it is no longer funny after primary years.

Families are folk groups, and chapters 5, 6, and 7 are about the folklore of families. Ethnicity is a folk category, a rich one that is considered in most of the following chapters. Religion is also a folk category. Each classroom is a folk group, and a class that has a strong sense of community will develop a rich folklore of shared references, jokes, and experience. Thus, inescapably, *we* are the folk, each of us participating in many folk groups.

What is the Lore?

Folklorists know what they mean by the term *folklore*, but the folk themselves generally don't recognize it as a separate and distinct cultural category. That is, they have no categories or labels for folklore's *parts*: they're aware of traditions and rituals, such as family reunions or annual Labor Day picnics; they know they tell jokes, that children play jump rope and house. But they tend not to think of these aspects of their lives collectively, as folklore. Hence, there is no folk category for folklore.

There is some consensus among folklorists about the content of their discipline. Perhaps the single most telling characteristic of folklore is that *it is passed from one person to another*. Methods of transmission vary. A major method is oral: telling a joke or a family story. Often transmission is by observation: children learn to play jacks or jump rope by watching others. Some folklore is transmitted by writing: chain letters, graffiti, and games or jokes that involve some writing, such as fortune-telling paper origami. Sometimes the origami are designed as "cootie catchers," devices to pluck pretend bugs or "cooties" off unsuspecting playmates.

A second characteristic is that *folklore changes when it is transmitted from person to person*, resulting in different versions.[4] The following tale, told both as a joke and legend, changes constantly:

> A woman was on vacation in Las Vegas, Nevada, and was staying in a hotel casino. One night she called an elevator to go up to her room. When the elevator doors opened, there was a big, mean-looking black man with a big dog in the elevator. The lady was frightened of being alone with this man but got in anyway. As the elevator started going up, the man's dog started pawing at the lady, which frightened her even more. The black man suddenly yelled, "Lie down, Lady!" The woman immediately dropped to the floor, crying, "You can have my money, but please don't hurt me." The man laughed and said, "Excuse me, ma'am, but I was talking to my dog." Later when the woman checked out from the hotel, the manager told her that her bill had been paid by someone who left a note. The note was from the black man. In it, he apologized for scaring her, and said it gave him such a good laugh, he decided to pay for her hotel bill. The note was signed by Lionel Ritchie [a famous pop singer].[5]

In his study of modern urban legends, Jan Brunvand has eleven pages on this legend, which he calls "The Elevator Incident" (1984, 18–28). Variations abound. The woman can be traveling alone or with companions. The city where the incident takes place is identified as New York, Boston, Philadelphia, Baltimore, Reno, or Las Vegas. The Black man is tall, sometimes well dressed, sometimes in a cowboy hat and jeans. The dog varies too. It is a doberman, a German shepherd, or sometimes a small dog the women don't see when they enter the elevator. The Black man has also been reported to be Reggie Jackson, Jesse Jackson, Wilt Chamberlain, "Magic" Johnson, O. J. Simpson, Larry Holmes, and Mean Joe Green. Sometimes he buys them breakfast, more often dinner; sometimes he sends them champagne; on other occasions he pays for their entire hotel bill. One way legends gain credibility is through details tying them to well-known local places. When the story is told in Rochester, for example, the women are from Rochester and visiting New York. But while legend changes as it is passed around, it remains recognizably the same. (So-called "fixed phrase" folklore has less variation. A proverb such as "Out of sight, out of mind" is a good example. Still, even fixed phrase folklore changes. "Spitting image," for instance, is a folk variation on the folk saying, "Spit and image," or maybe vice versa. Most folklore undergoes change as it is moved by the folk.)

Folklore is Traditional

Lifetimes of folklore items vary. The children's game known in America as jacks is very old—women are depicted playing a version of it in a Roman mural. The folktale "The Two Brothers" was known in ancient Egypt. Many fairy tales date back to the Middle Ages. Much children's lore has been known for hundreds of years. Iona and Peter Opie document the age of many examples of children's lore in both their collections, *The Lore and Language of Schoolchildren* (1959) and *Children's Games in Street and Playground* (1969). But folklore can be ephemeral too, particularly joke cycles spawned by a specific event. The morning after the American space shuttle *Challenger* exploded on January 28th, 1986, this riddle joke began circulating:

> What does NASA stand for?

The first answer was:

> Need another seven astronauts.

Variations followed:

> Now accepting seven applications.
> No aging survivors agency.
> Not a seal anywhere.

The original riddle was told all over the United States and was also reported in England, Scotland, Ireland, Iceland, Australia, and Switzerland. Yet, by May the space shuttle jokes had pretty much disappeared. The game of jacks is at least two thousand years old; by contrast the NASA joke cycle lasted only a few months.

Much Folklore Is Anonymous in Origin

The originator or the author of most folklore is unknown. There are exceptions, however. In some cases, an item enters the folk repertoire, and its origin is simply forgotten. Songs with known composers, like Woody Guthrie's "This Land Is Your Land," take on a folk life and often become detached from their originators. In other cases, the origin is known and remains known as the work of a particular folk artist. For much family folklore, family members know who started it and when and where it began.

The matter of anonymous origins seems to bother students, who often argue about it in class. The folk, perhaps also uneasy with anonymous oral origins, tend to create them. In time, they may take on the aura of fact. The origin of the children's rhyme "Ring Around the Rosy," for example, is often explained this way:

> In the Middle Ages people danced to ward off the plague.
> They carried sweet smelling flowers in their pockets.
> There's a nursery rhyme to remind us:
> > Ring-around-the-rosie,
> > A pocket full of posies . . .
>
> > > Gladys Perint Palmer,
> > > *San Francisco Examiner*
> > > June 15, 1986, page A-1.

Iona and Peter Opie, British scholars of children's literature and folklore, have researched the rhyme. There is an American version dating from 1790, but in it no one falls down:

> Ring a ring a rosie,
> A bottle full of posie,
> All the girls in our town,
> Ring for little Josie.

Falling down doesn't enter children's literature before 1881, hundreds of years after the plague. The Opies write:

> The invariable sneezing and falling down in modern English ver-
> sions has given would-be origin finders the opportunity to say that
> the rhyme dates back to the days of the Great Plague. A rosy rash,
> they allege, was a symptom of the plague, posies of herbs were car-
> ried as protection, sneezing was a final fatal symptom, and 'all fall
> down' was exactly what happened. . . . The foreign and nineteenth-
> century versions seem to show that the fall was originally a curtsy or
> other gracious bending movement of a dramatic singing game
> (1973, 365).

The story of the origin of "Ring around the rosy" has itself become a
folk legend.

In this century, the definition of folklore and the focus of its
scholarship has changed. The lore has broadened to include the traditions of the many folk groups. For example, folklorists now study
"xerography," the cartoons and other forms of humor that pass
through offices via the copying machines.[6] Currently, folklore scholarship is also changing its emphasis. In the past, it has tended to look
at items in isolation, out of context and as relatively static. Now the
thrust is toward folklore as "performance,"[7] where the process of
what is taking place can be more important than the product, the
item of folklore itself. (The change of focus from product to process
parallels in time the same change in the teaching of writing. See
chapter 2.) The focus of folklore studies is changing, but the corner-
stone of folklore remains tradition. Simon Bronner makes this point:

> Folklore studies has sought traditions before they were gone or
> missed and has explained how they came to be or why they arise
> anew. The center of folklore studies remains in tradition, in explain-
> ing human experience that takes the form of recurrent, expressive
> responses to social life and environment. In its choice of subjects
> and in its approaches, folklore studies continues to comment on
> changes and continuities in society (1986, 129).

Folk Culture

Folk culture may be best understood when compared to elite and
popular culture. The former includes the arts: symphony, ballet,
opera, poetry, theatre, painting, sculpture, and classical literature.
The works of elite culture are created by known artists and are
expressions of their individual ideas. These inventions do not go into
oral tradition and do not change or vary. Once a novel or symphony
is written, it remains fixed on the printed page. Elite culture is highly
valued, as it should be, although it is enjoyed by a rather small per-
centage of the population. It is that part of our culture which we want
our children to study in school.

Less highly valued, but with greater currency among the general population, is popular culture: e.g., television, movies, comics, light fiction, newspapers, and magazines. Like elite culture, these works have identifiable authors and are fixed in form, but while elite culture is generally considered worthy, popular culture generally is not. Since popular culture is less highly valued than elite culture, it plays a smaller part in formal schooling.

Folk culture, by comparison, is truly the creation of the folk. We pass it around among ourselves, all the while changing and altering it so that it continues to entertain and serve us. As a result—and this is a critical difference—folklore is not the voice of an individual but the collective and usually anonymous voice of all of us, the uncensored, uninterpreted voice of a people. Roger Abrahams writes, " . . . it puts into words the most important shared values of group life; folklore in this way reveals attitudes that remind us how life ought to be lived, cautioning us about the consequences of not following these precepts. Thus, folklore often provides the main patterns for the expression and enactment of group values and ideals" (1980, 371).

While it is appropriate that the schools pass on elite culture to the young, it is sad that we overlook folk culture, given its enormous potential for learning. The study of folklore is a unique entrance into contemporary culture. Our folk culture reflects the good, the controversial, and the bad, often in one item. The "elevator incident" is a good example. It entertains. People enjoy it; it has been around for years and shows no signs of disappearing. At the same time, it is a folk commentary on racism. At first it seems a simple reflection of racist stereotypes—the white woman, trapped and defenseless in an elevator with a Black man and his menacing dog. The white, middle-class setting of the legend is central, because it speaks to a particular form of racism experienced by middle- and upper-class Black males—the famous, as in the legend, and the nonfamous. No matter who they are, no matter how conservative and expensive their dress, in white, middle-class surroundings Black males are often treated as potentially dangerous criminals. However, the legend begins to reveal evidence of a change in the stereotype. In this narrative the Black man emerges as kind and generous, uncharacteristic in white folklore.

There is constant interplay between the various cultures. For example, the movie 10, starring the actress Bo Derek, is an example of popular culture. However, the rating scale of 1–10 from which the title of the movie is taken is folklore. Bo Derek tops the scale at "10." Jokes circulated about the movie. Here's one:

What is 10, 9, 8, 7, 6?
Bo Derek growing older.

From students, I learn much about the interchange of popular and folk cultures. The folk legend "The Babysitter" is the basis of at least two teenage Hollywood horror movies. And "The China Doll," a children's legend in which a doll murders an entire family, inspired or was inspired by an early episode of *Twilight Zone*, which is replayed periodically on television.

This back and forth between popular and folk culture is constant. The title of John LéCarré's novel, *Tinker, Tailor, Soldier, Spy* comes from:

> Tinker, tailor,
> Soldier, sailor,
> Rich man, poor man,
> Beggar man, thief,

the English children's equivalent of the American rhyme:

> Rich man, poor man,
> Beggar man, thief,
> Doctor, lawyer,
> Indian chief.

And Edward Albee got the title for his play, "Who's Afraid of Virginia Woolf?" from a piece of graffiti.

While students can spot the interplay between popular and folk culture, the connections between folk and elite culture are more obscure. If in their English classes they are reading, for example, Sophocles's *Oedipus the King*, I tell them that the story is a folk narrative, that Sophocles didn't create the tale. He'd no doubt heard it and used it as the basis for his literary version. If they want to know more, *Oedipus: A Folklore Casebook* (1984), edited by Lowell Edmunds and Alan Dundes, is a good resource. Several of Chaucer's *Canterbury Tales* are well-known folk tales, and Shakespeare's "King Lear" is based on a version of Cinderella.[8]

Folklore, then, is a layer of culture that influences and is influenced by popular and elite culture, but that is seldom singled out and appreciated in its own right. Folklore and folk culture are not taught in the schools because they are viewed as forming the lowest stratum of the cultural pyramid rather than what they are: a central—and vital—element in our culture.

Folklore: Truth or Error

The word *folklore* is often used as a synonym for fiction or erroneous belief. When a story or claim strikes us as being doubtful, we say, "That sounds like folklore to me," or "Oh, that's only folklore," hence unworthy of further attention. There are two issues here: first, the origin of an item—Did it really happen; is it true?—and second, the "truth" implicit in the message of an item regardless of its origin.

The elevator legend, as far as I know, isn't true. When interviewed, Reggie Jackson denied it, although he said he'd heard it many times. However, his agent, Matt Merola, while acknowledging that it had never happened (at least to Jackson), told a *Boston Globe* sports reporter: "I tell everyone it's true. It's a nice story, a good story, if you want it to be true, it's true. Whatever way you heard it, that's the way it happened" (Brunvand 1984, 20).

As Merola realized, the factual truth of the story has little relationship to the truth of its message. The origin of a legend is almost irrelevant. Some are based on known events,[9] many are not. But what is important is that they sound plausible, have the ring of reality, so that people can believe them. Based on real events or not, believed to be true or not (some people tell the elevator incident as a joke, not as a legend), it contains cultural truths important to both tellers and listeners. (Be warned, however, that the reverse is often the case. A subsequent section of this chapter, *The Functions of Folklore*, shows that folklore, when it acts as a safety valve, often defies accepted cultural truths.)

The Field of Folklore

As students grow curious about folklore, I tell them a little about how folklore scholars work and where folklore is studied. This information validates the subject, which students find compelling, but which at first blush seems nonacademic. I bring in copies of major folklore journals, such as *The Journal of American Folklore* and *Western Folklore,* and encourage students to browse. They find articles on diverse topics: bullfights, versions of "Hansel and Gretel" in Spain and Mexico, legends of occupational ghosts, (the airplane engineer who died in a crash and appears to warn pilots and flight attendants of trouble), and articles on joke cycles inspired by the Three Mile Island and Chernobyl disasters.

Two major resource indexes folklorists use when studying folk narrative are *The Types of the Folktale* by Antti Aarne and Stith Thompson and the *The Motif-Index of Folk Literature* edited by Stith Thompson. The former, usually referred to as the *Tale-Type Index,* contains synopses of all the known plots in Indo-European folk tradition and is therefore little used in the study of contemporary American lore. Occasionally, a student will have been told a traditional tale as a child, such as a version of the Tar Baby story, and will mention it as part of the folklore of his childhood. I then tell him about the *Tale-Type Index* and show him the reference for versions of the tale, pointing out the places around the world where the story was told.

The *Motif-Index* doesn't deal in whole plots. It is instead a resource for motifs or recurring story elements such as an object like the Tar Baby, or a magic sword, or a trickster character like Brer Rabbit, or an incident like a hero killing a dragon. Unlike the *Tale-Type Index*, the *Motif-Index* classifies motifs from the entire world. Since some motifs current in contemporary narrative, particularly in legends and jokes, are traditional, the *Motif-Index* is used by folklorists studying modern lore. A motif that comes up often in the study of modern urban legends (chapter 12) is the central incident in the legend of the Vanishing Hitchhiker, Motif E332.3.3.1 in the *Motif-Index*. Mary Duffey, of Livermore, California, heard the legend the first time when she was in junior high. It was told, as it often is, at a slumber party:

> On November 22, a long time ago, a man was driving through Niles Canyon alone at night when he saw a pale young girl, so pale, "it was almost like you could see through her," with long dark hair in a floor length white formal standing by the side of the road. He stopped, and asked her if she wanted a ride which she accepted. She got into the back seat, and because she looked as if she was cold he gave her his sports jacket to put around her shoulders. She thanked him, and they began talking. The girl told the driver her name, and that she had just come from a party for her birthday, which was today.
>
> They stopped talking for a few minutes as they came to a large toll bridge, so that the man could get out some money for the toll. Then the amazing thing happened. When the toll man asked how many were in the car, and the driver told him "two," the man looked surprised and asked who the second person was. The driver then turned around and found neither his coat, nor the girl in the back seat.
>
> Several days later the driver looked up the girl's parents (the girl had an unusual last name and he found it in the phone book). To his horror they told him that their daughter had died several years ago by committing suicide off the very same bridge he had stopped at to pay the toll. He couldn't believe it, so they told him where she was buried, and he drove to the cemetery. There lying across her grave he found his sports jacket.
>
> And to this day the pale young girl with the long dark hair is said to walk through Niles Canyon on November 22.[10]

In nineteenth-century versions of this legend, the revenant *[person who returns]* is picked up by people passing a cemetery in a horse and carriage. The longevity and the history of the legend intrigues students. But the point here is that folklorists have a system of classification for the study of motifs such as this one and thousands of others.

Students interested in learning more about folklore should know that they can study it at many post-secondary schools around the country, and that at the universities of Pennsylvania, Indiana, California at Los Angeles, and Texas at Austin, they can earn Ph.D's in the subject. All the topics in this book can be easily studied without formal training in folklore. It is, however, reassuring for some students to know that there is a serious academic (and therefore elite) discipline in the study of folklore.

The Functions of Folklore: What Does Folklore Do for the Folk?

After introducing students to folklore, I ask them why they think people have it. Invariably the answer is, "It's fun." Entertainment is, in fact, the first function listed by William Bascom in his "Four Functions of Folklore" (1954, 333–49). Entertainment, however, is just the beginning. This function is obvious; others are more subtle. Furthermore, different types of folklore serve different functions. When students answer the question above, they haven't yet discussed funeral rituals, for example. They are important folklore but not fun. Much, but not all, folklore entertains.

Verbal folklore instructs and educates, a second function. It is an informal education in group values, attitudes, behaviors, and beliefs. When a young child learns the proverbial rhyme,

> Finders keepers,
> Losers weepers,

he or she is learning a folk value. Or when young children on a playground chant the folk rhyme,

> We won, we won,
> We won the BB gun,
> You lost, you lost,
> You ate the applesauce,

they are learning what Vince Lombardi, fabled coach of the Green Bay Packers, knew: "Winning isn't everything. It's the only thing." (Or "Winning isn't everything, but losing is nothing," a version attributed to the California politician, Jesse Unruh.) While parents and teachers offer children alternative proverbs such as, "It isn't if you win or lose, but how you play the game," or even teach children this folk rhyme,

> The first the worst,
> The second the same,
> The last the best,
> Of all the game,

the collective wisdom of children nevertheless seems to be "Finders keepers"—winning counts.[11]

Even in technologically advanced, literate societies, children get a folk education as important as their formal schooling. Kenneth Goldstein (1971, 167–78) studied how children use counting-out rhymes like "One potato, two potato . . . " when choosing who will be "it" in a game. He asked them why they used the rhymes—why they didn't just choose someone to be "it." "Everybody has the same chance," or "It's more democratic," they told him. Watching the children, however, Goldstein noticed that many of them manipulated the rhymes so that "it" wasn't the result of chance, as suggested in the interviews, but was often carefully prefigured by the child doing the counting out.

These children live in a democracy and have been taught early that fairness and equality are key values. Having learned this they give the adult questioning them the expected answer and perhaps believe it themselves. But in fact when they are at play, they also cheat. Through their play, both a belief in democracy and a knowledge that it is open to manipulation are being taught and reinforced. (Not that the world of children is simply the adult world writ small. Jay Mechling writes, " . . . the folklorist does not view children as merely unsocialized adults whose main goal is to acquire adult worldview. Rather, the folklorist takes an approach that views children's folk cultures as if they were fully complex, developed, and autonomous" (1986, 93). For that matter, the same holds true for any folk groups.)

Folklore instructs and entertains, but it also does much more. Roger Abrahams warns that to see folklore

> . . . only from [an] instructive perspective . . . is to reduce such verbal formulations to the category of "kernels of wisdom," or worse, to clichés. However, on those occasions on which such playful forms as riddles, parodies, lampoons, jokes, and jibes are performed, the world view of the group may be given voice and tested—even turned upside down (1980, 371).

Abrahams goes on to observe that while "the study of the folklore of a group opens the possibility of revealing the deepest feelings of its members at the same time it may address their ways of . . . testing the boundaries of the community from within" (371). In other words, folklore validates culture, but it can also violate cultural norms, providing an avenue to break the rules, literally and symbolically. William Bascom called this the "basic paradox of folklore" (349).

The tricksters of folktales and jokes are symbolic rule breakers. Coyote in American Indian tradition, Anansi in African tradition, Brer Rabbit in Afro-American tradition, the Hodja in the Middle East, Yankee Doodle, even Popeye—all are tricksters. They are bad, unapprovable, yet more often than not they go without censure or punishment. Young children have a natural affinity for tricksters. In first and second grade they sing:

> I'm Popeye the Sailor Man,
> I live in a garbage can,
> I eat all the worms
> And spit out the germs,
> Cause I'm Popeye the Sailor Man,
> Toot, toot!

Popeye lives out their fantasies. He lives the way he wants to; no one tells him to clean up or what he must eat to stay healthy. And he can perform a miracle—eating worms and spitting out germs. This is Popeye's "cleanest" exploit; in other rhymes he goes on to have many explicit scatological and erotic adventures—even in second-grade lore.

Some folklore even affords the opportunity to perform a minor act of violence under its protection. One fifth grader, for instance, goes up to another and says, "I'll trade you a what for a slap." The second child doesn't understand, so she falls into the trap and says, "What?" asking for clarification, and gets slapped. The victim has no recourse because it is a joke. Normally her friend couldn't slap her but within the framework of the joke, she can get away with it as a trickster. In middle school and high school, too, folklore is an avenue for breaking rules: TPing (toilet papering) houses, playing Spin the Bottle and Post Office, and pulling off "senior pranks."

But, more often, folklore makes it possible to act out against social constraints symbolically. To tell a joke is to be a trickster. When a teenager tells a "sick" joke in which a mother kills a child, the teller is among other things symbolically rebelling against cultural taboos. Catastrophes have for some time been classic opportunities for mocking society.

Today catastrophes occasion joke cycles in which the sacrosanct is symbolically attacked. After the shuttle Challenger exploded, a joke cycle appeared. The astronauts, one target of the jokes, were symbols of National Aeronautics and Space Administration or NASA, itself a symbol of American global leadership. When teenagers and others told jokes like this:

> What was going on in the shuttle right before it blew up?
> The crew was freebasing Tang.[12]

two American symbols were being ridiculed. Tang, a health drink developed for use in space, is likened to dope. The astronauts, symbols of "the right stuff," of clean-living middle America, are portrayed as taking dope.[13]

While the symbolism in jokes, as in the example just given, may seem blatant to adults, students often don't recognize it until it is brought to their attention. Subtler symbolism, too, can be seen in the jokes about Christa McAuliffe, the teacher who died in the Challenger explosion. McAuliffe, a woman and a teacher, is a symbol of both; jokes about her can be interpreted as anti-teacher (or anti-school and anti-intellectual) and anti-female. In the jokes, she asks "dumb female" type questions, as in this one, reminiscent of the old moron jokes:

> What were Christa McAuliffe's last words?
> "What's this button for?"

She is also unable to learn:

> I can't believe it. Seven months of training, and she still went to pieces after takeoff.

There is the implication in the next joke that teachers are ignorant.

> How do you get rid of a teacher?
> Challenge her.

The point here is that folklore is a way to let off steam about cultural constraints. The Challenger cycle was primarily a way to relieve anxiety about the disaster. But a look at the symbolism in the motifs reveals that the cycle was equally a vehicle to deprecate American leadership, teachers, and women. The folklore of jokes allows us to act out against the very rules or values that are learned through the same medium. Hence, Bascom's paradox.

This cultural rule-breaking function is closely tied to a fourth function: offering relief from troubling matters. Freud observed in his work on humor that we tell jokes to deal with or address troubling matters. Joking belittles or ridicules the problem, and laughter defuses, at least temporarily, our concern or distress. As an example, by fourth grade a male concern has to do with homosexuality, and it is at about this age that boys begin using this joke: One says to another, "Stick out your tongue." The second complies. Then the first delivers the punch line: "Stick it back in when you think you're a fag!"

This short trick exemplifies the condensed nature of folklore; a lot happens in the four or five seconds it takes for this joke to be played out. Cultural bias against homosexuality is expressed, rules are broken, the taboo term *fag* comes into play, and the jokester accuses his victim of being a homosexual. Since both boys laugh, their fears of homosexuality are defused for the moment. The joke is both positively and negatively functional. It's healthy to joke about problems, to reduce them to manageable size. At the same time, the joke reflects and teaches a destructive bias. And this is just the beginning of understanding its function. A fuller analysis would take into account context, performance, and would also include commentary from the folk themselves. If, for instance, these boys don't know what a "fag" is, the folklorist then has to rethink the interpretation. On the surface, this joke reflects a fleeting moment in childhood; a deeper look reveals a clever and complex event.

Here is another example. On a visit to Chelsea Hospital, a retirement home for soldiers in London, our guide was an elderly pensioner. During the tour he talked about "the old boys" and how they were always dying. Then he told this joke:

> A man goes to a fortune teller and asks, "I want to know if I'm going to heaven." The fortune teller answers, "I have good news and bad news for you. The good news is that you are going to heaven. The bad news is that you are going at 2:30."

The pensioner had a good laugh at his own joke, at death itself. Death is a common occurrence at the Chelsea Hospital, and joking about its imminence helps. This would be a good enough joke in many other settings, but the context makes it both poignant and powerful.

Finally, folklore makes a group feel like a group; it bonds people, be they families or children at summer camp. One student, analyzing her memories of playing Spin the Bottle, noted ways in which the game promoted physical and social closeness, allowing her to kiss a boy she liked and helping shy persons by giving them the courage to kiss someone. She concludes, "Spin the Bottle can bring any group to feel close together, even if it is only during the time the game is being played."[14]

Bronislaw Malinowski called folklore "a mirror of culture." As such, it reflects all aspects of culture, the full spectrum of humanity—its wit, wisdom, and beauty as well as its grim and disturbing side.

Studying Folklore: Identification, Collection, Analysis

Studying folklore involves three steps: identification, collection, and analysis. In this book, students go through a similar process, but with modifications. One difference is that collection begins with the student's own experience. If the area of study is, say, teenage folk-lore, students begin by listing all the teenage folklore in their lives: dating rituals, legends about teachers, the groups in high school from the preppies to the jocks, etc.

Next, students choose individual topics and begin to collect. For some topics, the collecting of data is limited to personal experience. For a professional folklorist, this would be far too limiting, but it works in middle and high school grades where the purpose of study-ing folklore isn't to turn students into folklorists but to help them "visualize folklore, [and] come to appreciate its qualities and some of its implications" (Dorson and Carpenter 1978, 8). For other topics, the students look beyond themselves, collecting other versions or gathering more information through interviews of family members, friends, peers, or strangers. At all times, context and performance, remembered or observed, are as important as the lore itself.

The collecting dealt with in this book is quite basic, usually a matter of interviewing or observing. (Interviewing is discussed in some detail in chapter 4.) A pamphlet, *Folklife and Fieldwork*, avail-able through the American Folklife Center of the Library of Congress, Washington, DC, 20540, is a useful guide to collecting. For more information, there is "How to Collect Your Own Family Folklore," a chapter in Steven Zeitlin, Amy Kotkin, and Holly Cutting Baker's *A Celebration of American Family Folklore* (1982).

After collection comes analysis. Analysis is a challenge. It is here that students begin to see the value and function of folklore, and more importantly, begin to be convinced that their lives are indeed worth studying. The student who wrote of Spin the Bottle, for exam-ple, had not considered events in her own life to be culturally signifi-cant. But once the idea was planted she did a good job demonstrating that her own experience—and in this case her only data was her nar-rative—figured in an important American ritual. A high school junior, she first described the event:

> The bottle turned and spinned, slower and slower, until the end stopped, pointed at me. My heart started to beat faster and faster, as I looked up and saw him coming closer to me. Then he kissed me, the cutest guy in camp kissed me on the lips. Smiling a smile from ear to ear, I thought, "God, it's my turn to spin the bottle."

She began her analysis with the entertainment value of the game. "It is interesting to watch everybody's expression as the bottle spins around on the ground," she wrote. When it stops, there are "sighs of relief and disappointment." Next she looked at the ways the game violated social codes. "A kissing game is wrong in the eyes of society," she observed. "Usually a game like this is kept a secret from adults and is played somewhere isolated" because it allows teenagers to "kiss at an inappropriate age."

Studying Spin the Bottle, the student realized why she had been attracted to and felt guilty about playing the game. She also appreciated how clever the folk, her peers, have been to invent a game that permits them to experiment with kissing in a safe environment; lots of other kids are around—things won't get out of hand.[15] From her own experience Kerri wrote a paper full of insights into contemporary American youth culture.

When students interview parents and grandparents, their analysis becomes more complex. They can, for instance, document continuities and changes, a mandate in the study of folklore. One example of the latter in American culture can be seen in this 1920s jump rope rhyme about Cinderella, a condensed version of the classic fairy tale:

> Cinderella, dressed in yellow,
> Went downtown to get a fellow.
> How many kisses did she get?
> 1, 2, 3, 4. . . .

Cinderella, a symbol of female adolescence, with whom the jumpers identify, goes out to find a man, her "fellow," the symbolic Prince Charming. We assume from the rhyme that her quest has been successful and that they live happily ever after.

By the 1940s the rhyme had changed significantly:

> Cinderella, dressed in yellow,
> Went downtown to get a fellow,
> On the way her girdle busted.
> How many people were disgusted,
> 1, 2, 3, 4. . . .

Cinderella is still looking for Prince Charming, but now there are pitfalls. Because of her vanity (symbolized by the girdle) Cinderella has perhaps lost her chance to get the prince. The folk have begun to make fun of the tale, a classic metaphor for courtship and marriage.

By the 1970s the rhyme had changed again:

> Cinderella, dressed in yellow,
> Went downtown to kiss a fellow,
> Made a mistake and kissed a snake.
> How many doctors did it take?
> 1, 2, 3, 4,. . . .

More change, some continuity. Cinderella is still out looking for the Prince but instead encounters a snake. In western tradition, the snake is variously a symbol of danger, wisdom, masculinity, and death.

Since in this rhyme he replaces Prince Charming and deceives Cinderella, we can assume that he is male and dangerous. He radically alters the rhyme. In high school classes students often interpret the doctor as performing an abortion or delivering a baby.

Whatever the interpretation, the contemporary Cinderella is living in changing sexual times. The jump rope rhyme is no longer a modern version of the fairy tale; now it's a cautionary chant. Again, this interpretation lacks context. A fuller analysis requires observations of and interviews with young girls chanting the rhyme. It's likely children would interpret the rhyme literally, believing that Cinderella was bitten by a snake and needed a doctor.

Conclusion

For each topic presented in this book, students follow the route of the professional folklorist: they identify their topic, collect and observe, then analyze what they have found. Along the way they are learning something about analysis in the social sciences and literature, since folklore in America has its roots in both. Furthermore, the folklore they are studying cuts across all disciplines. Oral tradition influences how and what is thought and taught in all their classes. Folklore, as Alan Dundes reminds his students, is the one course on campus that touches on all the others they take.

After a workshop on folklore and writing, one teacher wrote:

> This was about us, and I saw us differently. We forget that we're making traditions now, and our everyday lives are as rich as the Greeks!

Modern folklore is about the students, which is why students like it. That is the beginning. But soon enough the study of folklore helps them see beyond themselves, to understand their roles and significance as members of their culture and their country.

Notes

1. A similar short introduction to folklore useful for students is "Identifying Folklore," the foreword to Richard Dorson's America in Legend: Folklore from the Colonial Period to the Present (New York: Pantheon, 1973), pp. xiii–xv.

2. The terms myth, folktale and legend have specific meanings to folklorists, in some ways different from popular usage. The narratives that folklorists call myths are those which tell of the world up to and including the creation of man and the world as we know them today. These narratives are

usually believed to be true by the people who tell them in traditional settings. Legends are narratives that take place after creation and in the real world. They are also usually believed as true stories by the tellers and listeners. Folktales, which begin with a frame like "Once upon a time. . . . " are understood as fiction. Legend is the narrative form told most often in the United States today. Legends and a subgenre, the memorate or personal narrative, are the narrative forms that dominate the chapters of this book. (These definitions are derived from William Bascom in "The Forms of Folklore: Prose Narratives," *Journal of American Folklore* 78 (1965), pp. 3–20, and refined by Alan Dundes.)

3. Since these narratives take place in the present and are generally accepted as true by the tellers and the listeners, a folklorist would classify them as modern urban legends, not as fairy tales or myths.

4. In folklore, the words version and variant have specialized meanings. When the changes from item to item are slight, they are considered different versions of the same item. A version that is substantially different, although recognizably related, is called a variant.

5. The singer spells his name Richie. Jenny Eskey, a student at the University of California, Berkeley, reported this legend in 1985 to Stephen R. Whyte. She said the story supposedly happened to a friend of the woman who told it to her. Berkeley Folklore Archives.

6. Alan Dundes and Carl Pagter, *Work Hard and You Shall Be Rewarded: Urban Folklore from the Paperwork Empire* (Bloomington: Indiana University Press, 1978) and *When You're Up to Your Ass in Alligators: More Urban Folklore from the Paperwork Empire* (Detroit: Wayne State University Press, 1987).

7. "Performance" here includes ordinary events of daily life such as a mother passing down a family recipe to her daughter, to large-scale cultural events such as festivals, to the performance of a folk artist crafting a statue or telling a story.

8. Alan Dundes looks at the folklore sources of King Lear, in "'To Love My Father All': A Psychoanalytic Study of the Folktale Source of King Lear," in Alan Dundes, *Interpreting Folklore* (Bloomington: Indiana University Press, 1980), pp. 211–22.

9. Since the early part of the century, a common urban legend tells of the discovery of a decomposed mouse (or cigarette butt, etc.) found at the bottom of a soft drink, often Coca-Cola. In "Cokelore and Coke Law: Urban Belief Tales and the Problem of Multiple Origins," *Journal of American Folklore* 92 (1979), pp. 477–82, Gary Alan Fine documents many court cases showing that foreign matter is often found in soft drinks. These events are probably the sources of the legends.

10. Told by Mary Duffey, age sixteen, to Carolyn Duffey in 1969. Berkeley Folklore Archives.

11. Proverbs are a genre not studied in this book. But students can collect proverbs from oral tradition, such as "What goes around, comes around," and "Different strokes for different folks." Also, in literature, for example,

Tom Sawyer's Aunt Polly thinks in proverbs " . . . old fools is the biggest fools there is. Cain't learn any old dog new tricks, as the saying is . . . Spare the rod and spile the child." (Mark Twain, *The Adventures of Tom Sawyer* (Harmondsworth, England: Puffin, 1974, p. 8). Although proverbs sound like folk knowledge, students soon notice that they can be contradictory. "Absence makes the heart grow fonder," sounds like a bit of collective wisdom, until you consider, "Out of sight, out of mind."

12. For analyses of the *Challenger* joke cycle see, Willie Smith, "Challenger Jokes and the Humor of Disaster," and Elizabeth Radin Simons, "The NASA Joke Cycle: The Astronauts and the Teacher, both in *Western Folklore* 45 (1986), pp. 243–77, and Elliott Oring, "Jokes and the Discourse on Disaster," *Journal of American Folklore* 100 (1987), pp. 276–86.

13. This joke may refer to the death of the popular singer Ricky Nelson, another aviation disaster that occurred around the time of the Challenger explosion. It was conjectured at the time that a fire in Nelson's plane that caused the disaster started when he and others were freebasing cocaine.

14. From a paper written by Kerri Hernandez.

15. Other students, however, pointed out that a slight alteration of the rules can radically change this. For instance, as one reported, the couple can be required to go into a closet and stay there for five minutes.

Chapter Two

Teaching Writing While Teaching Folklore

At the close of the semester, I often ask students to write in their learning logs their thoughts about what they have learned during the term. Arturo wrote:

> The most important . . . thing to me was the way we wrote a paper. To do it, we wrote our paper and then went over it once and again. Finally we wrote our last draft. I liked best the way our papers turned out after we had written them over. It made me feel good to do something to the best of my knowledge.

Arturo, a senior in an inner-city school, began the year uninterested in writing and often truant. During the semester, though, he and his classmates changed. The change was, I believe, a result of the combining of a content of interest to him (his folklore) and a pedagogy based on a process approach to the teaching of writing. This chapter offers an overview of how writing is integrated with the units described in this book. The first section deals with prewriting, drafting, responding, revising, editing, proofreading, and publishing, all stages of what has come to be generally labeled "the writing process." (For early and still excellent introductions to the theory behind the process approach to teaching writing, see Britton, Burgess, Martin, McLeod, and Martin, *The Development of Writing Abilities (11–18)* (1975). And for both the theory and practice see Moffett and Wagner, *Student-Centered Language Arts and Reading, K–13: A Handbook for Teachers* (1983).

Since the notion of writing as a process was new to the students in the classrooms described in this book, I wrote these terms on the chalkboard and briefly introduced them to the ideas presented in this chapter. When the stages are written across the top of the chalkboard, they appear to be clear-cut, predictably linear. The reality is different: stages overlap, the process is recursive and seldom the same from writer to writer. Throughout the term, students reflected on the complexity of writing in general and on their individual processes.

The second section of this chapter is a discussion of peer response groups, and the third details learning logs, a type of journal in which students learn, among other things, the connections between writing and learning.

Prewriting

Prewriting is any activity that precedes drafting. Prewriting can help students find topics. Once that happens, other aspects of prewriting can be brought to bear to help students in gathering information. Prewriting encompasses a wide range of activities from drawing to field trips to role playing. Here, only those prewriting activities used in this book—brainstorming, clustering, gathering information, interviewing, listing, and talking—are described.

The first type of prewriting, that which aids in selecting a topic, is critical; students typically need to explore possibilities to find an idea, an issue, or a subject they genuinely wish to pursue. If they don't, the writing will probably be forced, flat, lacking any genuine engagement with the subject; in short, "school writing." Because the units in this book are based on students' memories and experiences, brainstorming (nonlinear tumbling out of ideas and information on a topic) is a useful way to start. A subject, let's say children's folklore, is written in the center of the chalkboard, and students call out their associations. Their words are randomly jotted on the chalkboard. This initial brainstorming is when students often find their topics. (See Figure 12–1 in chapter 12 for a sample whole-class brainstorm on graffiti.)

Once students have chosen topics, they often like to do a kind of private brainstorming or clustering as a preparation for writing. A cluster is less random than brainstorming; it's where related items can be tied together. In Figure 2–1, Keith clustered his memories about telephone pranks.

In his cluster, Keith brainstorms a thought and then develops it. Note that the lower right cluster begins "fear of getting caught," which apparently sparks a string of associations: "your mom finding out," "people tracing the call," "praying to God you don't call anyone you know," and ending "call the same person over and over till they

Figure 2-1
Keith's Cluster of Telephone Pranks

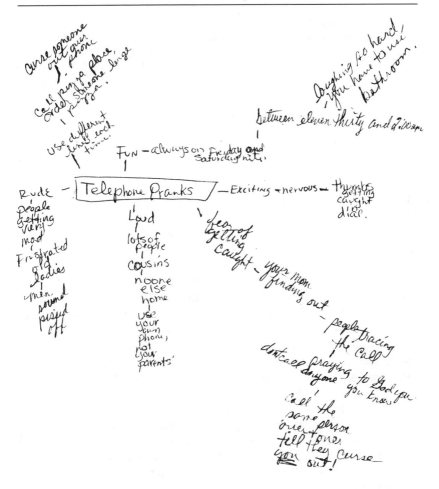

curse *you* out!" At first Keith is apprehensive, afraid his mother or
his victim will catch him. Then he becomes fearful of unconsciously
calling someone he knows and entrapping himself. Finally, he
reveals the thrill of pushing his victims too far: "call the same person
over & over til they curse *you* out!" (See Rico [1983] and Buckley and
Boyle [1981], for more information on brainstorming and clustering.)

In chapter 7 on family photography, students prewrote to choose
topics and to find ways into their writing once the topics—which
were to come from family photographs—were selected. They began
by going home and looking at photos. Some students did this alone;

others consulted with family members. Some knew immediately which picture they wanted to write about; others couldn't decide and brought in several. Those with more than one photo sought advice from friends in class, trying to decide which one to use.

Once students chose their photo, they were ready to prewrite again, this time to prepare for writing. First, the students studied their pictures for a few minutes, then listed all the words that came to mind.

After looking at the posed photograph of himself and his two brothers (see Figure 2–2), Ramiro wrote:

> Jalostotitlan
> Henry
> Ruben
> fresh hair cuts
> same style shirts/different patterns
> posing
> my little brother held a toy

Next, to elicit more associations and recollections, students discussed their photos and lists with classmates. Some students will end up describing the event in the photo or the photo itself; others will use it as a means of access to something beyond the picture itself, a catalyst for something else, perhaps a family story about someone in it. Ramiro's partner told him that he liked the phrase "fresh haircuts." And he wondered about the shirts: Why were they the same style but different patterns? Ramiro explained that his mother had bought the shirts for the occasion. They speculated that maybe the shirts showed how his mother thought of her sons, as brothers and members of the same family and therefore the same, but also as individuals. Before committing himself to paper, Ramiro had spent quite a bit of time on prewriting. It was time well spent. When he began to write, he knew that he had an interesting photograph and some good ideas.

The benefits of not rushing through prewriting are many:

1. Whole-class prewriting activities start projects off with a spirit of good will. The activities are fun, ungraded, and anyone can succeed at them.
2. It is during prewriting that students choose their topics. If they don't find a topic that connects with a real interest, they won't write well.
3. Success at the prewriting stage can help students gain confidence in their potential as writers.

Figure 2-2
Henry, Ruben, and Ramiro

Drafting

Drafting is tentative, exploratory writing, done for oneself or a trusted, familiar audience. It can be messy, boring, riddled with errors, for drafting is just a beginning, a place for writers to work their way into topics, to find out what they know and have to say, and to come up with questions.

Britton et al. (1975) call drafting "expressive" writing. Britton identifies it as the source or starting point, no matter what the final form of the writing will be. Learning about drafting, what it is and how it functions, often dispels student gloom about and resistance to writing. It also helps good writers become better ones. It truly gives students a boost.

My instructions to students about how to write drafts are adapted from Ken Macrorie's *Telling Writing* (1970). I ask them to write about anything that comes to mind about the topic, not to worry about sequence or form, to let ideas flow and feed freely into one another. Nor should they concern themselves about spelling, mechanical mistakes, or handwriting at this point. The draft won't be graded; it will get a response solely on the basis of the ideas and content. The only requirement is that it be legible. Most students are willing to give drafting a try. For those still resistant, I add, "If you hate the idea or are uncomfortable with it, it's fine to say so. You may write, 'I hate this topic, I have nothing to say'; the only rule is that you have to keep writing." Macrorie adds, "If what you write is bad or dull, no one will object." Another tip is to limit drafting time at first to five or ten minutes.

In an inner-city class about to start the study of children's folk-lore, Louis wrote a draft about shooting craps. His draft is fairly typical: it's relaxed enough to contain some humor and is a mix of reasonably okay writing and some confusing passages.

> Shooting craps is a game of luck and cheating. If you cheat good enough you don't need luck. First you need players, dice and money. The first man makes a certain number and in order to win you match your number. When people win they become happy, if you get that lucky, but when they lose, (crap) they get mad and sometimes fight. But there are dangers, if someone sees you playing, they might tell your parents. Once your parents find out, your dice throwing hand will be broken. Oh yeah, if you roll a one or a seven you crap. [Mechanical errors have been corrected in this draft.]

What's the value of this draft? First, Louis was a good talker but not much of a writer. His writing in school tended to be stilted, some-what voiceless prose. Drafting, where he knew he wouldn't be graded and where he could thus relax into colloquial language, allowed him to tap his oral skills and capture them in writing. It also helped him find a topic.

Like Louis, many students have never been taught to draft; they don't know it as an important stage in writing. Once they become comfortable with it, they learn that:

1. Drafting helps overcome starting problems.
2. It generates ideas, sometimes of the kind the writer had no ink-ling of when he or she began.
3. It's a chance to capitalize on oral language skills, since expres-sive writing is that closest to speech.
4. First drafts usually contain good writing that can be used in later stages of composing.

Responding

A response is a reaction to a draft. Receiving responses to their own writing and responding to the writing of others, young writers learn firsthand one major reason writers write—to communicate. When students write often and get responses to their writing, some, often much, of the writing will be enjoyed and appreciated by their readers. The students begin to understand the pleasures of writing and why people write. Also, by learning how to give, take, and act on response, students become better writers.

Many students have been trained to think first of form, to believe that the primary criterion for good writing is correctness. To help them see that content is preeminent, that it is served by form, the first responses are exclusively to content. Mechanics should be dealt with later. A response sequence used by many teachers starts with positive commentary on what is good and promising in the draft, follows with questions to clarify, amplify, and shape drafts and ends with a discussion of the purpose and the main idea of the writing.

Responding: Positive Commentary

Often students aren't sure they have anything to say in writing that anyone would care to read. Their self-images as writers begin to change when they are taught to look first for what is good in their work. Therefore, the golden rule of responding is to begin with something positive. Usually, it works like this. We all write drafts. Then I read mine to the class and ask the students to comment on what they like. From their observations, we make a list:

- a good idea
- a good incident
- humor
- a good choice of word(s)
- good description
- a good beginning or ending
- an interesting character

This activity has several purposes: first, by emphasizing what is good in their writing, it builds student self-confidence; second, it teaches students to look first at content, at what the writer is trying to communicate; and third, by identifying the good parts of their own work, students learn characteristics of good writing. Finally, the activity serves another purpose, which Anne Barrows, a writer and an instructor at the University of San Francisco, pointed out to me: it shows students how to receive praise for their writing. Compliments about their writing can make students, especially those with a low opinion of their writing, very uncomfortable.

There is a corollary to the rule of beginning with positive response; the response must be specific. Without specificity, the praise tends to be limited to phrases such as "It was wonderful" and "That's great!" While compliments like these may make students feel more confident, they don't help them identify what is good in their writing. When students praise each other, then, they are encouraged to give specific feedback. For example, in a class studying the folklore of family photographs, Miguel was praised for the humor of his opening sentence, "Posing for pictures is one of my better qualities." And Olga was commended for the poetic closing of the story of her visit to Mexico, where she spent a day with Tacho, her cousin: "After dinner Tacho and I went to sit on the door steps to receive the warm air of the night." Such positive reactions help students begin to think of themselves as writers, identify good writing, and concentrate on content.

Responding: Asking Questions

Questioning, the next step in responding, helps students begin to understand the needs of the reader. Although I think of questions as a second stage in response, during the time we are concentrating on positive response, students generate questions spontaneously. I model questions of two types: (1) those asking for more information, and (2) those asking for clarification of confusing text. Again, this is first done as a whole-class activity. I read a draft—mine or someone else's—and we pinpoint the areas we want to know more about and the parts of the writing that are ambiguous. (See chapter 7, pages 129–31, for an example of a class questioning a teacher's draft.) After the class responds with praise and questions a few times, students do it on their own in small groups. (See pages 56–57 for a brief overview of peer response groups.)

Responding: Main Idea

Now the focus shifts to the purpose of the writing. Again, we start with a whole-class activity. I read a draft and ask the students what they think the main idea or ideas are. We compare their responses with the author's and pinpoint the discrepancies, looking for clues in the writing to account for different impressions. Two important issues are raised. One is audience: How do readers interpret writing? The other is author responsibility: What does the author think he or she is writing about?

In one class, we began with Julieta's memory of playing marbles when she was little:

Marbles

I was living in Mexico. I remember I was about 5 or 6 years old. I used to take a bag of marbles because I like to play marbles in my free time at school. My mother was always getting mad with me because I played marbles. I used to hide my bag of marbles in my lunch bag. My mother was always getting mad because I was always getting all dirty.

At school I used to play with boys because my girl friends didn't like to play marbles. They used to go and play at the swings. They used to say, "Julieta you look like a boy." I didn't lisent to them. I keeped on playing. I used to be a good player.

I remember one day, it was Sunday. My mother told me not to go outside to play marbles because I was going to get my new white dress dirty to go to church. I didn't lisent to my mother. I went outside and told the guys to play. My friends name are Pedro and Juan. They were about my age. I like to play with them because I always win them. They used to get mad because I was always the winner. Juan and Pedro said, "We can't play right now because we are going to go to church," and I said, "come on are you chickens to play with the pro?" They got mad and started playing. First we made a circle with a stick, then we put a lot of marbles inside the circle. Each one of us had about 5 marbles. If we shot and hit the marble inside and it comes out of the circle that marble is his. Whoever got more marbles was the winer and when someone didn't have any marbles left to shot he was out of the game. We use to have small marbles and big ones. They were different colors like black and brown. Some had three colores. We didn't win nothing just the marbles. I used to sell my marbles to other friends because I needed money to buy candies. Pedro said, "Julieta you be first" and I said "Why me.' He said because the first one always get bad luck." I said, "that is not true." I lose my first turn. I was mad. They started laughing but I was winning when my mother came outside and said "Julieta look at you, you are all dirty. Go inside the house and take a bath right now." She was mad. I thought she was going to hit me but she didn't. The only thing she did was to hide all my marbles where I wouldn't find them. When I was all clean and dress I was looking for my marbles. I couldn't find them. My mom told me she has hidden the marbles away because I didn't lisent to her and because I was not a boy to be playing with marbles. I started crying because that was the only game I played.

The class found much to praise in Julieta's draft. Then the members of the class wrote on response sheets their understanding of the main idea. The girls tended to agree with Rosie, who wrote:

The main idea is that she didn't care what people told her about playing marbles because only boys would play that game. She did what she was good at.

Julieta, the author, agreed, but she added a second theme—disobeying parents. She wrote:

> I think the main idea was to show that not only boys can play marbles . . . girls can play too. Not lisenting to your parents.

Lupe interpreted the draft exclusively in terms of Julieta's secondary theme:

> The main idea of Julieta's paper is playing marbles behind her mother's back.

The boys, by contrast, never mentioned that marbles was a boys' game. For them, the focus of the piece was on Julieta steadfastly playing marbles. Arturo wrote:

> The main idea of Julieta's game as a child is that if you like to do something you'll do it no matter what.

Ramiro agreed:

> Looks like she would do anything to keep playing marbles.

Julieta was pleased with the results. The girls understood what she was writing about, and the boys were on the right track, although their perceptions seemed to be colored by their sex.

Responding: Student/Teacher Conferences

Not all response is from peers. For writing that will go to a final draft (roughly one out of six first drafts will be polished into a final draft), students have a conference with me. It is my impression that, for most students, a conference has more effect on their writing than my written comments, and conferences take less time.

Responding: Some Concluding Thoughts

Response is critical for young writers. It is through praise received for their writing that students begin to feel like writers. When they look for what is good in each other's writing, they are learning the characteristics of good writing. In their peer groups, students are learning to talk about writing, which will in turn improve their writing.

Marian Mohr, who has made a study of her students' written reflections on their own writing, found that students lacked confidence in the pivotal skills of giving and receiving comments. One reason is that they lack experience and strategies for thinking about writing, but equally important is how they feel when others discuss their writing. Mohr has some excellent advice: "When you are giving comments, keep in mind how you feel when others comment on your writing. Listen for feelings" (1984, 117). The manner and content of the responses in the classroom set the tone for the classroom community.

Revising

Response is preparation for revision. In responding to writing, students learn to reperceive their work through the eyes of another and thus to reconsider their drafts. As a prelude to revision, the whole class responds to a draft and then talks about how the writing could be revised, keeping a list of the suggestions. Typically a list looks like this:

1. Add dialogue.
2. Add new information.
3. Add description.
4. Delete some text.
5. Rearrange some text.
6. Start in a different place. (Students and myself, too, often write our way into a piece, sloughing off the original paragraphs.)
7. Change the focus or point of view.
8. Change the form, for instance, from a narrative to a play.

Students then experiment with their first revisions. In the beginning, revision can be tentative; acting on suggestions, students add a few words or a sentence. As students gradually begin to internalize the concept of revision, their changes become more complex and global. An example of revision by Arturo, a senior in an inner-city school, follows.

Arturo's class was studying the folklore of family photographs. He had chosen to write about a cherished photo of himself from the sports section of a local newspaper. It is a dramatic photo; Arturo, high in the air, has just kicked the ball. His first draft was short (see Figure 2–3) and was written late in the term when Arturo knew that first drafts could be messy. (Arturo's draft also shows the recursive nature of writing. He is revising as he writes his draft, crossing out false starts and correcting grammar. He first starts to write "Falcon" with a small *f* and corrects the placement of the word *jumped* but in the process misspells it as *jupped*.) Arturo's response group found the game and the false call by the referee of interest and encouraged

Figure 2-3
Arturo's First Draft

I remember that it was the championship game. We too lost, but we were cheated, I have never said I never like give excuses when it comes to playing soccer, but if we loose, o.k. we lost, but in this game which we played Piedmont high we were cheated. We were cheated by an oficial or Referee, when the ball up kicked by José Quintero a former Italian passed the goal line. This counts as a goal (1 point), but it didn't. It was doubting because the ball when went over the goal line slowly and as this happened the goaly jumped (their golie) jupped on the ball and pulled it back towards himself F out of the goal fox.

him to revise. They also had four questions for him, which he wrote down like this:

- What was I thinking?
- Who was winning?
- Where was this game played at?
- Was the game hard?

As Figure 2–4 (see pp. 48–49) shows, Arturo's revision benefitted from the response he got. He now believes that this is a story worth telling. Compare the weak opening line of the first draft, "I remember that it was the championship game," with the confident opening of the revision, "'We were cheated,' were the only words I could hear after our soccer game for the championship against Piedmont High School." His group asked him what he was thinking, and he tells them. During the bus ride to the game, he plans the game as if he were the coach. He has thought about the formations, the team strategy, and feels that his ideas are better than the coach's. However, he keeps his own counsel. Arturo also takes the other questions to heart and answers all of them in his revision. He gives a bit more setting by telling where the game was played; he includes the score as it develops; he shows it was a tough game and that he was giving it his best.

Revision is hard work, and at first students balk. However, when they've done it often enough to see that it works, that they can improve their writing through drafts, they begin to appreciate its value.

Editing

When they edit, students shift their focus from content to style. Although the editing stage is devoted specifically to style, it is not the first mention of style. During responding, it is often style that students single out for praise. But for a more global look, I like to put student writing on the overhead and have the class identify aspects of style such as sentence structure, paragraphing, similes, metaphors, and parallel construction. Students play with changing and improving style.

Here is the revised but unedited opening for Martin's teenage folklore paper.

Substitute

One day I walked into my American Government class. Suddenly, I saw a paperball zoom a few inches away from my nose. Immediately, I knew we had a sub. Then I tried walking to my chair when a little wet ball of paper struck me in my cheek. Disgusted, I took it off. I managed to servive the trip to my desk without any other flying objects hitting me. I saw the sub, she was an old lady in her 60's with glasses that looked like binoculars.

The teacher began taking role, paper planes started swarming through the air, guys were slam dunking paperballs into the garbage can, some were asking the old lady, "Where's the beef?". . . .

We start with the stylistic strengths. In the first paragraph, the students like the image of the spitball zooming a few inches from Martin's nose and sticking to his cheek. They like "the flying object" as the metaphor for the spitball or paperball. They like the simile of the old lady's glasses looking like binoculars. The opening sentence of his second paragraph has effective parallel construction and strong verbs: the planes "swarming" through the air, the guys "slam dunking" the paperballs.

Martin's introductory paragraph is good, but I suggest some stylistic changes and have the class debate whether or not they improve the writing. To me the opening sentence does not do justice to the whole piece. I'd like it to be stronger. "What about dropping

Figure 2-4
Arturo's Revision (Part 1)

"We were cheated," ~~was~~ were the ~~only~~ words I could hear after our soccer game for the championship ~~is~~ against Piedmont. The game was played at ~~Berkley~~ Berkeley High school. On our way over ~~it~~ I was thinking of the way that we were going to play against their formation. I didn't like our formation that we were going to use but I wasn't the coach. I've always liked the offensive formation or the counterattack formation, but never the defensive formation. I knew this wasn't going to work, but I kept it to my self. Butterflies were in my stomach till we got there.

¶ Finally the game started, ~~Usually I'm~~ I was dropped back to defend ~~which~~ wich I didn't like. ~~The~~ Piedmont was always on the attack and had us pinned to the wall. First half ended with the score tied 1-1. Our coach noticing the mistake he had done tried to fix it, but it was to late, because they knew

Figure 2-4
Arturo's Revision (Part 2)

that we were going to chage our founation. Second half started, after 15 minutes of playing they scored for the second time and the score was now 2-1 in favor of Piedmont. We didnt give up, we tried and tried to score. Our chance didnt come till about 5 minutes before the game ended, when José Quintero, a former Falcon, took a shot from about 30 yards out. The ball was kicked so hard that it slipped out of Piedmonts golie hands and slowly went over the goal line. If tthe ball goes over the goal line, it counts for one point. As soon as we saw this we jumped with joy, but the referee said that it was'nt a goal. We all argued so much that we were about to be thrown out of the game. Everyone said it was a goal even some of Piedmonts players after the game, but the referee didn't think so. In this photo of me, I had kicked the ball to my teamates, It shows how tired and nervous I was. I think we played good in this game, but cheated by the the referee.

the original opening sentence and starting with the second sentence?" I ask. The class argues. Some feel that the setting would suffer; others suggest alternative openings. They continue through the piece, making suggestions and judging the effects. A class-edited version of the first paragraph might look like this:

> A paperball zoomed a few inches away from my nose. Immediately I knew we had a sub. I tried walking to my chair when a little wet ball of paper struck me in the cheek. Disgusted, I took it off. I managed to survive the trip to my desk without any other flying objects hitting me. Then I spotted the sub, an old lady in her 60s with glasses that looked like binoculars.

Martin, as the author, was free to accept or reject any suggestions.

Although I try to keep editing and proofreading separate in my mind, students naturally edit and proofread all along. When they revise, for example, students reread drafts, catching usage and syntax errors along the way.

A major source of appreciation for all aspects of writing, including style, comes from reading. I encourage the students to bring in whatever they are reading for pleasure, and I do too. We look at it all, from teenage romance to the local sports columnist, for content and style, and we study it as we do our own writing. A serious interest in style seems to develop after students have been writing for a while, have published a few times, and have become more sophisticated readers.

Proofreading

Sometimes when students are getting ready to publish, I read their drafts and underline grammatical errors. The students figure out what is wrong; I encourage them to ask friends and family for help. The burden for this method, however, is on the teacher. A second method is to have students proofread one another's papers in small groups. When using this method, it is important that at least one member of each group be a competent proofreader.

I like to keep proofreading separate from editing for two reasons. First, its placement in a late stage of writing puts mechanics in perspective, following content. Second, when proofreading is a separate stage and time is devoted to it, it is evidence that correctness is valued.

Publishing

The word *publishing* is used in a loose and general sense here. Publishing is reading a piece aloud to a class; it is also pinning finished work on the classroom bulletin board or in the corridors, making a display of writing that travels around the school, duplicating a book of polished student writing, placing a piece in school or local newspapers. Any type of "going public" with writing counts.

Publishing gives students new audiences and can have a profound effect on budding writers, but like everything else in the process, it can take time before many students understand and appreciate its significance for them. The initial go-around is often a struggle. The first time we publish in class, I feel as if I am slogging through a swamp, pushing heavy, reluctant animals before me. For many students, publishing takes on meaning only after the fact. It works like this. I announce with great enthusiasm and excitement that the students will choose one of their favorite drafts to publish. The first time I make this announcement, the students are often more tolerant than enthusiastic.

There are moments along the way to the final publication, however, when students may get interested. For some, it is the day we choose a title. For the artist in the class, it can be the day he or she designs the cover. For others, it is the day when all the papers have been duplicated (mimeographed or photocopied) and are spread out all around the room waiting to be collated. And yet for others, it is only upon seeing the product, the book.

I make a ritual, a ceremony that becomes part of the folklore of our class, of the reading. We all place chairs into a giant circle. Students read their writing aloud (although shy ones may have a friend read). When each reader finishes, there is often a hush, a moment of silent appreciation. It is followed by students telling the reader what they've enjoyed in the writing. It is at this moment that many students begin to understand in the larger sense that writing is a special type of communication very different from talking. In chapter 7, I discuss the evolution of interest in publishing that I noticed in a particular class. Few were interested or voluntarily read aloud in the circle from their first book on their childhood folklore. By the second publication on graffiti, there was more enthusiasm for the project. But by the fourth unit, students were asking, "Are we gonna make one of them books?"

Learning Logs: Connections
Between Writing and Learning

In learning logs, the entries are first-draft writing. They are usually less than a page in length and are written in class. Learning logs are not private; they are read by the teacher and other members of the class. Although there is no set rule, students average about one or two log writings a week.

Among the many functions learning logs serve, three are discussed here. First, learning logs provide an avenue for easy, non-judgmental communication between students and teacher. This is a social as well as pedagogical function that contributes to the sense of the classroom as a community. Second, learning logs offer teachers an unparalleled view into what is happening in students' minds as they learn (or fail to learn). Third, learning logs are a place where students can experience the power of writing as a learning tool. In logs, students restate in their own words the ideas and information being taught, internalizing the content and learning it. Logs are a place for students to make informal, personal connections to content, and for them to get ideas from these connections. They are a place for students to learn to use writing to solve problems and raise questions.

A Sample Log

On the first day of school, I hand out the learning logs, small composition books. If these aren't available, individual sheets of paper will do. I briefly explain how the logs will be used in class and why I use them. In the logs, students will be writing to one of three audiences: themselves, classmates, or me. The logs will never be "corrected," but will usually get a response from me or other students. I explain that logs are for expressive or first-draft writing and request as a first entry something like this: "Introduce yourself and tell me something you would like me to know about you."

Kerri, a bright young woman but an average student, was a junior in a suburban college-track class. Samples from her learning log over a five-month period illustrate both her development as an expressive writer and the functions and value of learning logs. Her initial entry was written at the end of the first class:

> My name is Kerri and I am 16 years old. I'm into anything that I don't have to do homework in. So far this Folklore stuff sounds interesting. I really don't know what you want to know so I don't know what to write.

Except for the humor in the second sentence, Kerri is taking no chances. She says explicitly that she doesn't understand what I want, so she is not writing. In answer to her entry I wrote, "I like your honesty—there will be homework, although not a lot." I wrote enough so that she would know I'd read it and was responding to the content of her message. For a week or two in the beginning of the term I write back to the students in their logs to encourage them and to show that I am reading the logs and responding to individual ideas. But by the end of the first month, I adopt a strategy I learned from Verda Delp, a junior high school teacher in Berkeley, California. I underline the good parts of logs and put a star next to excellent parts, writing only a word or two. This way I can read a class set of logs in twenty to thirty minutes.

In Kerri's class, the students started their response groups in the first month. After the first meeting of groups, I wanted a reading of how they had gone. Kerri's entry is still brief but less guarded:

> Those writing groups are ok I guess. Though I don't know why we need so many copies of the paper we wrote. [I had asked the students to come with four copies, one for each member of the group.] Yesterday I got stuck tring to tell Teresa what was good and everything in her paper with no help from Margaret. Oh well.

From this entry I learned that Kerri's group was trying but floundering. She didn't understand why I wanted each member of the group to have a copy; maybe I hadn't explained that clearly. I wrote back:

> Kerri, helpful comments. Although you were frustrated, you are on the right track. Praising and questioning are not automatic. Trust me, you and the others in your group will get better with practice.

I checked Margaret's and Teresa's logs for their reactions and made a mental note to sit in on this group.

About six weeks into the term, we planned to do a few days' study on the folklore of Halloween. I began the unit by telling the class to write anything they knew about Halloween—any questions, reaction, memory, or thoughts they had about the occasion. Kerri's logs are by this time getting longer and more fluent. She is comfortable with expressive writing, unselfconscious about such slang as "bummed out."

> Within the past 5 years Halloween has been bummed out. Parents don't let the kids go out trick or treating anymore for fear that they might get kidnapped. I remember we use to go trick or treating all night sometimes to see who could get the most candy. But now the parents and the media has taken all the fun out of it. I feel sorry for all the kids now who don't know what it's like to really go out and trick or treat. Last year only 5 kids came to our house.

As Kerri gains experience writing logs, they begin to work as a place for her to get ideas. She makes an important personal connection with the topic and through it taps into a serious change in American culture in her lifetime: many Americans, even in suburbia, no longer trust their neighbors. Since the purpose of a log entry like this one is to collect student knowledge, classmates share entries in small groups, pooling their information and asking questions. This information is then reported to the whole class and perhaps recorded on butcher paper. The information and questions from the students form the foundation of the unit.

Individual logs can also be a beginning point for a paper. Kerri, for example, may want to further explore the changes in the ritual of trick-or-treating in the last ten years and speculate on why the ritual has changed. Or she might want to explore how this change in the celebration of Halloween reflects other changes in American society.

In November, Kerri's class did an abbreviated version of the study of the folklore of names (see chapter 5). Since their writing was going to end with a first draft and a response, I told them to write the draft in the logs. By now, several months into the term, Kerri has grown into a skilled expressive writer in her log. She knows that she will get ideas as she drafts. In fact, her ideas are now coming faster than she can write; she doesn't always complete thoughts; she is much less careful. She is using the log as a place to do early thinking about a subject:

> Having both a Spanish middle and last name can get confusing when you have a 1st name like KERRI. KERRI MARIA HERNANDEZ. What a dumb name for someone who lives in the U.S. I guess. Mother chose my first name, Kerri, after some aunt on her side of the family. She's been long dead, even before I was born. I don't know how she figured on spelling it like it is since there are so many ways to spell it. I really don't care for the name Kerri because its just so blunt. Plus no one can say [it] that is all the little kids, so they call me Lisa since she's my sister and Lisa is easier to say. Now MARIA, my dad named [me] because my grandmother's name is Maria. My mom usually goes around calling me Kerri Maria or Merry Kerri or I think you spell [it] Mary Kerri, since Maria means Mary in English. It all depends on what kind of mood I'm in I guess. I hate Hernandez because when you 1st see this on a piece of paper you think, Spanish, [illegible word] something like that. My mom is always saying that she wants to change our last name to Davis, her maiden name, because people discriminate against it but Kerri Maria Davis does not sound too hot.

This is a poignant draft. It has humor—the little kids calling her Lisa and her mom playing with nicknames. It shows her history, how she was named by both parents and carries names from both sides of the family. It shows her discomfort with a Spanish name in a predominantly Anglo setting. She closes with a significant sentence. Kerri Maria Davis doesn't "sound too hot." She is feeling the pressure of discrimination in response to her Spanish surname, but she is also beginning to resist, to rise above it. She is not ready to give up her name, a brave step in her milieu.

About halfway through the semester, I wanted the students to reflect on the content of our study. What did they think about spending time on folklore in their English class? I asked for a log entry on their thoughts.

> Folklore is very interesting. I think I can get into the subject in fact I think I already have. It beats the same old English stuff we would be doing. It's something new and it's kind of fun. It makes you realize things that you haven't really noticed before like the children's games and the names.

Although short, this is a meaningful entry. In her own words, Kerri is beginning to articulate the realization that through exposure to folklore she has become aware of aspects of her culture that she had previously overlooked.

Kerri didn't like all topics equally. By the time we got to graffiti, she felt free to tell me so in her log:

> I don't like graffiti because it makes everything look dirty and slum-like. It's ok if you write it on your book cover but anywhere else it isn't right. Who cares if you love someone, you don't have to go and write it all over the place. The only time I like it is when a whole wall is painted, like in San Fran, with scenery.

In Kerri's class, as in all classes, there is a wide range of opinion about graffiti. Often, to begin class discussion about graffiti, I read from students' logs (with their permission). Using the logs as a starting point, students discuss graffiti. Is it just writing on walls, or can it be writing on book covers and city murals? Is it folklore? What value can there be in studying it?

While most of her classmates found some aspect of graffiti compelling, it never captured Kerri's interest. Her entry evaluating the unit was short and clearly shows that she was not engaged:

> Graffiti isn't really all that interesting. It's fun to read it and everything but when I have to write about it it's not that interesting.

Not surprisingly, her graffiti paper was not as good as her others.

The final unit in Kerri's class was on heroines and heroes. Kerri and many of the students balked at the topic in the opening discussion (see chapter 9), rejecting it as childish or dated. To find out why they were uneasy with the topic and to give them some space to let off steam about it, I asked for a log response.

Two things happen in Kerri's log. First, she states her annoyance over the topic, but then a most interesting thing occurs: she writes her way into the subject and finds her topic. A refrain from the writing workshops of Mary K. Healy, research and training coordinator of the Puente Project, is "The act of writing itself generates ideas and solves problems." Kerri's log is a perfect example:

I, personally don't have a hero. I never really believed in that kind of stuff. It just doesn't appeal to me I guess. I guess if I had to admire someone it would be someone who had it all together. Their life was perfect, and had everything for themselves. The person thats worked hard to get where they are now. The only person I can think of would be my neighbor Vickki. Her life isn't perfect but she has come a long way and is doing the best she can. I like to just go up and talk to her sometimes. I've known her for 4 years and she's like an older sister.

Kerri wrote her paper about Vickki.

Summary: Connections Between Writing and Learning

Most writing in American schools is done specifically for evaluation. This leaves students little room to explore writing as an instrument of learning. But the ungraded learning log is different. In the non-judgmental space of her log, Kerri made early forays into the content. The connections were made through personal experience, e.g., her observations about the change in Halloween ritual and community discrimination based on names. She solved problems, as is shown in her writing on heroes, where she moved from rejecting the subject to finding a person to study. In the course of five months, Kerri's writing voice changed from the tentative student who wrote in her first log, "I really don't know what you want to know so I don't know what to write," to a writer in touch with her opinions and ready to state them. Finally, Kerri's writing voice grew stronger as the year progressed. Students often lose their voices when they move from expressive to expository writing. One way to keep their personal voices alive is through regular log writing.

Peer Response Groups

Peer response groups met often in the classes discussed in this book. The groups consisted of two to five students working independently, responding to one another's writing in the classroom. These groups, which need careful training, can transform classrooms. They encourage student talk (and talk for teenagers is synonymous with *life*) in the classroom; they help create a community in the classroom. Writing can be an isolating, lonely activity; groups help a class begin to feel like a collection of writers sharing common problems. Groups provide a new (and more meaningful) audience, an alternative to the teacher. Using groups entails handing control of the classroom over to the students. In order to become proficient writers, students must write often; teachers can't respond to all or even most of it, but peer groups can.

Before students go into groups on their own, I model how groups work. First, the whole class acts as a response group reacting to a piece of writing I read. Then four or five students volunteer to role-play a group in front of the class, and the class critiques the performance. When they move into their groups, I remind the students of the procedures:

1. In the group, the writer reads his or her draft; the others listen.
2. The listeners will have more information for feedback if they take notes or just jot down a few words while listening, to help them remember what they liked.
3. If the listeners get so involved that they forget to take notes, they can ask the reader to read the draft a second time.
4. When the reader is done, the listeners tell the reader which parts they liked best. The reader can underline them.
5. The listeners can either ask and discuss their questions with the reader, or they can write them down for the reader.

A generic writing response sheet looks like the one in Figure 2–5. The third entry is an open slot often filled with a question about main idea or focus, but it can direct the student's attention to any aspect of writing. Peer response sheets can be designed to fit many purposes at different stages of the writing process. For example, during the proofreading stage some teachers have students use grammar checklists in their groups.

Figure 2-5
Writing Response Sheet

Date: _____

Your name: _____

Writer's name: _____

Topic: _____

1. Positive comments! This always comes first. What did you like about this writing?
2. What questions do you have for the writer?
3.

Conclusion

There is a lively student and teacher folklore about papers. Students tell of teachers who fling the papers down a flight of stairs and grade according to where they land: A's near the top, F's at the bottom. They tell of others who weigh papers. They tell of the student who handed in a brilliant first and last page with pages from the telephone book in between and got an A. And teachers tell of peers who, faced with a mountain of uncorrected papers, threw them out or burned them.

When I first started teaching, only after a few glasses of wine could I confront class sets of papers. At the time, I didn't understand why I dreaded them; I just felt guilty. But now I know. They were boring. Often they were correct in form but the content was too often lifeless prose.

The sheer number of student papers will always be a problem for teachers. So even today it isn't quite true to say that I always look forward to reading them. The difference is that now I honestly enjoy reading *most* of what my students produce, for their writing is energetic and filled with strong voices tackling issues that matter.

Chapter Three

"Bloody Mary"
Introducing Students to Folklore

In their first encounters with the study of folklore, students begin to realize that old, familiar parts of their lives are about to be seen from a new perspective, one that will challenge their impressions of the commonplace. In this chapter, two lessons for introducing folklore are presented. The first, which focuses on memories of a childhood game, can be done in one period. The second, which opens with three genres, takes about two periods. In both lessons, students define folklore and folk groups and are introduced to function, context, and performance in folklore.

Introductory Lesson One: The Legend/ Game/Ritual "Bloody Mary"

The setting for this lesson is an eighth grade inner-city classroom. The students, primarily Black, are thirteen and fourteen years old and are mildly curious about me, a visiting adult who is going to talk about folklore. After introducing myself, I tell them that we will begin with some folklore from their childhood. Usually I do this lesson using the game Hide and Seek, which may be the single most widely-known game, crossing socio-economic, ethnic, and national borders. However, through teaching other folklore classes in this school, I learned that when they were in the elementary grades, most of the girls and many of the boys played a game/ritual that they call "Bloody Mary." Even the students who didn't actually play knew about it. "How many of you," I ask, "remember playing 'Bloody Mary'?"

They don't expect this question; it catches their attention. Then they all start talking at once.

"Yeah. I did!"

"Oh, yeah."

"Yeah, I used to get sca—red!"

"Okay," I say, "One at a time, tell me what you did."

"First we turned off the light, and everybody say [and this the student says slowly, her voice breathy and ominous], "B-l-o-o-d-y M-a-r-y one . . . " Before she can finish, she is interrupted by a chorus of kids who suddenly remember the specifics of the game. "Yeeaahhhh!" they shout in chorus. She continues, "B-l-o-o-d-y M-a-r-y two, B-l-o-o-d-y M-a-r-y three, and then we would go up and up and then, and then, everybody would say, 'Look she in the mirror, she in the window!' and they'd scream!" The student has a captive audience. When she finishes, the class laughs and shouts as they remember playing the game.

I interrupt. "What did you think Bloody Mary was going to do?" The answers come quickly.

"We thought she was gonna come and get us."

"And scratch us."

"Yeah, and scratch you up."

A male student offers his version. "We didn't do it quite the same way. We'd turn out the light. We'd be in a really dark and room and ummm . . . we'd sit in a circle, and then my cousin, you know, and everybody, all of us would say, 'B-l-o-o-d-y M-a-r-y,' and once my cousin screamed and scared everybody. . . . we had to close our eyes and everything."

Another student recalls her version. "We used to go in the girls' bathroom in school." The girls who had played it in school lavatories nudge each other and laugh, enjoying the memory. The student starts again, "We used to go in the girls' bathroom, close the door, cut the light off, and then we'd start screaming, and we would lock the doors, and everybody would run into the bathroom and grab each other and all this stuff."

"What was your fear? What did you think was going to happen?" I ask.

"I thought Bloody Mary was a ghost or something [and] probably would come up there."

"How would you describe her?" I ask.

"I think she's a lady with a long gown on. . . . with big red finger-nails."

"I used to think she probably had a white dress on with blood spots on it. . . . blood over it."

One girl suddenly remembers being skeptical. "I used to think she was a made-up person." The rest of the class disagrees; they were believers.

"I did [believe]," they all shout.

"I was scared!" another adds as proof of belief.

I ask a few more questions. "How did you learn about Bloody Mary?" The answer is so obvious they wonder why I ask.

"Friends."

"From my sister, she used to do it when she was little."

"Friends tell friends, they just pass it on."

"Who do you think made up Bloody Mary?" When I ask this everybody starts talking at once, for they all have theories and much to say. "I think a person made it up and told someone and then it went on and on—"

"I had thought maybe it came from Halloween or something—"

"Some guy could have made it up and told the next person who probably exaggerated and as he told the next person he exaggerated—"

"There was probably a lady who wrote a book about herself or something—"

"It's probably an old lady who doesn't like kids messing with her so she got irritated so—"

"When I was really little I had thought it was like a lady who had passed, who had died, and her spirit had become—"

"There was this lady. She had a whole bunch of cats. Everybody used to call her 'Cat Lady,' and everybody used to be scared of her, they'd run past her house, and she'd be peeking out the window—"

Everyone seems to know the Cat Lady. As the noise level rises, I break in. Now it is time to look back on the discussion.

Defining Folklore

Information taken from the students' discussion can be used to define folklore. For instance, the student's observation on how she learned to play the games—"Friends tell friends, they just pass it on"—becomes point one on the board: 1. *Folklore is passed from person to person, often orally.* One dimension of folklore is "that part of culture handed down" (Thompson 1951, 12). In this book, the concentration is on verbal folklore, which is usually oral. There is, however, written folklore, such as chain letters and graffiti. We also discuss other ways folklore is transmitted, for instance, by watching. Children learn many games by watching and studying other children at play, and players often provide direct instruction. A point to remember is that this is voluntary. No one is told to pass folklore along; folks of all ages do it on their own.

2. *Folklore is traditional.* Stith Thompson wrote, " . . . tradition . . . [is] the touchstone for everything that is to be included in the term folklore" (11). "Tradition" has multiple meanings. Dan Ben-Amos (1984) has identified seven, four of which are particularly germane here: tradition as the actual items of folklore, as a canon of belief, as the process by which folklore is passed on, and as the performance of folklore. With students I stress at first simply that "traditional" means that the item has existed for a period of time. There is, however, great variation in the lifetimes of folklore. For example, a joke about a current event comes and goes quickly. Fads, such as green (or is it yellow?) M&M candies making you "horny," last for years. And some folklore, such as the game of Hide and Seek, is over a thousand years old. Pollux, an Egyptian Greek lexicographer, (c.170), describes Hide and Seek, which he calls *Apodidraskinda:*

> . . . one player shut his eyes, or had somebody covering them to ensure that he did, while the others ran off. This player then proceeded to look for them, while the object of each of the hiders was to reach the seeker's place and become seeker in his stead (Opie and Opie 1969, 155).

The game is often mentioned in European writings, for example, in Shakespeare's *Love's Labour Lost,* IV: iii and as "I Spy" in William Wells Newell's *Games and Songs of American Children* (1963, originally published in 1883).

Pieter Bruegel's painting *Children's Games,* dated 1560, offers students a chance to see what games looked like in sixteenth-century Europe. A reproduction of this painting provides a class with impressive evidence of continuity and change in children's games in western civilization. In the painting are such recognizable activities as leapfrog, rolling hoops, jacks (played with knucklebones), riding a hobby horse, walking on stilts, and playing with tops. There are also unrecognizable games. Students can speculate about what is happening in the unfamiliar games and about why some games have lasted and others have not. Folklore, therefore, is traditional but with wide variation in the longevity of its specific items.

Matters of age catch students' curiosity. In this class, they begin to wonder about the Bloody Mary tradition: How old is it? Folklorists don't know, I tell them, but we can do a little research on the question. As a start, their homework is to ask family members—older siblings, parents, grandparents—if they too played Bloody Mary.

3. *Folklore usually has variation.* In this class, there are almost as many versions of Bloody Mary as there are students. As children pass

the game along, they alter it, tailoring it to their needs and the context. I read to them a description of the ritual in Mary and Herbert Knapp's, *One Potato, Two Potato: The Folklore of American Children* (1976, 242). The game is widespread and also known as Mary Worth.

4. *Folklore is often of anonymous origin.* The students make good guesses about the origin of the Bloody Mary legend. They help make an important point: usually the origin of verbal folklore is unknown. The students have many theories, but no one knows for sure where Bloody Mary comes from. Students often argue that they have started a joke or know a friend who has. I ask them to check their sources. Folklorists, I tell them, would be delighted to have a documented source for a joke. Once students try to track the origins, they find themselves with plenty of clues but no single source. It takes time for them to develop an appreciation of the power and complexity of oral tradition.

Roger Abrahams defines folklore this way:

> The term *folklore* has come to mean the accumulated traditions, the inherited products and practices of a specifiable group. . . . Not only traditional texts of performance and material objects are studied but the process of making and doing as well (1983, 345).

In this first class I want the students to get a taste of what Abrahams calls "the process of making and doing." So we have general discussions on what they feel about the function or purpose of Bloody Mary, and we discuss content and performance as well.

Some Functions of Bloody Mary

"Why did you play Bloody Mary?" I ask. They answer, "It's fun." This is a good start. There are more functions[1] of the game, but they are hidden under the entertainment. I press them to think of other things they learned or did while playing the game, and they search for less obvious meanings. One student remembers sprinkling ten drops of water on each child's head. I suggest that perhaps the game is a child's imitation of a religious ceremony. Another student counters that the game was more like magic and witchcraft. The students talk about the excitement and power they felt as children when they conjured up Bloody Mary. They talk of the terror of her impending appearance, and of the contagious quality of that terror. They also note that the game had an aura of illegality about it, that it was something adults would not approve of—and that this definitely added to its attraction. A related issue surfaces: Who or what is

Bloody Mary? I direct them back to her physical description—the bloody dress, her fingernails. "She's a vampire," someone shouts out. Others like this interpretation and liken her to Dracula.

The students are getting at some of the game's other, less apparent functions. I ask them to think about what they may have learned playing Bloody Mary, if the game may have been about fears, such as fear of the dark, and why their parents would have disapproved of it. They are also prompted to consider why it seems to be predominantly a girls' game.

Context, Performance, and Folk Group

Context, performance, and folk group can all be introduced through Bloody Mary. The students remember playing the game in dark spaces—often, but not always, in bathrooms, which were ideal because they could easily be darkened, and Bloody Mary could appear in the mirror. It was played elsewhere too—in hallways or any convenient room. Bloody Mary could appear in windowpanes or emerge out of thin air. Darkness was important. Playing Bloody Mary required not only a specific context, performance was also important. The students remember that some children were masters at summoning up the apparition, others limited their participation to squeals, and still others were afraid even to play.

The folk group that plays Bloody Mary is elementary school children, usually girls. A folk group is literally any group of people, from a family to a marching band, that has something in common—traditions or conventions—or that connects them as a folk group. To reinforce the concept of folk group, we spend a few minutes listing those to which we belong (see the discussion of folk group in chapter 1, pages 13–17, and give an example of folklore from each one. If time allows, this can be done in small groups.

For a class like this, many of them doing poorly in school, there are a number of benefits. Most students, no matter what their skill level, participate; they realize that here is a subject they can be good at. They can use their past experience to advantage, and I can honestly praise their insights, such as their speculations on the origins of Bloody Mary and their intuitive linking of her to the "Cat Lady," another folk character.

What Is and Is Not Folklore?

Before the period ends (depending on the class, the lesson may extend into a second period), I want the students to get a perspective on folklore and where it fits into culture in general. I give a brief explanation of elite, popular, and folk culture with examples of each (see chapter 1, pages 20–22). Then I give the students a list of items. In small groups, they identify and explain why each one is *elite, popular,* or *folk culture.*[2] Here is one such list:

1. "The Cosby Show"
2. Beethoven's *Fifth Symphony*
3. Monopoly (the Parker Brothers game)
4. children playing house
5. holding up the index finger to indicate you're "Number One."
6. Snoopy
7. Shakespeare's *King Lear*
8. slumber parties
9. Disneyland
10. Homecoming
11. the movie, *The Rocky Horror Picture Show*
12. tying a shoelace
13. Chaucer's *Canterbury Tales*
14. cheerleading
15. video games

We then discuss each item. Some are easy: (1) "The Cosby Show" is popular culture and (2) Beethoven, elite. But (3) Monopoly causes confusion. Some students think we don't know the inventor and so call it folklore. But in fact we do know. Others recognize that the game is commercial and therefore popular culture. However, when people play, they often invent their own rules and variations—that part is folklore. So it's both. (4) Playing house and (5) the "Number One" gesture are both folklore—in fact, gestures in general are folklore. (6) The comic book character Snoopy is popular, although some students argue for comics as folklore, and (7) Shakespeare is unquestionably elite (and gets a round of boo's in this class, as does Beethoven). (8) Slumber parties are easily folklore, but (9) Disneyland is controversial.

At first glance, students often consider Disneyland folk culture. In the discussion that follows, some students point out the folk characters one sees at Disneyland, while others note the film and comic book characters such as Mickey Mouse, who are part of popular culture. Although there is something about comics, perhaps their low cultural status, that makes some students at first see it as folklore, Disneyland is, of course, popular culture with some folk influence. (10) Homecoming is a folk ritual. (11) While *The Rocky Horror Picture Show* is popular culture, the rituals that surround it are folklore. (12) Tying a shoelace is a folk skill. (Remember how you learned?) (13) *The Canterbury Tales* are elite, although Chaucer was heavily influenced by folklore. Many of his tales turn up in *The Types of the Folktale* (Aarne and Thompson 1961) (see chapter 1, pages 23–24).[3] Students who have read a bit of *The Canterbury Tales* may recognize some of Chaucer's stories as folk tales. (14) Cheerleading was originally folklore and still is, although it has developed commercial (popular culture) dimensions, such as summer cheerleading camps. (15) Video games are popular culture. At the end of the second version of the opening lesson described below, this activity is repeated.

Introductory Lesson Two: Three Forms of Folklore

The difference between this lesson and the first is that the students discuss three genres of folklore instead of one. They are:

1. paper airplanes (folk material culture)
2. jokes
3. games

In class it works this way: First the students make paper airplanes and have a contest. Anyone who wants to compete lines up against a wall and launches his or her plane.

Next comes joke telling. Natural settings for these sessions are slumber parties, the bus ride to school, or lunch time, not the classroom. Therefore, I prime the pump with a few jokes of my own to set the mood. If I am uneasy about the content of a spontaneous joke-telling session, I have the students write out jokes, and then I can select the ones to be told.

Third, the class reminisces about playing Hide and Seek (also known as I Spy and Kick the Can), much as the class above recalled their experiences with Bloody Mary. We share memories spurred by questions such as: How did you play? How was "It" chosen? How did it feel to be "It?" Did you cheat? If so, how? What chants do you remember? Did you shout, "Olley, olley, oxen free" to free the base? How did "It" let the other players know he or she had finished counting? Did she shout, "Anyone round my base is it!" or "Apples, peaches, pumpkin pie, who's not ready holler I!" or "At three the base is on fire! One, one and a half, two, two and a half, THREE!" Where was your favorite hiding place? How did you count? What memorable things happened to you playing Hide and Seek? Students often remember the dilemma of the perfect hiding place; it is so good that no one finds you. The game ends, the players go home, and you're still hiding!

Hide and Seek is often played at dusk and on into the dark. For many children, playing Hide and Seek is a small rite of passage; it is the first time they are allowed out alone at night without an adult. This is probably one reason that students have vivid memories of the game.

The paper airplane activity works best as a whole class activity, but the joke-telling session is better as a small group activity, with the students reporting their best jokes back to the class. The Hide and Seek reminiscence can be done orally with the whole class, orally in small groups, or in writing. If students write a draft of their memories of Hide and Seek, they then read it in peer groups and report the details of the game back to the whole class.

Defining Folklore

Next the students generalize about the three activities: What do they have in common? What makes them folklore? The first characteristic they notice is usually that it's passed along. It is the most obvious, and it is proof of the value of folklore to the folk. Students conclude this activity by speculating on the commonalities among the items. It is a good activity for small groups. After students have developed a definition of folklore, I tell them how folklorists define it, and we compare the results. I also tell them that folklorists themselves are not in agreement, that the definition is a slippery thing, and that as we continue they should continue to question it. (The concepts of folk group, functions, context, and performance can all be introduced as they were with Bloody Mary.)

Common Questions in the Opening Lessons

Students who come to class with some knowledge of traditional folklore need to make sense of their notions vis-a-vis what is happening in class. They often ask questions like the three discussed below.

1. *"What about things like Mother Goose Rhymes?"* Questions like this one and about myths, fairy tales, and fables come from students who especially want to understand the relationship between traditional folklore and the paper airplanes, and jokes of today. Nursery rhymes and the like fit the definition of folklore, but they are not *living folklore*; that is, they were long handed on from person to person by word of mouth, but today we know them primarily from books. Some families still have nursery rhymes in oral tradition, but generally they are not in current folk usage as is the folklore studied in this book.

More specific answers about nursery rhymes can be found in *The Oxford Dictionary of Nursery Rhymes* (Opie and Opie 1973). The rhymes are old; the Opies estimate that 24 percent of known rhymes existed in oral tradition before 1599. By about 1825, the majority had been written down. Nursery rhymes are different from the children's folklore studied in this book in that they are passed from parent to child. That is, they are *adult* folklore for children, while the children's folklore studied in chapter 4 is for and by children, passed from child to child, usually without adult involvement. Consequently, the messages and the functions of nursery rhymes are different from that of children's folklore. (An interesting project would be to compare the nursery rhymes students remember from childhood with their childhood games.)

2. *"What about superstitions?"* Superstitions are folklore, although folklorists call them *folk beliefs,* a gentler, nonjudgmental term. Today we continue to perpetuate traditional inherited folk beliefs, but we also make up new ones. An example of a new folk belief was reported by an Asian immigrant student. She and her friends believed that a breakfast of one sausage and two eggs before exams would give them a perfect score on an exam. They placed the sausage first on their plate and followed it with the two fried eggs, making a breakfast of an imitation of the number 100, a perfect score. Folklorists call this *homeopathic magic,* magic analogous to a metaphor. We use such folk beliefs in situations where we are concerned about outcomes we can't control.

Students are experts on superstitions. In any class they can come up with a long list. There are omens like black cats, broken mirrors and umbrellas opened indoors. There is divination, e.g., plucking the leaves from a daisy while saying, "He loves me, he loves me not." There are good-luck charms and four-leaf clovers. In one suburban class, a freshman girl surprised her classmates by telling them, "I heard from my sister that it's good to cut your hair at a full moon because then it grows faster." The students laughed, but I pointed out that hers is an old belief. Farmers used to (some still do) plant certain vegetables during what they call the "dark" of the moon, the time from the full moon to the new moon, believing they would grow better.

There is no chapter on folk belief in this book, but it can easily be included following the same model of other chapters. After identifying the genre, students can begin with memories of their own experiences with folk beliefs, or they can collect the folk beliefs of others. Then they would analyze when, where, why, and how the beliefs are used.

3. *"What about Paul Bunyan?"* Paul Bunyan, the American schoolchild's symbol of American folklore, was a minor folk character. The Paul Bunyan students learn about in school is actually more a product of popular than folk culture. He was the creation of William Laughead, a publicity agent for the Red River Lumber Company from 1914 to 1930. To publicize the company, Laughead wrote and distributed Paul Bunyan stories. Children's authors have been writing about him ever since. Richard Dorson (1959) has christened Paul Bunyan tales "fakelore," popular culture stories written in a folk style but that never had much oral currency. Dorson adds that the Bunyan tales that did exist were not the "syrupy confections" we know but tales like these:

> The Blue Ox used to look fancy when he went out with nine bales of hay stacked on one horn and seven bags of feed on the other. Every time he'd crap it'd take the crew three days to swamp around the pile. During the Winter of the Blue Snow, one of Paul's men climbed a tree and couldn't get down. It was so cold that Paul told him to pass water. He did, it froze, and the jack slid down on the icicle (222).

Conclusion

These lessons are a beginning; comprehending what folklorists mean by folklore takes time. As noted in chapter 1, that part of culture folklorists call folklore has no name in our society. To a folklorist, paper airplanes, Grimm's fairy tales, and note-passing in class are all part of the same discipline. But since English doesn't have a common term identifying folklore, it takes a while for students to understand what that discipline encompasses. After studying several types of folklore, they begin to grasp the commonalities among different forms and come to appreciate the power of folklore in our lives.

Notes

1. For a discussion of functions of folklore see pages 25–29 in chapter 1.

2. I got this idea from Robert H. Byington, "Introduction to Folklore," *Teaching Folklore* (Buffalo, New York: Documentary Research, Inc., 1984), p. 25. Byington asks his students to identify which are folklore and which are not and to explain why.

3. Also see Carl Lindahl, *Earnest Games: Folkloric Patterns in the Canterbury Tales* (Bloomington: Indiana University Press, 1987) and W. F. Bryan and Germaine Dempster, eds. *Sources and Analogues of Chaucer's Canterbury Tales* (New York: Humanities Press, 1958).

Chapter Four

"My Name Was Carlos"
The Folklore of Naming

For all parents fit names to their children as soon as these are born, so that there is no one so poor or so gentle that he is nameless.

Homer, *Odyssey, Book viii*

On this Earth everybody has to have a name or they are no one.

Verena, seventh grade,
inner-city student

He who steals my purse steals trash, but he who steals my good name steals everything.[1]

Folk saying

Names define us; without a name, we are no one. When parents choose names, they are influenced by the folklore of naming. Southerners are more likely to give children double names; Northerners generally stick to one. Jews name after the dead; many Catholics give their children a saint's name. During the Civil Rights Movement many Blacks took African names and/or bestowed them on their children. For many years, the most popular girl's name in this country was Jennifer; currently it is Ashley. In some families, the children have the same initials, or first names starting with the same letter.

Identifying the folklore of naming can be a little tricky because people are often unaware that they are following folk traditions when choosing names. Usually, however, they are following regional, religious, ethnic, political, historical, national, or family naming traditions. All of them are folklore, passing from person to person, having multiple existence and variation. Occasionally, the giving of a first name is not folklore, as when parents choose a name from one of the what-to-name-the-baby books or when they simply like the sound of a name.

In studying this topic, students think about the meaning of their names and nicknames, consider their origins, and think about how they are and are not defined by their names. Furthermore, the study of naming folklore can provide clues to familial and societal values. As Alan Dundes (1973) writes:

> It is probably universally the case that the bestowing of a name upon an individual has ritual or symbolic implications. Whether a person is named for an ancestor or for an event or for the day on which he was born, the name selection process is almost certainly in accordance with a conscious or unconscious cultural pattern.[2]

This unit works well at the beginning of the term. Students get acquainted and learn each other's names, and I in turn learn a little about the students' families early in the year.

Day One: Introduction to the Folklore of Names

Often I introduce this topic with my own name, as in this ninth-grade suburban class. I tell the students that names are important, that they not only define us, they also contain our family histories. Interviewing someone about her name will reveal her family naming folklore and her family as well. As I write all of my names, past and present—ELIZABETH JANE RADIN SIMONS—on the board, I challenge the class, "Try and find out as much as you can about me by asking questions about my name."

The first student to speak is confused. "What's your *real* name?" he asks. I laugh; it's a good question. They are all my names, but when I married, I dropped Jane. Tait, whose mother has been married three times, smiles and says, "It's a good thing my mom didn't keep all her names from the past."

"What other names did your parents think of?" Brian asks.

"If I had been a boy my name would have been Edward," I say.

"Didn't anyone ever call you Peaches or something like that?" Susan wants to know. Everyone laughs.

"Alas, no one ever called me Peaches, but I do have a nickname, Liz, and when I was a child I was Lizzie." Susan isn't satisfied with this; she wants something "crazy." And at that moment I remember one of my father's pet names for me, "dear, dear Elizabeth." My father had coined it—the first "dear" was because he loved me and the second because I was so expensive! "Dear, dear Elizabeth" isn't quite "Peaches," but Susan seems satisfied.

"Why did you drop the Jane instead of the Radin?" Brian wants to know. Allison has an answer: "No one ever does that." A hot discussion ensues about keeping last names after marriage and divorce. And Michele (who was named after the Beatle's song "Michelle") brings some closure to the discussion with this observation: "Just because she got married, she didn't want to forget where she came from." A beautiful point. Michele understands that my name, a symbol of my past, is something I might want to keep after marriage as a way of maintaining my ties to my family—where I came from.

The folklore of women's surnames after marriage has changed in this country since the feminist movement. Women began to view themselves differently. One manifestation of the new self-image has been the establishment of options for surnames after marriage. Now women have choices: keeping their maiden name, hyphenating the husband's and wife's last names, making up a new name, or taking the husband's name. The first three options are new. No one legislated this; it came directly from the people, an example of a spontaneous change in folklore reflecting a change in society.

The girls are interested. "I'm going to keep mine," some murmur to friends. "Why do they [married people] take guys' names instead of girls' names?" Allison asks indignantly. Then she answers her own question: "It shows that men are more important than women."

One student mentions that when parents get divorced, the mothers often keep their married names because of the kids. "What does keeping the name do?" I ask. It makes them closer, they are more like a family, the students answer. They are beginning to understand the power of names (and the importance of naming folklore). Having the same name is a statement of closeness; it is bonding.

"Why were you named Elizabeth?" Eric asks, returning to my name on the chalkboard.

"I'm Jewish," I explain, "and the Jewish naming tradition is to name after someone who has died." The students, none of them Jewish, want to know why Jews have this tradition. I give them the answer I learned from my father. It is Jewish folk religion. Jews, he told me, do not believe in life after death. When we bury the dead, we simply say, "We now return to the earth that which we have received from the earth." The dead are remembered when a baby is named for them.

Then I tell the rest of the story behind my first name. "I was named for my grandfather, who had died seven years before my birth. His name was Elijah. My parents are first-generation Americans and when they named me, they had two concerns: they wanted to carry on Jewish tradition, but they didn't want my name to sound too Jewish, perhaps because they had known discrimination and didn't want it to happen to me. So they took my grandfather's name, translated it into Hebrew and back out again into English and came up with Elizabeth. They felt they had preserved our heritage but hadn't burdened me with a Jewish name."

I tell this story whenever I teach the folklore of naming. Recently, I saw my parents and told them my little speech about how I got my name. They looked at each other and started to laugh. "Liz," my father said, "the grandfather you were named after was Jacob!" Now I tell both stories to my students because both versions—my parent's and mine—are equally important; both are family folklore.

"Do you have any brothers and sisters?" Danny asks. He wants to know their names and if they were named after people who had died. He is looking for family naming patterns. My brother and sister were both been named for relatives, people my parents had loved and missed.

"What about your middle name?" someone asks. Jane was a common name when I was born; many women my age are named Jane. "What are the faddish names today?" I ask. One student knows. "David is the second most popular name. I got that from the *Book of Lists*." Names in vogue or name fads (oral folklore) reflect the culture. For example, in the late 1960s through the early 1980s, there was a national preoccupation with roots, which was reflected in the popularity of Biblical names. Joshua, Jonathan, Rachel, Sarah, Daniel, and David were common.

Cristina and Deepika have something else on their minds and turn the discussion to last names. "My last name is from my great-grandfather who was from France," offers Cristina Olivet. This led Deepika to observe, "Some families have a coat of arms."

What's in Your Name? The Importance of Naming Traditions

"What have you learned about me from looking at my naming traditions?"

"You're Jewish."

"Your grandparents were Russian."

They have learned my family history while questioning me about my name. I have also told them a little about my grandparents' lives in Russia and their arrival in America, and about my parents' lives as young people in New York City.

"You had to have a name so that your family knew who had died and the name passed on." When she said this, Allison was trying to articulate the idea that I was named according to Jewish naming traditions. We talked over the values and concerns of my parents as first-generation American Jews and how what they did was typical. We traced the Jewish naming traditions into the second generation and looked at how I named my children. They too are named for deceased grandparents, but the grandparents' names are their middle and therefore less important names, a clear sign of both assimilation and dilution of Jewish tradition.

To further dramatize the significance of the folklore of names, students look at traditions radically different from their own. Chapter 1 of Alex Haley's *Roots* (1977, 11–13), is the story of the naming of the hero, Kunte Kinte. The naming folklore of the Mandinka tribe reflects their intimate knowledge of tribal history, of their desire to perpetuate it, and of their beliefs in the great importance of a newborn, a new addition to the tribe.

An extended discussion of a person's names (the source can be any student or adult who is knowledgeable about his or her name) usually touches on the folklore surrounding names and naming:

- the oral traditions or folklore of choosing first names (naming after the dead, naming fads)
- the folklore of choosing last names when marrying
- the history of last names (both folk and nonfolk histories)
- the folklore of nicknames
- family, religious, ethnic, regional, and national naming traditions
- the folklore of naming after famous people (traditions of using them and avoiding them)
- the folklore of the namer (who does the naming in the family— mother, father, grandmother?)
- the folklore of specific names (when you hear the name Sarah or Bertha or Sam, who do you envisage?)
- the power of names (mothers keeping names after a divorce to bond the family)

Important concerns are intimately related to this folklore. One is identity.

Students Interview Each Other About Their Names

Next, the students interview one another about their names. If it is the beginning of the year, I have them work in pairs. In an inner-city class, this is the first unit of the term; the students are not skilled interviewers. The purpose of the activity is to help them gather ideas connected to their names.

Before they start, Maria protests, "If I write my name, they gonna laugh." I advise Maria to choose a partner whom she trusts. "I won't laugh at your name," Raul reassures her.

"Testing *uno, dos, tres* . . . " Carlos says, testing the tape recorder I have put on his desk to record his interview of Theo. The boys play with the tape recorder for a few minutes, figuring out how to put the tape recorder on pause so they can edit the tape.

"Okay, fella, Theo, what's your name?" Carlos begins.

"Theodore Vargas."

Carlos is surprised and asks, "You ain't got a middle name?"

"Uh-uh. That's it, man, that's on my birth certificate." Carlos is incredulous and asks again to make sure. "You ain't got no middle name?"

"No, [I've got] a nickname," Theo offers in lieu of his missing middle name. Carlos is annoyed. "I know you have a nickname."

I overhear this discussion and tell Carlos and Theo that there are conventions for people without middle names. In the army, for example, it is NMI for "no middle initial." When I leave, Theo proudly tells Carlos, "Theodore NMI Vargas."

Carlos moves on. "How did you get your first name?"

"Well, I got my first name from my dad's uncle, man. The home-boy [buddy] got shot so he named me after him." Theo laughs and Carlos asks, "Got shot? Your father's uncle?"

Theo confirms it. "The homeboy got shot."

Perhaps picking up on a subtle cue from Theo, Carlos asks no further questions about Theo's first name.

"Do you know anything about your last name?" He asks.

"It's just one and only. There's only one. Did you ever look in the phone book and see Vargas? It's the one and only."

They both laugh at Theo's joke; Vargas is a common name.

"Did you ever trace your roots?" Miguel persists. "What's your grandmother and grandfather's last name?"

Theo's grandparents have a different last name. And Theo explains, "My dad had to change his name because the FBI was after him."

Again Carlos does not follow up. Instead, he asks, "What are your nicknames?"

"Mr. Vargas," Theo jests at first, and then says, "Theo."

"How did you get it?"

"From my mom; it's short for Theodore."

"Who can use it?" Carlos wants to know.

"Family, personal friends, people who know me well, and all the sexy ladies."

"Do you like your name, Mr. Vargas?"

"Yes, I do. Definitely."

"Why do you like your name?"

"There's hardly anyone named Theodore, it's something that's different, different from all the other people out there in the world."

"Are there any other people with your name?"

"Theodore the Great," Theo informs Carlos. "That's from olden times. I'm serious."

But Carlos will have none of Theodore the Great and tells Theo, "It sounds like a magician." They both laugh; then Theo begins to interview Carlos.

Day Two: Role Playing—"What To Name the Baby?" and First Drafts on Names

Many students have taken part in or observed adults discussing what to name a new baby. Two or more students role-playing parents choosing a name for their child is not only a great deal of fun for them and the class, it also dramatizes the folklore of naming. The role play simulates reality. Students argue about which side of the family the baby will be named for, which relatives will be pleased and which ones offended. Such acted-out family conflicts surrounding the naming of a child are significant because they often signal a clash in traditions, as can be seen in Pam's naming story:

> My mother and father have always told me and my sisters how we got our names. My father named all of us. All of our names start with P, all our middle names with a D and all our last names with a W. There was one mistake with my sister under me. Her name is Thelma. My father said my mother's mother (my grandmother) beat him to the hospital and named my sister after herself. My father was mad. . . .

Pam explained that in her neighborhood, grandmothers often did the naming. Her dad was breaking the rules and her grandmother was fighting for her rights. The rest of the class, observing the role playing, can identify folk traditions and anything else that's noteworthy in the discussion. For instance, it is an honor to have a baby named for you.

When it comes time for first drafts, I encourage students to tell the stories of how they were given their names. Students who don't know the origins of their names can write about other aspects of their names. They can write about their nicknames—how many they have, how they got them, and who is free to use them. They can describe

how they feel about their names. Do they like them? Why or why not?
They can write about changing their names (a phenomenon that
becomes almost epidemic in junior high, when students are trying
out various adult persona and experiment with the spelling of their
names and with new names); what new name did they want and
why? They can make up a story of how they got their name. They can
write about being teased about their names or about common jokes
centering on them. Many students begin with the story of how their
names were chosen and then write on the other questions as well.
Teresa, who was born in Zamora, Michoacan, Mexico, was named by
her godparents, as is the custom there. She writes:

> At first I didn't like my name because people, especially young
> people of my age, used to make fun of it. An example is that my
> name rhymes with things such as *ceresa* (cherry) and they called me
> *ceresa*. Another example is my mother's last name which is Barajas.
> Whenever I said it, people laughed at me because it means poker
> cards. Things like that really made me ashamed of my name.

"Now," she continues, "everything is changed." Upon moving to
America, Teresa dropped her mother's last name. (Spanish naming
traditions include keeping both parents' last names. When students
move to America, they often drop their mother's name.) Her name is
now Teresa Avalos. As for her first name, she shares it with two other
Teresas she admires, her Aunt Teresa and the famous Catholic nun,
Mother Teresa. A curious thing about the power of names is that
students (as well as many adults) often feel an almost magical connection with famous people who share their name.

Beto, a junior who had done little writing in school, wrote this
first draft after much cajoling:

> My name is Humberto Delgado Cruz it is a name I think I will never
> like, because most [non-Spanish-speaking] people cannot say it.
> They call me Humbert, Hamburger, Umbert and all kinds of differ-
> ent things. So what I do is I tell everybody, "My name is Beto." Most
> people can say it better than my real name.
> Sometimes my name causes problems. I have gotten in a lot of fights
> because of my dumb name. On one occasion one of the guys that
> called me hamburger just kept saying it over and over and I got real
> mad and hit him in his eye and we got into it. But like it was in P.
> E. the teacher broke us up and we both got a three day suspension.

Even though he didn't know how he got his name, Beto wrote a
good first draft and brought up an aspect of naming not yet mentioned: how we feel when our names are mispronounced. Efrain and
Raul have Beto's problem; Anglos do not pronounce their names
properly. Furthermore, Efrain complains that teachers misspell his

name as well. The class talks about how painful it is when your name is mispronounced. And I notice that Raul is in the process of changing his name to Ralph.

For homework, the students read their drafts to their parents. If the parents don't know about writing process, students explain that this is a first draft and that what they need now are some positive reactions (no criticisms; this is a work in progress). They also encourage their parents to reminisce about the choosing of their names. These discussions will provide details and new information for students to use in their revisions.

Day Three: Response and Revision

In class, students read their drafts, which they will revise for homework, in their response groups. A basic revision technique is adding new information to a draft. Naming drafts are perfect for demonstrating this. First, the students have new details and anecdotes that they have learned from their parents. And second, since students are genuinely curious about one another's names, they tend to ask questions that draw out more information when they are responding in their groups.

Martin's draft and revision are an example:

> My name was Carlos. When I was young, I got very ill. My parents took me to hospitals all over Mexico. All the doctors gave me shots in my behind and that didn't do any good. I got worse, my family didn't know what to do. They thought I was going to die.
>
> One night my mother had a dream that I was going to get better. Early in the morning my mother took me to a nearby church. In a corner of the church was a Saint named San Martin de Porres. My mother put me in his open arms and prayed for hours. When it got late, she took me home. As days passed I started getting better. My father thought it was a miracle, so they renamed me after the Saint, Martin.

Martin was asked three questions by his response group, and he made small changes in his draft in answer to them. How old were you when it happened, they wanted to know. So Martin changed his second sentence from "When I was young . . . " to "When I was two years old . . . " They wanted lurid details about the shots. Martin responded orally but didn't want to write about it. Instead, he added the sentence, "All it did was give me problems lying in bed." Because of his reticence to give the details, the revision was limited. They were also curious about the statue of San Martin de Porres. Martin changed the phrase from "a Saint named San Martin de Porres" to "a stone figure of San Martin de Porres." This was the students' first time with revision, and Martin's are beginning efforts, but they improve the writing. His readers can now envision a little two-year-old lying in the stone arms of a statue.

Martin got his additional information from his parents. When students share their drafts at home, it provides parents an opportunity to tell them how they felt when the children were born and what went into the choosing of their names. For many parents and students it's a lovely exchange. Conversely, it's wise to plan for students being unable or unwilling to interview parents. They can do the first writing about their names, but when it comes to interviewing, they may want to change their focus and study someone else's name, that of a friend or a teacher.

Day Four: Reading Final Papers Aloud and Looking at Naming Traditions

Public reading sessions are serious, frightening at first for some students, yet very rewarding. To establish an atmosphere of equals, I put the class in a circle. Everyone, myself included, reads aloud and receives one or two comments of praise. Then we discuss the content. In naming papers, we look for two things: naming folklore and kernels of ideas imbedded in the writing that could be the basis for another piece based on the naming narratives.

Sample opening paragraphs from different classes show the richness of this activity, both as a subject for writing and as a source for further research. In a junior suburban classroom, Trish wrote:

> My parents and grandparents named me this [Patricia Kathleen Day] because my parents are first generation from Ireland! so they wanted the first born to have a full Irish name! . . .

Trish's family naming folklore maintains cultural heritage. Trish could write about this tradition: Why do people practice it? What connections does she feel to Ireland through her name?

Lisa's writing introduced another tradition:

> Before I was born my parents decided what my name was going to be if I was a girl. Like most Catholic families, they chose my name after a Saint. Saint Isabella and Mother Mary were the saints my parents chose. They changed Isabella to Lisa and Mary to Marie. I now have the name Lisa Marie Richnavsky. I feel happy with my name because it also belonged to two other beautiful women. . . .

In an article on names, Byrd Howell Granger writes, "Saints' names have long been used in the pious hope that those bearing the names might not only emulate their patron saints, but also gain their protection" (1961, 28). The students noticed that Lisa's parents didn't let religious tradition override aesthetic concerns: they changed the saints' names to names that pleased them.

A Chinese student, who asked to remain anonymous, wrote:

> In my language [his name] is a name of a tree which lives the longest of all among other trees in the forest. Because of its meaning, my uncle got this wild idea about naming his nephew a name which describes the lifespan of his nephew. Of course as you already know, younger people can't disobey whatever their elders tell them to do; so therefore, my dad agreed with his older brother, my uncle, in naming me—since it means that I shall live a long life. . . .

Even from this brief paragraph, we see a Chinese cultural respect for elders, including older siblings. We also see some Eastern naming folklore: naming done by the eldest male in the family, and naming from nature, using words that embody desirable qualities like long life.

In an inner-city class, Miguel, a talented artist, wrote:

> My name is Miguel Angel Hernandez. My first and middle names were picked by my mother and father from Michelangelo the famous painter, but . . . they used the Spanish term for it rather than the Italian. . . .

Another tradition is to name after famous persons: artists, actors and actresses, characters from books. Often the person is a hero or heroine to the parent at the time the child is named. Miguel's classmates wanted to know if his parents had wanted him to be an artist. Had his name shaped him?

In Theodore's writing, the value of the prewriting interview is evident.

> My name is Theodore "Theo" Vargas. How did I get my name? I got it from my dad who tried to honor his older uncle by naming me after him. I really don't know anything about my uncle because my father doesn't like talking about him. My grandmother said he was a bad man and was killed for being bad. Me, I think maybe when I was born, my father thought I was going to be bad like my uncle, so he named me after him.

The students shied away from responding to Theo's last sentence, although they listened carefully when he read. They talked in general about the power of names to determine character. It is a good issue to discuss and write about: Does the name make the individual? Or do we make names for ourselves?

Rhonda wrote of the fun she and her friends have nicknaming one another.

> All of my nicknames fit my description, for instance Lil Ms. Butterworth (big behind), Crazy Girl, CG (everyone thinks I'm crazy), Sparkle (in my eyes, smile, personality and attitude), Looney Tune (funny person). I received those nicknames from friends and cousins. They usually don't call me those names unless we're laughing about them or I don't want someone to know my real name like when meeting a stranger walking down the street.

Students can study and write about the origins and functions of nicknames. Nicknames make an interesting comparison to given names because often they are acquired later in life and are descriptive, unlike names given at birth. Nicknames, however, can also define and mold us.

When parents give a child a name in vogue (oral folklore), they seldom realize they are choosing a popular name. In fact, they often believe they are choosing an unusual name. Monica's mother had this experience:

> My mother chose the name Monica Marie because no other person in our family or neighborhood had that name. Now my mother slightly regrets the name because I have two cousins with the same name. I also have three friends who come over my house with the same name.

How is this possible? When parents choose such a name, it is already popular in oral tradition, but they are unaware that they have learned it by hearing it frequently. People don't pay much attention to oral tradition as a source of information. Consequently, parents believe they are choosing an unusual name, only to discover later that it is a fad.

After the papers are read, students look for class-wide family, ethnic, regional, or religious patterns. In one instance, students noticed that while sons were often named after fathers, daughters were seldom named after mothers. They speculated on the meaning of this tradition: more evidence that males are more valued? Some students were named after movie stars, a common American tradition and evidence that movie stars are heroes and heroines in our culture.

Black students see that they carry an amalgamation of naming traditions, reflecting different strands of their history. Black male students are often named for their fathers. There are more "juniors,"

"II's" and "III's" among Black students than in other groups. Juniors, II's and III's are western culture traditions. On the other hand, many Black students have unique invented names. Black American language is noted for creative word play, and many ascribe invented Black names to this alone. But some West African tribes, the tribes of the slaves, invented names to celebrate the uniqueness and individuality of the newborn. There's a good chance that Black families are carrying on this tradition. Other West African tribes, the Yoruba, for example, name the young for heroes. When Black Americans name children for heroes, which they commonly do, they may be carrying on an ancient African tradition as well. This, however, is also a western European custom. In short, Black naming traditions are drawn from several sources.[3]

By reading papers aloud, especially at the beginning of the year, students get to know one another, have some fun, and begin to feel comfortable about sharing writing. Furthermore, the study of the folklore of names can be a positive way into the study of different cultural and ethnic groups. Naming traditions herald and welcome the newborn and reflect important, positive values of the family or other folk groups. Students can identify the traditions and the functions of these traditions in their families. When they are given family names, for instance, they are being bonded into the family. When they are given unique names, their individuality is also being celebrated. If students want to generalize about these values, they will have to expand their research beyond their nuclear family, finding out how cousins, aunts, uncles, grandparents, and family friends of similar background got their names.

Day Five and Later: Further Activities

The folklore of naming can conclude with the class reading and discussion just described, and it can be a beginning of another project. Students can follow their naming narrative with another writing based on an idea from the narrative. Beto, for example, could explore the implications of living in a country where the majority cannot pronounce your name. Another topic is the prophetic power of names; do they believe, as a *Time* essayist suggested, that " . . . a boy named John will grow up differently from one named Cuthbert"? Naming narratives can also be the beginning of a larger study of family names. Some teachers do a unit including a family tree, interviewing other family members for their naming stories, designing a family crest based on what has been learned. It can become a small research project with students using library sources to discover the history and historical meanings of their names. Other teachers use naming as the beginning of autobiographical work or oral histories.

"In this Earth everybody has to have a name or they are no one." Verena might have continued, "but once a name is bestowed they become someone." The names we are given define us and stay with us for our lifetimes. At first glance, the folk traditions behind the giving of these names seem a small commonplace matter, but they are not.

Unit in Brief

Day One: Introduction to the Folklore of Names

- Log entry topic: "On this earth everyone has to have a name or they are no one." (This is not discussed in the chapter, but it is a nice alternative opening. If you use it, plan on an extra period for the writing and discussion of the writing.)
- Whole class discusses the folklore of names focusing first on the name of the teacher or one of the students.
- Students interview each other about their names.
- Homework: Read chapter 1 of Alex Haley's Roots. It describes an African naming ritual.

Day Two: Role-playing—"What to Name the Baby?" and First Drafts on Names

- Compare and contrast the naming traditions in Roots with those from the class. What do the Mandinkas value?
- Role-play: "What to name the baby?"
- Students write first drafts on their names in class.
- Homework: Students read the drafts to parents and ask for positive response and also for more memories from the parents of what went into their naming.

Day Three: Response and Revision

- Students read drafts in groups, get responses, and revise drafts for homework.

Day Four: Reading Papers Aloud and Looking at Naming Traditions

- Students read revisions aloud in class. Others give them positive feedback. Everyone identifies the naming folklore in the writing, discusses its meaning and the values it implies, and looks for naming trends in the class.

[Short version of the topic ends here.]

Day Five and Later: Further Activities

- Moving to expository writing: students use ideas embedded in naming narrative as basis for expository writing.

- For a longer unit that begins with the folklore of names, students
  —interview parents, cousins, aunts, uncles, grandparents, and family friends about their names and identify and analyze family naming patterns
  —research the history and historical meaning of their names
  —do a family tree
  —design a family crest
  —write an I-Search paper (See chapter 8) on names

Notes

1. Perhaps Shakespeare heard it, or perhaps he is the source. In *Othello*, Iago says:

> Who steals my purse steals trash . . .
> But he that filches from me my good name
> Robs me of that which not enriches him
> And makes me poor indeed. (III.iii)

2. From the introductory note to Newbell Niles Puckett's "Names of American Negro Slaves," in *Mother Wit from the Laughing Barrel*, Alan Dundes, ed., (Englewood Cliffs, New Jersey: Prentice Hall, 1973), p. 156.

3. See Sheila Walker, "What's in a Name?" *Ebony* 32 (June 1977), pp. 74–76, and P. Robert Paustian, "The Evolution of Personal Naming Practices among American Blacks," *Names* 26 (1978), pp. 177–91.

Chapter Five

"When I Was a Little Girl . . . "
The Folklore of Childhood

Day One: Introducing Children's Folklore

When I start this topic, the students have been introduced to folklore and know what it is. I start by saying, "Tell me some of the games you played as a child, ones you learned from other children." Some classes answer in a big competitive rush; others take their time as they warm to the subject.

"Jacks?" Rosalba asks tentatively; she is not quite sure what I am after. "Good," I say, and then because this is a prewriting as well as a brainstorming session, and I want to encourage details to use later in writing, I ask, "What do you remember about playing jacks?"

Lorenzo interrupts and starts laughing, "You start from 'onesies' and 'twosies'?" Everyone joins his laughter at the memory of "onesies and twosies." Maria suddenly remembers "Cherry in the basket!" and laughs. "What else do you remember?" I prod.

No hands are raised, but from somewhere in the back of the room I hear a tentative suggestion. "Jump rope?" "Good," I encourage, and ask, "Do you remember any jump rope rhymes?"

"Teddy bear, teddy bear," Olga chants, imitating a young child, and everyone laughs again. Gradually, the girls begin to remember their jump rope rhymes. "Windy, windy, weather . . . " "I was born in a frying pan . . . " "Ice cream soda, with a cherry on top . . . " "Apple on stick, makes me sick . . . " Rosalba is getting impatient with the jump rope rhymes; she wants to talk about something else. "I don't remember what it was called with the hands." Lorenzo helps her out, "Patty clap." The class remembers the elaborate handclapping games

87

the girls used to play. In some classes, more extroverted students will try and demonstrate the handclapping. Often when they try, they cannot remember the words and have forgotten the intricate hand-clapping patterns, although they enjoy the memory.

The reminiscing continues. Lorenzo suddenly remembers a popular playground game and shouts out, "The boys against the girls." The class is laughing again when someone quips, "We still do that!"

The opening discussion introducing children's folklore is a pleasure. High school students are nostalgic about childhood, perhaps because childhood, so strong and sweet and poignant, seems so far away that it makes them feel adult. Left to their own devices, students would happily reminisce for days about their childhood. A strong appeal of this unit is that it allows students, for a few weeks, to relive it.

After the entire class does some preliminary brainstorming on children's folklore, the students break up into groups of four—usually at this time I segregate the sexes because many of the games of childhood are sex specific, and on this topic they seem to do better brainstorming in a same-sex group. I give directions first. "In each group," I tell them, "try to remember as many kinds of games and play as you can that you did as children. Each time you mention a game, talk about it. Remember as many details as you can." Each group has a scribe. As games are mentioned, the scribe writes them down.

Here, a group of five male students remembers the folklore of their childhood. Miguel asks, "Gentlemen, what are we going to talk about today?" and offers the first memory: "Brother, I played soccer all my life." Lorenzo teases Miguel, making a pun on soccer, "Sucker?" The group laughs and banters the words "soccer" and "sucker" for a few seconds; then Miguel moves them back to the subject: "We used to throw things at this old guy and he used to tell us 'Get out of the grass!'"

Miguel turns to Lorenzo and asks, "How did you play *La Cuca-racha*?" Lorenzo is not interested and answers laconically, "Mexican sombrero, you throw it on the floor and go around it." Changing the subject, Miguel tells the group, "We used to play guns man, like we used to have a little—"

Ralph gets interested and interrupts, "BB guns—" Miguel stops Ralph, explaining, "Not all of us could afford BB guns, man, some of us had to use sling shots. We used to hide up in the trees and shoot people, you know, they didn't know we were across the street. *Ptttuu* [Miguel makes the sound of a missile being fired from a sling shot]."

Everyone laughs. Martin changes the direction of the talk. "Kick-ball—"

Tony agrees enthusiastically, "Yeah, I used to play kickball."

Now the group gets down to work and seriously lists ball games they played as children: volleyball, basketball, dodgeball, baseball. Lorenzo, the resident comic, changes the mood by bringing up "Play-[ing] 'Doctor' with the ladies." The others agree and comment, "Yeah, we still do that!"

The pace of their talk quickens as they begin to remember more. They interrupt one another as new memories come to mind. "Slap Jack," Ralph remembers. Miguel recalls, "We used to play Spin the Bottle." In chorus the others add, "Yeah, we did that." Martin is thinking along different lines and remembers, "In Mexico we used to shoot lizards."

"Run Down and Smear the Queer," Miguel suddenly adds. And then everyone is talking at once, sharing memories of "Run Down," such as "I used to aim for the head and then say, 'Oh, I'm sorry.'"

Not all groups get into remembering with such ease. To spot those that are floundering, I circulate and listen in. If the memories aren't flowing, I drop a few hints. For a group of girls I might ask, "Did you play with Barbies?" or "Did you have slumber parties?" or "Did you play with dolls?" For groups of either sex I mention Door Bell Ditch and prank telephone calls. I ask Miguel and his friends if they had ever played telephone tricks. Tony remembers. "You'd say, 'Is your refrigerator running? Well go get it!'" Martin tells of a telephone prank of his own invention. "I called up somebody, I had a whistle, and I put it up to the phone." Martin demonstrates how when the person at the other end picked up the phone, he blew into the whistle with all his might. "Oh man, that was mean." Ralph flinches at the thought.

In their group, the boys had enjoyed themselves and worked well. When they were finished, they had seventeen examples of children's folklore. Listening to the tape, I noticed that the boys were making some analytical observations that would be useful later in the unit. Toward the end of the session, for instance, Ralph commented on the violence in many of their games. Several times Miguel spoke with pride of the inventiveness of poor children. When someone mentioned water pistols, he sniggered, "Water pistols? We used to get those Windex things 'cause we didn't have water pistols." When someone suggested Monopoly, Miguel told him disdainfully, "No, those are board games. . . . We used to play from scratch, man!"

Day Two: Master List of Children's Folklore

The next day, we make a Master List of Children's Folklore. (See the end of this chapter for an example.) These lists usually contain between 100 and 150 items. Speculative talk accompanies the making of the list. Students discuss, for example, which games they think their parents and their grandparents played. (This can become a historical study of children's folklore in a family, with students interviewing parents and grandparents about the games of their childhood, looking for similarities and differences. They could, for instance, test Brian Sutton-Smith's claim (1968) that children's games are now more individualistic and competitive than they were fifty years ago.

As we make the list, we talk about girls' and boys' games and the ages students were when they played them. I ask about context—where the game was played, and about performance—who was good at it. We also speculate a little about function; why do children play these games? This discussion is preliminary, relaxed, exploratory talk about issues that will be more fully addressed later on.

What Is and Is Not Children's Folklore?

As new items are added to the list, they are tested. Most are clearly folklore, games and play that children teach each other in generations lasting a year or two. But some items raise questions. Commercial games such as Checkers and Ouija Boards are popular culture. However, when people begin to play the games and start making up their own rules, folklore enters. (Some commercial games, such as Battleship, were originally folk games.) Many of the material items children play with are commercially made, e.g., Hot Wheels, dolls, GI Joe dolls, Barbie and Ken dolls, toy trucks, etc. These are products of popular culture, but when children use them to make up their own games, as they invariably do, that is folklore.

Day Three: Choosing Paper Topics and Writing First Drafts

Students choose from the master list a game they liked to play when they were young, preferably a game they played often and can remember in some detail. After choosing, the students do some prewriting on it, maybe a cluster, or they might talk their memories over with a partner. James, a senior, came up with a cluster on shooting craps (see Figure 5–1). It delighted his classmates. Notice the headings for each cluster, "How to Lose," "How to Cheat," "How to Win," "Betting Money," "How to Get Beat Up," and "How to Get Arrested."

When it is time for first drafts, I say, "Write down everything you can remember. If you are writing about 'levitating' at a slumber party, for example, try to remember the details, such as what you chanted. Was it 'Light as a feather, stiff as a board'? If you were levitated,

Figure 5-1
Shooting Craps

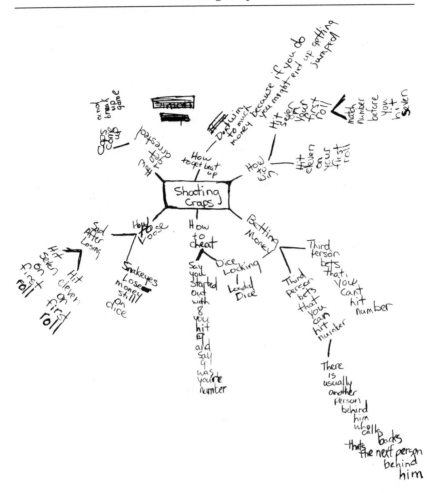

describe how it felt. Describe the context or setting and the performances of the different participants." I remind the students that this is a first draft and not the time to worry about producing polished writing. Ralph wrote the following first draft about learning to play the card game 21:

> I remember when my brother taught me to play 21 at the house, he must have wiped me out. After that day I would watch his hands and what was his strategy. After teaching myself the rules and everything else I would call up my friends and we would play for

money and everytime we played I wound up winning. We would
play in my backyard, behind the school, and sometimes we would
skip Sunday school and go play cards at a nearby park, but best of
all I would love to play my brother and beat him at his own game.
As I grew older I would watch my dad play cards and I wound up
teaching myself how to deal from the bottom of the deck and tell if
a person has a good hand by their facial expression.

Ralph's response group liked his draft and identified strongly with
the experience. Listening in, I learned how important a pastime card
playing is for these students. I was also impressed by how effectively
Ralph had taught himself to be something of a master card player and
mentioned it to the group. They disputed my point; learning, as they
conceive it, takes place in the classroom. Ralph doesn't consider
himself to be a good student. In the discussion, I tried to show him
that on the contrary, when motivated, as in learning to play 21, he
was an excellent student.

In a suburban classroom studying children's folklore, Jane Juska
and I team-taught. For this assignment, she stipulated that the memory should be written in first person and in the present tense to create
a sense of immediacy. One student, Lynn, wrote of playing Red Light,
Green Light:

Coming home from grade school, I can't wait to change out of my
school clothes and into a pair of jeans, grubby, old and faded. It
seems the whole neighborhood is in the same state of excitement for
everyday at approximately 2:30 pm we kids meet in the park by the
drinking fountain, dressed in play clothes and ready to play "Red
Light, Green Light." Standing in a circle, our fists thrust into the
center we wait as a boy, his brown hair messy from running, counts
out, "Eeine—Meine—Miny—Mo." This is one game when everyone
wants to be it. Calling out "Green light" and watching the pack of
kids scrambling forward to tag you before you yell "Red Light" is
always fun. We play until the sun sets in the west and we're weary
and rosy cheeked from running in the cool autumn air.

Before my arrival, Ms. Juska had been teaching cumulative sentences
and descriptive writing. In many of the drafts like Lynn's, the students were testing their new skills, playing with description and sentence structure. Kay, who forgot the injunction about first person,
wrote about "dressing up." She began:

Putting on her mother's bright red shoes, the little girl smiles, orange
lipstick smeared from ear to ear, she looks in the mirror at the image
so grown up in her eyes.

Susan, who was not yet as descriptive in her writing as some of
the other students, still writes effectively, showing the concentration
and thoroughness of little girls playing with their Barbie dolls:

I remember playing with my barbies from morning till night. I had sacs & sacs full of junk. Barbie clothes, Barbie furniture, Barbie cars & motor homes & of course I had my Ken doll. I had a blond and a brunette Ken doll, I always preferred the brunette, which is kind of funny because I still prefer brunets today. I would make my houses for my dolls very early & it usually took me 3–4 hours . . .

These early drafts are valuable. From them, I learn about the lives of the students and folklore new to me. Students who grew up in a poor Black neighborhood taught me about folk characters who were rapists. Discussing them in class, Pam explained, "Billie Do, he was a rapist. They used to call him that. We used to get scared at night time [we'd be] walking down the street and they'd say, 'Billie Do behind the bushes!' and everybody'd start running."

"I thought he was the Dickie Man," Robert interrupted her. Rhonda remembered being warned not to stay after school or else the Dickie Man would come and mutilate or kill her. "If you saw the Dickie Man, you were supposed to pray, then you could be saved," Rhonda explained.

I also learn about regional and ethnic variations on traditional folklore. Olga, a Mexican-American student, wrote a draft about hopscotch. "In the middle of the street I would start drawing the game while Rose got a bowl of water and thread," she wrote. "Why a bowl of water and thread?" I asked. "We played with the water and thread because it was easier for wet thread to land on the number, not like other little objects that you throw which bounce and roll away." I told Olga about the small, flat stones that I used as a child and called "potsies." The thread and water is a nice variation.

These drafts, the memories of childhood play, usually make good reading. The content is compelling. Students like the subject and are in control because the material comes from their own lives.

Day Four: Responding and Revising

The memory writing will be incorporated into a larger paper on childhood folklore. But now, students read their drafts in small groups, get responses, and do a first revision. They then store the papers in their writing folders.

Brief Alternatives

In one alternative, students revise their writing and complete the unit now. The purpose of the unit would simply be writing a memory piece. For a longer alternative unit, the memory piece can be a source of ideas for an expository essay. These memory pieces have seeds of ideas that can be explored further. Ralph, for instance, could use his paper on learning to play 21 to investigate what is meant by "learning."

A fuller study of children's folklore, however, requires at least another week, entails some research in the form of interviews, observations, if possible, and some analysis of the folklore.

Day Five: Starting the Research—Interviewing

To study children's folklore, students need more information than their memories provide. Folklorists gather much of their information through interviews. The students interview three people: an older person who remembers playing the game as a child; a peer, who also remembers the game; and a child who is still playing it. When possible, the student researcher observes the child.

Students create an interview questionnaire discussing what type of information they want to gather (see Figure 5–2). Each student makes up several questions. (I offer a few hints, such as avoiding questions that can be answered "Yes" or "No.") From these the class selects the best ones and creates a questionnaire. If the class doesn't suggest numbers one through five on the questionnaire, I add them. Beyond these, the students decide what to include. Students first practice in class. Two volunteers conduct an interview in the front of the room while the class watches and takes notes. Afterwards, they discuss what worked and what needed adjustment.

Lorenzo, who was studying the game Smear the Queer agreed to interview Miguel. Before they began, I asked which interviewers they liked on TV. "Barbara Walters," Lorenzo answered. "Good," I told him. "Pretend you're Barbara Walters."

"I got to stand up right here?" Lorenzo asked, beginning to have second thoughts. Miguel asked helpfully, "You got your list, man?" Increasingly uncomfortable, Lorenzo asked, "My what? I have to stand up here by myself?" I suggested that he invite Miguel to join him at the front of the room.

"I have to stand up too?" Now Miguel was having doubts. Lorenzo hit upon a solution, "Here, get a chair, man, can we get a chair? That's the way Barbara Walters—" Before he had finished speaking, everyone was laughing.

Lorenzo was not at ease. To mask his embarrassment, he spoke in stilted, mocking tones, imitating formal interview style. "Umm, Umm, Umm, Umm, what is your name?" He began. The class laughed. Miguel played it straight, however, and the interview proceeded.

Figure 5-2
Children's Folklore Interview Questionnaire

1. Interviewer's name _____
2. Interviewee's name and age _____
3. Date and place of the interview _____
4. The topic *(Hide and Seek, for example)* _____
5. How did you learn to play? _____

_____

The rest of these questions come from different class interview sheets. Not all questions will be appropriate for all types of play and games. For instance, questions about competitive games don't apply to playing school.

6. If you remember, what happened the first time you played?
7. What did you like best (least) about the game and why?
8. What things or objects are needed to play?
9. How many people are needed to play?
10. Tell me about the people you played with.
11. Describe where you played.
12. What time of day did you play?
13. How often did you play?
14. Describe the good players and the bad players.
15. Did you get into any fights or arguments? If you did, tell about them.
16. If the game had a person who was "It," did children want to be it or not? Why?
17. Describe how it felt to win or lose.
18. Is it a boys' game or a girls' game? Why?
19. Why do you think children play this game?
20. What kinds of things do you think they are learning when they play?

M: Miguel.

L: How old are you, Miguel? [laughter]

M: Seventeen right now.

L: What nationality are you? [laughter; everyone in the class is Latino.]

M: Mexican-American.

L: Okay, do you remember the first time you played?

M: Played what?

L: Smear the Queer.

M: Yeah, in junior high.

L: Why?

M: 'Cause everybody else did it.

L: How did you learn?

M: I was—I watched my friends do it.

L: What was the best part of it, of playing Smear the Queer with your friends?

M: Hitting somebody . . . hitting somebody . . . hitting somebody you didn't like.

L: Do you still play this game since you are older now?

M: No.

L: What do, oh . . . did you get in fights or arguments?

M: Yeah.

L: Why?

M: [Laughs] 'Cause somebody thought they'd hit 'em on—you know, somebody'd get hit, and they didn't have the ball or something.

L: Go on. Is that it?

M: That's it.

L: What did you gain by playing this?

M: Bruises, bruises, brother. [laughter]

L: Did your mother approve of this game?

M: No [laughs] she didn't know about it, actually.

L: How many people played?

M: I think it was about ten guys.

L: Did you guys play with a football, softball, can, or pillow?

M: No, we played with a football.

L: How does it feel to hit somebody, I mean just really hit em? [laughter]

M: If it's somebody you don't like, it doesn't matter, it doesn't make a difference.

L: How did it feel when you got hit?

M: When I got hit man, I felt like hitting somebody else.

L: Was it fun?

M: Yeah, sometimes when there wasn't any fights.

L: Is it for boys and girls? And why?

M: One girl played, she got stuck [slang for "hit"], though. [laughter]

L: So you're saying this is only for boys.

M: I'm not saying that; I'm referring to the fact that [laughter] that ladies can play, but they have to take it like everybody else, not just like a man but like everybody else does.

L: I agree with you. What kind of people did you play with? You know, were they older than you?

M: No, they were my age, but they were like . . . they were big.

L: How often did you play this game?

M: Oh, I think every day—at lunch.

L: Did you ever get in trouble playing this game, with the principal, or you know—

M: No, the security guards stopped us from playing like that.

L: Did you guys go to jail?

M: Never.

L: Have you ever been convicted of a crime?

M: No. [laughter] You're getting off the subject, man.

When the interview was over, the class critiqued it, starting with what they liked about it. "The fun!" Martin said. Good point. I elaborated by telling the class to try to enjoy interviewing, to make it fun for themselves and at the same time to help the interviewee relax. We complimented Lorenzo. I noted that several times he had departed from the list of questions, which is good, for ad-libbed questions can be the heart of an interview. Lorenzo added these questions: "Did your mother approve of this game?" "How does it feel to hit someone, really hit them?" "Did you ever get in trouble [playing Smear the Queer]?" These questions elicited relevant information. They added to the interview, because Lorenzo really was curious about the answers. By comparison, his last question was not appropriate. He had a dilemma; he didn't know how to end the interview gracefully, so he resorted to the playful way he and Miguel normally relate. However, Miguel wouldn't let him get away with it and gently brought him back to the task at hand.

During the study of children's folklore, some of the students joked about being poor as little kids. They were proud of their ingenuity and creativity, so when Lorenzo asked, "Did you play with a football, softball, can, or pillow?" he was referring to their improvisations, and his joke was appreciated.

While Lorenzo had asked a few spontaneous follow-up questions, he had overlooked other good opportunities. For instance, Miguel mentioned that he remembered the first time he had played the game, but Lorenzo didn't follow it up. During the class discussion of the interview, Miguel did talk about it.

Well, my friend, one of my friends, told me to come in and play 'cause he used to just watch me sit there, watching them play, so he told me to go out there and play, and I was scared at first because most of them guys were pretty big. But then, so I went there, and after you hit somebody, you know, you get used to being hit. So, I was cool, but when I got hit, I got mad—

Maria interrupted, "I have a question: Did you guys hit each other hard?"

"Friends we didn't hit them that hard, we just kind of bumped them and that's it, but people we didn't like, we stuck 'em," Miguel explained.

Since I wanted the students to be constantly thinking about following up promising answers, I pointed out two others that I would have pursued with more questions. I was curious about the girl who played. I also noticed that during the interview Miguel mentioned fighting, often joking about it. It seemed an important part of the game, but when asked what made a good game, he said that a good game didn't have any fights. I would have asked Miguel to explain this contradiction.

In the discussion that followed the interview, no one brought up the game's title. The game, a common one, is widely known as Smear the Queer but has other names, such as Kill the Pig and Get the Man with the Ball. The game is best played with a group. One player throws the ball, another catches it and then tries to break away from the pack and avoid being tackled. The player who catches the ball is the "queer"; if he fails to get away, he gets "smeared." (For a study of Smear the Queer see Dundes 1985, 115–29.)

Part of the appeal of folklore in the classroom is that it is about life in the real world. Smear the Queer is a good example. The boys learn something useful about playing football, but they also learn a pejorative label for homosexuals from the title. It is helpful to discuss the meaning of the game and the title. The game needs to be evaluated in terms of the subtle ways in which prejudices permeate society; how they are learned unconsciously by children playing games. When, for instance, do they learn that "queer" is an epithet for homosexual? One ten-year-old, when interviewed, said that a queer was someone who was retarded or weird. He and his friends called a homosexual a "faggot." An interesting contradiction to consider is that when the "queer" gets away from the pack, he is the hero. All the boys want to catch the ball and successfully pull away from the crowd.

Homework for the next two nights is to conduct three interviews; these can be eye openers. Rhonda, for instance, discovered that her friend's recollection of Simon Says was at odds with hers. Rhonda's memory of the game was dominated by the competitive pressure she felt while playing. She remembered:

> When playing the game, I tend to get a little tense, tight, stiff, also a bit of a headache from carrying out commands, from the sunshine beaming down on the top of my head, from the fear that I might lose and from the excitement that I might win.

Her friend remembered violence. She explained, "Simon would say, 'Simon Says slap Jane Doe,' and you would have to slap her or be out of the game."

Day Six: Scholarly Analysis of Children's Folklore

In preparation for the analysis of their folklore, students look through the analytical works of professional folklorists. This serves two purposes: the writings are, of course, models for what the students can do, and at the same time they legitimize the study of folklore.

A book to start with, *The Lore and Language of Schoolchildren*, by Iona and Peter Opie and noted earlier, comes from England. The Opies' work is unusual—a scholarly work that is also a successful popular book. (They do, however, shy away from sensitive areas of scholarship, such as scatological and erotic lore.) The Opies' presentation of British children's lore includes many examples of closely related American lore. The reader not only enjoys a well-written book but also gets a good feel for the variety and volume of children's lore. The Opies also do a commendable job tracing the historical roots of the lore. Another useful collection that also offers some analysis is Herbert and Mary Knapp's *One Potato, Two Potato . . . The Folklore of American Children* (1976).

These two books can be sources for students in search of variations on the folklore they are studying. Edward, a Black student, was concentrating on the children's legend, "Johnny I want my eyes back." In Edward's version, Johnny's mother sends him to the store to buy some black-eyed peas. But Johnny spends the money on candy. On the way home he cuts through a cemetery, pokes out the eyes of several corpses, and presents these to his mother instead of the peas. That evening the corpses rise up from their graves in search of their eyes. Ever so slowly they walk down the road, turn up the path to Johnny's house, mount the stairs, and enter Johnny's bedroom, chanting, "Johnny I want my eyes back, Johnny I want my eyes back." In *One Potato, Two Potato . . .* , Edward found a version where the liver is stolen from the corpse. (See also "Gotcha!" by Sylvia Grider [1980, 12]). Edward and his classmates were amused by the Afro-American twist to the black-eyed peas legend, although they didn't mention the pun. Edward assumed that only he and his friends knew the story and were further surprised to find that it is a modern variant of a traditional folktale, "The Man from the Gallows" (AT366—Aarne Thompson Tale-Type Number, see chapter 1, pages 23–24). In the traditional tale, a man steals the heart or liver or stomach from a person who has been hanged and takes it to his wife to eat. Later, the ghost arrives to claim his stolen part and carries the man off.

The books by the Opies and the Knapps are essentially collections. These are useful, but students need to see analytical studies as well. Sometimes I have them read articles; sometimes I give a brief talk about several articles so students can see how different folklorists approach the same subject. One talk deals with three articles on telephone pranks. (See also Knapps, 100–104).

The talk begins with Norine Dresser's article, "Telephone Pranks" (1973), which is a good model study for students. Dresser's data was collected by teachers in eleven classrooms. Four hundred juniors and seniors were interviewed. Dresser feels that the most popular pranks served the social needs of "making positive social contacts [and] . . . releasing hostility and frustration with a minimum risk of retaliation" (122).

Dresser first discusses nonhostile pranks, those which allow for positive social contacts. Some are done to peers. Boys and girls, for example, call someone they know, usually of the opposite sex, giggle, and hang up. In others, adults are the targets, as when a number is dialed at random, the caller asks for Grandfather, and sings "Happy Birthday" to him. Most of the calls Dresser discusses, however, are hostile and directed against adults.

Dresser discusses two-victim calls, telephone company calls, obscene calls, phony contest winner calls, the formulaic call, and survey calls. Of the two-victim calls, the best known is the "Pizza" call—calling and ordering several pizzas, often for a neighbor. In one version of the telephone company call, the callers identify themselves as telephone repairmen working on the line. They tell the victim not to answer the phone for the next half hour because it would be dangerous for the repairman. Then they ring the number over and over, until finally out of desperation the victim answers. The callers then let out bloodcurdling screams, pretending they are being electrocuted. Phony contest winner and survey calls are parodies of the real thing. Formulaic calls are probably the best known of the pranks and include such classics as

> "Do you have Prince Albert in the can?"
> "Yes."
> "Well, let him out."

As to the source of the hostility behind telephone pranks, Dresser writes:

> The best possible explanation would appear to be linked with the age of these callers (11–15). . . . They are at the onset of adolescence, when the first stirrings of rebellion against adult rules are beginning (129).

The anonymity of the phone call, Dresser observes, is essential. The victim and the perpetrator are unknown to one another. "The protection of anonymity," Dresser explains, "provides a very safe method for releasing hostility or frustration and with little fear of retaliation" (128).

Dresser concludes:

> It would appear then that the telephone pranks serve a very important social need for the adolescent, and are a valuable means for expressing and communicating his ideas and his conflicts (129).

At first the students are incredulous that a folklorist would bother to study their telephone pranks and is condoning, even praising them. Students agree with much of Dresser's work but have some questions. In a footnote, Dresser suggests that telephone pranking does not begin in earnest until eighth grade. Her article was published in 1973. Students now report starting as early as fourth grade.

Dresser suggests that students with better language skills tend to improvise on established pranks and even make up their own. Students liked this idea and began to vie with one another for the best invented prank. Maria told us that when she was very little, she and her friends called the operator and pretended they were being robbed. Within minutes, they heard police sirens. Before the police arrived at the door, Maria and her friends were escaping over the back fence.

To demonstrate that there are different ways to tackle the same subject, I also tell the students about Marilyn Jorgensen's article, "A Social-Interactional Analysis of Phone Pranks" (1984), which focuses on the types of dialogue used and its formal features, such as rhymes, alliteration, polysemy (words with multiple meanings), and puns. Jorgensen contends that one reason for the continued popularity of telephone pranks is the verbal play. There are, for instance, formulaic parodies of the way businesses answer the telephone. She mentions

> Morgan's Morgue
> You stab 'em, we slab 'em.

Pranks that depend on double meanings of words are also popular. One involves calling a market and asking:

> "Do you have pop in a bottle?"
> "Yes."
> "Well, let him out. Mom wants him."

Or,

> "Do you have chicken legs?"
> "Yes."
> "Well, wear long pants and they won't show."

To show yet another perspective and disagreement about interpretation among folklorists, I also mention Trudier Harris's "Telephone Pranks: A Thriving Pastime" (1978). She notes, as the others have, that the pranks are probably as old as the telephone. Her focus is different; she categorizes the pranks according to commercial and residential calls. And she disagrees with Dresser, maintaining that the purpose "is always the same—make an idiot of the person on the receiving end of the prank. . . . " (138). She adds another point of interpretation; an important appeal of the pranks is that the callers enjoy the power they have over the anonymous adult on the other end.

All three, Dresser, Jorgensen, and Harris, identified the genre, collected versions, and then analyzed their data. Dresser focused on the functions of the jokes, Jorgensen looked more at verbal play, and Harris at the longevity of the pranks. They were all trying to figure out why children play telephone pranks.

I finish by telling the students that they will all have something not found in scholarly works—their first-person narrative accounts of the folklore. Furthermore, I point out to the students that no analysis is ever final. They can always ask new questions, bring in new information, and develop new theories. They can see already some gaps in these three studies. There is no mention of the ethnicity of the players, and no attempt is made to see if there are any male/female differences in the types of pranks played. Each writer seems to assume that all American children play the same pranks the same way and for the same reasons.

From the articles or the lectures, students should learn the steps involved in folklore research: identifying, collecting, and analyzing the folklore. They should learn that there is more than one way to interpret the data. And finally, they should see their own experiences as valuable data and a source of analytical ideas.

Day Seven: Student Analysis of Children's Folklore

Although the students have discussed earlier some of the functions of folklore, we review them:

1. Some folklore teaches the rules of society—values, attitudes, beliefs, and how to behave.
2. Some folklore offers relief from troubling matters.
3. Some folklore makes it possible to violate the rules of society.
4. Some folklore entertains.
5. Some folklore makes people feel closer together.

Once the students have chosen their topics, written their memories of the topic, and done several interviews, they are ready to tackle analysis. As a prewriting activity, students sometimes exchange their memory papers. At the end of the papers, readers write down their impressions of the functions of the particular folklore discussed. For example, Judy had written about Red Light, Green Light, her favorite childhood game, played in school at recess and also nightly in her neighborhood. Tom read her paper and wrote:

> I think you were learning to take risks. When someone called, "Green Light," you ran as fast as you could, taking the chance that when they called, "Red Light," you wouldn't be still moving. It was also a form of entertainment because it took up much of your time. It brought you close together with your friends and neighbors.

Trisha had written of playing Hide and Seek. Jennifer read her paper and wrote this note:

> Hide and Seek has the functions of entertaining the people who are playing it and it could be that it teaches you to hide from something bad or scary, because if you are hidden it can't find you, and if it can't find you, it can't hurt you. It also teaches kids to cooperate because they have to decide on certain rules. It's a game of strategy because you have to figure out where to hide and if there's a base, how to get back.

Jeff wrote of Capture the Flag, which he had called War. Twenty boys were divided into two groups. Each team had a flag. The object was to capture the opposing team's flag without getting "killed." Jon read his paper and wrote back:

> War was played to teach you to be patriotic and proud. It helped bring out the male dominance role that is programmed in society.

Sissie wrote of playing a neighborhood game of softball and got this note:

> Sometimes when friends get together, just sitting around talking can be uncomfortable. Finding a favorite game that everyone likes can bring you closer together so you really have a great time.

When Ron was little, he looked forward to day care where every day he and his friends played in the yard with toy "army men." They shot at each other's "men" with rubber bands that "acted like high power rifles tearing off arms, legs and heads." He got this suggestion:

> I think it is teaching you to be tough, to be a man. Also you are breaking some of the rules when you tear off the army men's legs, arms and heads.

Another prewriting activity is partner or small-group talk. After hearing a paper, students can offer their answers to questions such as, "What did you learn playing the game which is still important?" and "What was important about the game just at the time you were playing?" When the students write drafts of their analyses, some incorporate the suggestions of their classmates, others do not.

Last Days: Writing the Final Paper

The final papers in this unit vary. Students without much experience in writing can successfully complete the unit with three separate pieces of writing: the childhood memory, the interviews, and the analysis. More skilled writers can take their data and reformulate it into a paper that includes their memory, describes the folklore, and analyzes it. Within a given class, especially a heterogeneously grouped one, there is a wide spectrum of final products. The papers of Robert, Pamela, and Ava, three students from an inner-city class, are examples of the diversity within one class.

At the end of the school year, we published a booklet of student writings. Most of them had never seen their written words in print before. Robert, one of the least skilled students, chose to include his essay on playing Doctor. He rewrote it five times before it was ready. It opened with the sentence, "The game Doctor reveals all closed doors." He went on to describe how he remembered playing:

> First I pretended to examine her reflexes. I hit her knee. I grabbed her hand and touched her breast and looked in her eyes and said, "They're okay," and checked her lips and kissed them, and said, "They're okay," and giggled a little.

Robert was proud of his writing. The class joked about their own memories of Doctor playing days.

The next piece was written by Pam, a capable senior with little interest in school. In folklore class, however, she turned out to be a fluent writer. Her children's folklore paper was on jump rope:

> Jumprope has been around forever. I played it, my mother played it, her mother and her mother played it. When I was little about 12 girls played jumprope with us. The more we had, the more fun it was. The only thing I hated was when my socks fell down. The way we played was 2 people held the ends. Whoever got out had to hold the rope and the previous rope holder got in line. You could jump with one or more persons if you wanted, but whoever got out, held the rope. We didn't have steady enders because everyone wanted to play. What I loved the most was when it was time out for Kool Aid. We always had plenty and even today I still drink it every day.

> I didn't know that the game was originally a boy's game [this
> information was in one of the readings]. When we played, boys
> always teased, grabbed the rope and made us miss. They would
> jump in and jump out and laugh and tease us about our songs.
>   You can learn from jumprope too. We learned how to get along
> and take turns. We learned rhythm. We jumped to music, singing and
> sometimes to our own humming.

Pam's classmates appreciated the details of her socks falling down,
the memory of "steady enders," and the description of the boys dis-
rupting the game. They liked her interpretation that by playing jump
rope the girls were learning to cooperate. They also liked the mention
of rhythm in the game. The syncopation of African-American musical patterns was a critical part of their childhood play that they
delight in recalling and reenacting.

One of the best students in the class wrote a more analytical
paper, five typewritten pages on telephone pranks. Ava, who had
been playing telephone pranks for years, discussed her own pranks
and those she learned about while interviewing friends and family.
Studying her data, Ava noticed something not mentioned in the three
articles. At different ages, she had played different pranks. She traces
her developmental stages as a telephone prankster:

> First came the sort of "starter" pranks—ordering flowers and food
> (Chinese and pizza).... another early prank was calling to say
> "hello" or just to bother somebody. ... My version of this was to call
> and try to chat at 2 o'clock in the morning.

These were followed by more complicated pranks such as those
requiring a series of calls:

1. Is Lisa there?
   No.
2. Is Lisa there?
   No.
3. Is Lisa there?
   No.
4. Hello, this is Lisa. Have there been any calls for me?

Next, Ava describes illicit pranks she graduated to:

> "Hello, I'm calling from a local market whose name cannot be
> revealed to you, but we would appreciate it if you took part in our
> survey. How often do you shop?"
> "Three times a week."
> "What is the average total of your bill?"
> "Thirty dollars."
> "What brand of peanut butter do you buy?"
> "Jiffy."
> "How long does it take you to reach orgasm?"

In her article, Dresser mentions that the primary audience for phone pranks is the caller's friends, not the person being called. While Ava agreed, she also made some interesting additional observations. As she got older, she got more interested in the reaction of the person called. When she was younger—she played from age seven to fourteen—she hung up immediately, never waiting for a response. But as she got older, she began engaging people in longer conversations.

Ava's paper emphasized power. She felt that the dominion the telephone gives kids over adults at the other end of the line is the key to understanding the appeal of the pranks. Ava also mentioned historical changes in the playing of telephone pranks that she had noticed in her research:

> To my parents' (or perhaps grandparents') generation, the form of the prank was much different. Instead of calling to say something, they listened in on the party line, only occasionally saying something to bewilder the other people.

She concluded with the observation that today's popular culture emphasis on sex is reflected in the game. Telephone pranks by students her age (fifteen) today are mostly about sex. Finally, she predicts that telephone pranks are here to stay unless "video phones" come in.

Robert and Pam, students who had relatively limited writing experience, depended more on their narratives. Ava, with a stronger writing background, incorporated her experience into a paper that focused on analysis.

This unit in children's folklore takes roughly two weeks and accomplishes much. First, the study of childhood folklore gives students great pleasure. Not only is it just plain fun to reminisce about childhood, this study takes the mundane events of their early lives and elevates them into valuable studies of American culture. Students learn about how cultures subtly and constantly inculcate values in the young from an early age. They also see cultural beliefs in a new light and a new setting. Equally important, the information from their folklore helps the students mature academically as they write narratives, conduct interviews, and write analytical essays.

Unit in Brief

Day One: Introducing Children's Folklore

- Whole class reminisces about childhood folklore.
- Small groups make lists of their childhood folklore.

Day Two: Master List of Childhood Folklore

- From the lists made the previous day in small groups, class compiles a master list of children's folklore.

Day Three: Choosing Paper Topics and Writing First Drafts

- Students choose paper topics from the master list.
- Prewriting: students do brainstorms on their topics.
- Students write first draft of memory of childhood game or play and finish the drafts for homework.

Day Four: Responding and Revising

- Students respond to first drafts in small groups.
- Students begin to revise drafts and finish the drafts for homework.

Day Five: Starting the Research—Interviewing

- Whole class creates interview sheet.
- Students practice interviews, first the whole class, then in pairs.

Day Six: Scholarly Analysis of Children's Folklore

- Students review books and articles on children's folklore.
- Students read selected articles and discuss in small groups.
- Teacher lecture on scholarly analysis of children's folklore.

Day Seven: Student Analysis of Children's Folklore

- Students help one another to understand the functions of the folklore they are studying.
- Students read one another's papers and comment in writing or
- Students discuss papers in small groups and offer suggestions.

Last Days: Writing the Final Paper

- Students write the final paper.
- Students publish and read papers. If the papers are short, this can be done orally with a general read around, followed by discussion. If the papers are long, several can be read aloud to the whole class and discussed, parts of papers can be read aloud, or students can read each other's papers silently and then discuss them.

Optional Final Evaluation: Closure on the Unit

- Log entry on the unit: for example, what were the best parts? The worst parts? What did you learn? Suggestions for next year?

Or

- Write any comments or observations you have about the study of children's folklore

Or

- Any other log writing that will bring closure to the unit.

Master List of Children's Folklore: Inner-city Class

Batman and Robin
Bloody Mary
Billy Bo
Bogeyman
Bubble Gum, Bubble Gum in a
  Dish
Chicken
China Doll
Chinese Tag
Cigarettes
Club houses
Coffee, Tea, Milkshake, Pee
"Comet, It Makes Your Mouth
  Turn Green . . ."
Cooties
Cowboys and Indians
Crossed Fingers
"Cub Scout, You're Out . . ."
Dickie Man
Ding Dong, Long Gone
Doctor
Dodge Ball
Dolls
Door Bell Ditch
"Down, Down, Baby, Down by the
  Rollercoaster . . ."
Duck, Duck, Goose
"Eenie, Meanie, Miny, Mo . . ."
"Engine, Engine, Number
  Nine . . ."
Fat Momma
Father, May I?
Four Square
Freeze Tag
"Fudge, Fudge, Tell the Judge . . ."
Go Carts
Hambone
Handclapping
Hide and Go Get It
Hide and Seek

Hide the Belt
Holding Breath Until Dizzy
Homemade Forts
Hopscotch
HORSE
"I'm Rubber, You're Glue . . ."
Jacks
Jumping Rope
"Kings"
Knock, Knock, Boom, Boom,
  Zoom, Zoom
Knocking on Wood
Knuckles
Kung-Fu
Lead Pencils
Lizzie Borden
Marbles
Mother, May I?
Mud Pies
Mumbly Peg
"Not Last Night but the Night
  Before . . ."
"Oh, Mary Mack . . ."
Patty Cake
Peekaboo
Pencil Fights
Pitching Pennies
Playing Cards
Playing Church, Funeral, House,
  School
Popcorn
Red Light, Green Light
"Red, Red, You Peed in Bed . . ."
Ring Around a Rosie
Scary Stories
Seven-Up
"Shake, Shake, Shake to the
  'Rithmetic . . ."
"Shoe Counting"
Shooting Craps

Some of the folklore on this and the following list is idiosyncratic to the neighbor-hoods where the students grew up, influenced by ethnicity, region, and setting. The majority of children's folklore, however, is known in cities, in suburbs, and in the country.

Simon Says
Slingshots
Smear the Queer
"Step on a Line . . ."
"Sticks and Stones . . ."
String Figures
Superfriends
SWAT

Table Football
Tag
Telephone
Three Soul Bears
TIME
Tree Houses
Truth or Dare
Yoyos

Master List of Children's Folklore: Suburban Class

ABC Games
Arm Wrestling
Around the World
Baby Dolls
Barber
Barbie Dolls
Baseball
Basketball
Battleship
BB Guns
Blind Man's Bluff
Bloody Knuckles
Bloody Mary (Mary Worth)
Board Games (which can become
　　folk games)
　　Bingo
　　Checkers
　　Monopoly
　　Ouija Boards
　　Scoobie Doo
　　Shuffle Board
Boys Chase the Girls and Girls
　　Chase the Boys
Building Blocks
Building Forts
Cap Guns
Card Games
　　Go Fish
　　Old Maid
　　Poker
　　War
Card Houses
Charades
Chicken
Chinese Jacks

Colored Eggs
Cooties
Cops and Robbers
Cotton Balls
Cowboys and
　　Indians
Doctor
Dodge Ball
Doorbell Ditch
Dressing up
Duck, Duck, Goose
Egg in the Mouth
Evil Kneivel
500
Flame Thrower
Follow the Leader
Food Fights
Food Race
Football
Four Square
G. I. Joe
Handball
Handclapping
Hide and (Go) Seek
High Jump
High Water/Low Water
Hit and Run
Hopscotch
HORSE
Hose Fights
Hot Lava Monster
Hot 'n Cold
Hot Potato
Hot Wheels
House

Master List of Children's Folklore: Suburban Class, cont.

Hula Hoops
Hyperventilating
I Spy
Indian Ball
Jacks
Jump Rope (Chinese Jump Rope)
Keep Away
Kick the Can
Kickball
King of the Mountain
Leap Frog
License Plate Games
"Light as a Feather . . ."
Limbo
Little People
London Bridge
Mailman
Marbles
Mercy
Monkey Bars
Monkey in the Middle
Mother, May I?
Mud Pies
Murder in the Dark
Musical Chairs
Motorcycle Racing
Paper Airplanes
Paper Boats—Gutter Boating
Paper/Scissors/Rock
Pencil Fights
Pickle
Pillow Fights
Pin the Tail on the Donkey
Ping Pong
Pitching Pennies
Play Dough (homemade)
Poison
Post Office
Puddle Stomping or Walking in
    Puddles or Splashing in
    Puddles
Red Light, Green Light
Red Rover
Ring Around the Rosie
Sandcastles
School

Seances
Sharks and Guppies or Minnows
Shoes
Simon Says
Skipping Rocks
Slap Ball
Slumber Parties
Smear the Queer
Snowball Fights
Soap Bubbles
Spin the Bottle
Stick Ball
Tag:
    Ball
    Bicycle
    Body
    Cartoon
    Flashlight
    Football
    Freeze
    Line
    Marco Polo
    Newspaper
    Shadow
    Tunnel
    TV
Tarzan
Tea Parties
Telephone Pranks
Tetherball
Three Flies Up
Tic, Tac, Toe
Tiddly Winks
Towel Whip (Fights)
TPing
Treasure Hunts
Trick or Treat
Truth or Dare
Twenty Questions
Tug of War
War
Water Balloon Fights
Water Pistols or Squirt Guns
Weed Bomb Fights
"Who Stole the Cookie . . ."
Yoyos

Chapter Six

The Cat Burglar
Family Folklore I—Stories Our Families Tell About Us

In an inner-city classroom, we devoted four days to one genre of family folklore: stories that our families tell about us. Rosie, a gregarious, playful member of the class, wrote "Peeking Rosie." Rosie opens her paper with background to a family story her mother likes to tell about Rosie. When she was a little girl, her family moved in with her aunt. At first, Rosie was timid, afraid of the new house and her aunt and uncle. She slowly got to know her relatives and their house. One day, Rosie watched her aunt put towels away in a closet she had not noticed before. Later that same day, a friend of her aunt's arrived from Mexico. This is what happened next:

> The lady asked, "Is it all right to take a bath?"
>
> "Sure," my aunt replied, "Our house is yours." My aunt was always the hospitable type.
>
> The lady took hours and hours in her bath. I was getting impatient, pacing back and forth. When I heard the water click off, I thought to myself, "Oh good she's done. Now I can take a bath myself."
>
> I opened the closet door to get a towel and to my surprise I found a small door next to where the medicine and toothpaste were. As a child of six, I was curious. I stuck my hand to open it and to my astonishment as I clicked it open I saw the lady taking a bath in the total nude!
>
> As soon as I opened it I closed it. I don't think the lady saw me, but my aunt caught me! . . . I felt a headrush of shivers.

Later, whenever the lady spoke to her, Rosie was embarrassed and "felt shy to respond."

Rosie's story is family folklore. Her aunt and mother still tell the story and now, years later, Rosie tells it too and likes it. "I have always been described by my mother as being a curious brat and not afraid to take a chance," Rosie tells the class.

Stories like these which I learned about from Gail Siegel, a teacher in Ross, California, help to define us, to place us within our families. They are evidence that family and friends noticed us as children and that our childhoods and connections to the family are memorable and ensconced in the family's lore. Such stories can also be quite personal. Therefore, this unit is best undertaken well into the semester, when the students know one another and are comfortable in the class.

Day One: What is Family Folklore?

Family folklore is material that is handed on by tradition either by word of mouth or custom or practice. Like other folklore, context and performance are critical to understanding what is being communicated by the lore. Family folklore includes treasured objects (material folk culture) passed down through generations, ways of celebrating birthdays, holidays and weddings (folk customs), and the vast verbal folklore of sayings and stories. Like other folklore, it gets transmitted through generations, changing as it passes from person to person. One big difference with family folklore is that it tends to be adult folklore passed around among adults and down to children. This is different from childhood and teenage folklore, where transmission is almost exclusively among young people. Another difference is that the origin of much family folklore is known.

Steven Zeitlin, Amy Kotkin, and Holly Cutting Baker have written a popular book on family folklore, A Celebration of American Family Folklore (1982). I often begin the study of family folklore with their opening chapter, "Family Folklore: The Creative Expression of a Common Past." Here is the first paragraph:

> Families travel light. As the greater part of our experience slips beyond our reach, we clasp a mere handful of stories, expressions, photographs, and customs. Our photo albums, attic trunks, even our memories can only hold so much: Aunt Ida's fading wedding photo or a pair of unused tickets for the fateful voyage of the Titanic may be all that remain of whole generations in a family. From countless incidents, families choose a few stories to pass on, the funniest or perhaps the most telling. From all of the garbled baby talk, a single

utterance may become a family expression. Yet these time-honored images do more than recall scattered people and events; they come to represent the unremembered past, the sum total of a family's heritage (2).

Most families do travel light. We don't keep much from our past, but the few items we do hold on to are symbols of our history and our heritage. The table of contents of *A Celebration of American Family Folklore* is a list of types of family folklore. The chapter titled "Family Stories" has tales of heroes, rogues, mischief makers, survivors, innocents, migrations, lost fortunes, courtships, family feuds, and supernatural happenings. There are chapters on "Stories for Children," "Family Expressions," "Family Customs," "Family Photography," and "Other Ways of Preserving the Past." I read the contents to the class so they can get a feel for the dimensions of this folklore. And we spend the period talking about them and making lists.

Family artifacts, material folk culture, tangible items passed down from generation to generation, are good examples. To start discussion about family artifacts, I talk about my grandmother's brass candlesticks, part of her dowry from Russia. When I was a child, my mother promised me I would inherit them. In a suburban freshman class, students begin to list their family treasures. One student talks about a set of wooden baby blocks that had gone through generations. Another tells of her grandfather's trunk from Germany. Yet another describes her grandfather's medals. We talk about why these are saved—what they mean to their families. One student wants to know about his father's souvenirs, one of which is a pennant from a Minnesota Vikings Superbowl game. Is it an important family artifact? We debate this; are modern souvenirs "family artifacts"? Can they be considered folklore? Some students resist and argue that these items will not last, will not be passed on. In the end, I suggest that as long as the souvenir is valued by the family and is being saved, it is a potential family artifact. However, items that stand the test of time and last through generations are probably more important. Family artifacts are discussed in "Other Ways of Preserving the Past" in *A Celebration of American Family Folklore*.

From the chapter on "Family Expressions," I read several examples and give a few from my family. A favorite of ours is "Vespicio," an imperfect acronym for, "Vice President in Charge of Pest Control." When I was little, my brother Arthur was the family insect killer. He was fearless when it came to bugs. Whenever anyone spotted a pest, we called for "Vespicio," and he exterminated it. The students share family expressions, those known only to their own families, and also more widely known ones like the ominously familiar admonition, "This is going to hurt me more than it hurts you."

The biggest chapter in *A Celebration of American Family Folk-lore* is "Family Stories." Here are tales of family folk characters including heroes, rogues, black sheep, mischief makers, survivors, and innocents. There are stories about legendary events in the histories of families such as migrations, lost fortunes, courtships, family feuds, and supernatural happenings. As we talk in class, I list all the types of family folklore on the chalkboard, and students share examples and get ideas for what they will write about. Usually, I let them choose from any type of family folklore. They might write about how their family celebrates Easter (Mom cooking for days in preparation, new clothes, early morning Mass, and egg hunts), or write a description of a valued family artifact, giving its history and significance to the family.

Although I have stated a preference for the type of family lore the students will write about, if students are uncomfortable with the topic (perhaps they don't like the family stories told about them), they may write about any aspect of family folklore.

I model family stories with one I tell about my son, Daniel.

> When my son, who is now in college, was little, he went to the Prince Nursery School. One day, Mrs. Griffin, the teacher, telephoned me. "Mrs. Simons," she said, "Daniel has brought some money to school today." Well, you don't need money in nursery school, so I said, "Thanks for telling me, just take it away from him." Then she said, "I thought you should know about it. It's a rather large sum of money." "How much?" I asked. She said, "Daniel has thirty-five dollars!"

The class begins to laugh and I continue:

> He had gone into his father's wallet and taken out the thirty-five dollars in case any emergencies arose in nursery school. When he came home, he felt contrite. To make amends he gathered a present for me. He went next door and picked every single lemon off an ornamental miniature plant my neighbor had been carefully tending. As a parting gesture that night, just before he went to bed, he gave himself a haircut on one side of his head.

Since we are going to both gather family lore and study its functions, students need to look beyond the narrative or the artifact. They need to place it in a context: Who tells the story? when do they tell it? how do they tell it? what do the listeners (especially the subject of the story) think? And they need to consider the purpose of the narrative: Why is it told? Or if they have chosen an artifact, who keeps it? Why is it treasured? When is it mentioned or discussed in the family?

Placing the narrative about Daniel in context, I explain that I am the only one who tells this story. I tell it when Daniel starts lobbying for an expensive item—a camera, an elaborate ten-speed bicycle, expensive stereo equipment, top-of-the-line skis and boots. Even at three, Daniel was showing one side of himself—that he loves money and what it can buy. The rest of the narrative shows how much trouble Daniel can get into in one day—all the while well intentioned.

"How many of you can think of a story that is told about you in your family?" I start.

"I ain't got no long one," Lorenzo informs us.

"Let's hear it," I prompt.

"I killed my brother's bird, when I was—"

Lorenzo is interrupted by laughter. By this time in the year, we all know him, and this story has the earmarks of a typical Lorenzo story.

"My mom and dad said I went inside, I got in the cage and just choked it."

Looking for some perspective and analysis, I ask Lorenzo why the story is told. "Is there a kind of rivalry between you and your brother?" Lorenzo doesn't answer my question but says, "My brother killed my sister's bird." This brought down the house. "Maybe it's just a family tradition," someone suggests.

Other students want to tell their stories.

"When I was little, I didn't like to have my picture taken," Lupe tells us. "I always used to put my head down." Her family tells this story, Lupe explains, when she acts shy today. Olga says that when she was little, she was never home. Instead, she was outside playing with her friends. Her father still talks about it, and we laugh because Olga is one of the most social members of the class. Araceli talks about beating up a neighborhood bully. We laugh again. Araceli is still her own mistress.

The purpose of this lesson is to introduce the spectrum of family folklore types and talk about the importance of folklore in defining and bonding families. Homework for students is to come up with a few stories about themselves from their own recollections. They are to go home, tell the tales to their parents, and ask them for their own versions. If the students don't know any such stories, they are to go home and get some. As well, students who have chosen other aspects of family lore get started on them.

Day Two: Kathryn Morgan's "Caddy Buffers"

Folklorist Kathryn Morgan's short book, *Children of Strangers: The Stories of a Black Family* (1980), is a study of family folklore. In her work, students have a fine example of what one folklorist has done with lore from her own family. In the preface, Morgan explains its function: "Our folklore was the antidote used by our parents and our grandparents and our great-grandparents to help us counteract the poison of self-hate engendered by racism" (xiii).

The heroine of *Children of Strangers* is Morgan's great-grand-mother, Caddy. Caddy was born free but sold into slavery at the age of eight. She started the tradition of storytelling in the family. In her stories, she "stressed family solidarity, self-respect, decency and dignity. . . . " (11)

To illustrate the value of family stories like the "Caddy" legends, the students read a few and discuss them both as family folklore and as American history. The first legend, called simply "Caddy," was told by Kathryn Morgan's daughter, Susan, when she was ten. Caddy was her great-great-grandmother.

Caddy

Sometimes you think it would be nice to be a slave girl where you wouldn't have to be worried about financial problems and things. But when you hear this story I believe that it will change your mind. It's about a girl named Caddy. Caddy was my great-great-grand-mother. She was only eight when she was sold on the slave block. After that she was always being sold. She had to be sent from plantation to plantation because she would always run away and sass the mistress. She would even sass people who weren't her mistresses. Well, she grew to be a beautiful young girl and that made all the white women hate her out of pure jealousy. The white masters loved her and sometimes she was taken into the big house to live. That didn't make any difference to Caddy. Big house, little house, great house, small house, it was all the same because they were just taking her in so that she would be more convenient for them. Sometimes she would run away so that she wouldn't be a convenient little handy hand, but was usually caught and then she was taken into the barn and hung up by her thumbs and whipped across her back with a cat-o'-nine-tails. It would hurt real bad but do you think Caddy would cry? Ah, you bet not! It would take more than a cat-o'-nine-tails to make Caddy cry in front of poor white trash. Maybe they were rich in money, but they were poor in brains. Caddy hated trash, black or white. Usually they had to sell Caddy because she was too hard to handle and would always be running away. (17)

Kathryn, who was not allowed to use "bad" words unless they were attributed to Caddy, delighted in the following legend, which is also told here by her daughter, Susan.

What Caddy Did When She Heard That Lee Had Surrendered

Caddy had been sold to a man in Goodman, Mississippi. It was terrible to be sold in Mississippi. In fact, it was terrible to be sold anywhere. She had been put to work in the fields for running away again. She was hoeing a crop when she heard that General Lee had surrendered. Do you know who General Lee was? He was the man who was working for the South in the Civil War. When General Lee surrendered that meant that all the colored people were free! Caddy threw down that hoe, she marched herself up to the big house, then, she looked around and found the mistress. She went over to the mistress, she flipped up her dress and told the white woman to do something. She said it mean and ugly. This is what she said: "Kiss my ass!" (18)

After reading the family legends, students discuss them in small groups. They respond to legends as they would to their own writing, first identifying the parts they like. They then ask questions of it: What parts aren't clear? What would you like to know more about? Next, they discuss it as family folklore. Morgan calls the legends "Caddy buffers," because they were folklore that acted as buffers for the Morgan family when they were faced with racism. Students speculate on who would tell these stories and when they would be told in order to function this way.

For other readings on the subject, there are five chapters in *A Celebration of American Family Folklore* describing family folklore in detail. One chapter is about the *kazatske*, a Russian dance still performed at weddings of Jews of Russian descent. The author tells of the meaning of the dance in his family. A second describes the best storytellers in a family where characterization is the skill most valued in storytelling. Another tells of the use of a proverb, "Getting butter from the duck," in his African-American family. A fourth chapter is about a mother's memories of the folklore generated by her two sons. They include a song written to commemorate a birth and spontaneous sayings that have become family lore. And the fifth author writes about storytelling in her Pennsylvania German family on special occasions such as weddings, funerals, and holidays.

For the next class, students are to bring in a first draft of their narrative, which includes the setting or context and the performance, that is, who tells it, and how it is told.

Day Three: Why Is This Legend Remembered and Retold?

In this class, students will read their drafts in response groups. The first part of the response will be as usual—positive assessment and questions. The second part is new. The students will ask one another questions that will help them with the analytical sections of their papers.

To model this for the class, I read a brief narrative of a story that is still told about me as child. Before my father and mother tell it, they usually preface it by saying, "Remember the time Liz ate all the cherries!" and they laugh. This happened on a humid midsummer day on Long Island, before air conditioning. We were sitting on the front porch trying to catch stray breezes when the grocery man appeared, delivering a cardboard carton of fruits and vegetables. In the carton was a small bag of deep red Bing cherries, my favorites. I spotted them and plotted. I took the bag, ate a cherry, and made a face. "No good?" my mother asked. "Sour," I told her. While my family watched, I ate all the cherries, complaining all the while. When I finished, I confessed that they were delicious.

Following our usual routine, the students first tell me what they like and then ask questions. Next we move to analysis. I ask them what more they need in order to speculate about the function of this story in my family. They want to know who tells the story, my mother or my father. When do they tell it? To whom? Do I ever tell it? How do I feel about the story? (Another direction would be to think about how the person in the narration is being depicted.)

I answer that it is usually my father who tells it because he likes it and because he is the family storyteller. My father likes the story because it portrays me as he remembers me as a child—as someone who played tricks and who is a little selfish. Now, he tells it on occasions when he feels that I or one of my children has acted too much out of self-interest. Although the story isn't flattering, I still enjoy hearing my father tell it, maybe because it depicts me as being shrewd and spunky. Of course, I think I've outgrown playing tricks and being selfish, but since he tells the story, apparently he doesn't.

The students go into their groups and talk about each other's drafts, responding and questioning much the way they did with my paper. From the second part of the response, each student should have some ideas for analyzing his or her narrative. Homework is to do a final draft that will include a revised narrative and the analysis.

Day Four: "Publishing" by Reading Aloud

We don't make a booklet of the stories, but we do spend a period reading them aloud and enjoying them. The students marvel at how accurately the childhood stories describe who they are today. Occasionally, though, we are surprised. Ramiro, for example, is quiet and seldom speaks in class, but his writing reveals another side:

> Back in Mexico my mother loved to raise chickens. She must have had about twenty of them. One day I needed some money to buy

rubber bands to fix my sling shot. Instead of asking my mother for it, I went into her chicken coop, took a few eggs, sold them in the store and bought my rubber bands.

Ramiro went into business; his mother couldn't understand what was happening to her eggs. First she blamed the rooster, then rats. When she discovered Ramiro's secret cache of eggs, she asked him, "What were you going to do with all of these eggs?" "I was going to eat them!" he told her. She didn't believe him.

Miguel told of the time his mother and sisters went to visit their family in Mexico for two weeks. He and his fourteen-year-old brother stayed home alone while their father worked. They decided this would be good time to teach themselves to drive. Miguel described the raw terror he felt when his brother took him for his first ride around the block. Alba described herself as a three-year-old playing Tarzan. She followed her older siblings who, bellowing like Tarzan, jumped out of a window. Alba, inexperienced at the game, landed on the pavement and broke both her legs. Martin wrote about himself as the "Cat Burglar":

> When I was eight years old, I lived in Los Angeles. I used to go around and steal people's cats, take them back and get rewards. That idea came to me one day while watching cartoons. The cartoon was about a bulldog that stole cats. He kept them for a while until the owners got worried. The owners would put ads in the newspapers with rewards for the return of their cats. The dog then took the cats to their owners and received rewards. I thought the dog was a genius.

This last line brought a good laugh. The class followed closely as Martin told how he grew quite rich in his new profession and how his mother found out and closed his business. Martin concluded:

> Today my mother still remembers. She brings it up at parties, family gatherings and every time she sees a cat.

The analyses were as interesting as the narratives. Olga wrote about her father's anger at her when she was little for always being outside playing. His first question when he arrived home from work was always, "Where is Olga?" Once he was so angry he spanked her, Olga writes, "from the front entrance all the way to the patio." The next day she was out with her friends again.

But there was another side of Olga: although she was often out playing with friends, she was a good daughter. She always did her chores and helped her mother, who began countering her husband's complaints with stories telling of Olga the girl who was very social but also very good. "I *am* very social," Olga explains, "and sometimes

I'm out a lot, but I always get my chores done. . . . My mother tells these stories so my father won't be angry at me."

Conclusion

"Hearing people talk about me," Arturo's piece began, "makes me feel good." These stories do indeed make us feel good because they bond us to our families and enhance our self-esteem. We must have been important, after all, to be the subject of such tales. The stories can come from any family member—a parent, grandparent, aunt, uncle, sibling, or a family friend. Furthermore, most students can find a story told about them that depicts them in a flattering way, a way that portrays them as they like to think of themselves. Finding the right story is a chance for students to define themselves. In this unit, students also exercise several language arts skills: they interview relatives, collect stories about themselves, think about which one they prefer, write a narrative, and reflect on its significance to them.

Unit in Brief

Day One: What is Family Folklore?

- Class reads from *A Celebration of American Family Folklore* and shares family material folklore, family expressions, and family stories.

- Homework: students interview someone from the family (parents, grandparents, siblings, aunts or uncles, or a family friend) and collect stories told about them (the students) as children.

  Students who prefer can collect and write about another aspect of family folklore—family artifacts, family customs, family expressions, or stories about another member of the family. Each of these topics is also fine as a whole class unit.

Day Two: Kathryn Morgan's "Caddy Buffers"

- Students read and discuss "Caddy Buffers" as an example of family stories. Readings could also be taken from the "Five American Families" section of *A Celebration of American Family Folklore*.

- Homework: Students write a draft of their family story, including narrative, setting, and performance.

Day Three: Why Is This Legend Remembered and Retold?

- Class responds to a draft, discussing how to make meaning of the family stories.

- Small groups respond to first drafts and make suggestions for analysis.
- Homework: Students write final paper.

Day Four: "Publishing" by Reading Aloud

- Students read papers aloud in class.
- Students evaluate the unit in whole class, small-group discussion, or in a learning log entry.

Chapter Seven

Nuestro Pasado (Our Past)
Family Folklore II—
Family Photography

Day One: Getting Started

Bringing in the Photographs

"Can you guess which one is me?" Raul asked, while Alba peered at a photo of two little boys in cowboy costumes standing next to a display of Halloween candy. Nearby, Olga had five photographs spread out on her desk. She was asking Norma which one she should use—the one of the ancient pyramid she had visited with her cousin Tacho in Mexico, or the one of her as the Virgin Mary holding a real baby "Jesus" in her church Christmas pageant. Norma looked over the photos of her *quinceañera* (a coming-of-age church ritual)[1] and beamed. She was the focal point of every picture, resplendent in a white ball gown and crown, holding a bouquet and accompanied by her *damas* and *chambelánes* (male and female attendants, young friends and relatives, elaborately dressed in matching colors, who start the dancing which follows the Mass at the *quinceañera*).

Shy Luz smiled quietly while looking at the picture taken at her first family picnic in America. Lupe and Julieta had photos of birthday parties. Miguel was showing Lorenzo a picture of his family at Christmas. In it, Miguel, his father, two sisters, and brother grin in front of their tree, but Miguel confided to Lorenzo, "I always hated those pictures!" Lorenzo liked it: "It looks like a Mexican 'Brady Bunch'," he quipped. This first day, the students, junior and seniors, predominantly Mexican-American, were already involved in the unit.

123

For this day, students need to have family photographs in hand. About two weeks before, I'd begun asking students to bring them in. At first, only a few comply. But as photos begin to appear, we devote a few minutes at the beginning of class to discussing them. This breaks down resistance; once the photos are shared, they quickly become a hit, generating plenty of talk and questions. By the morning the unit begins, most students have already brought in their photos. A few forget and pull one from their wallets or try to beg one from a friend, but even these most reluctant students bring photos in by the third day.

Family photographs can take a writer in many directions: historical, analytical, autobiographical, anecdotal, and folkloric. I wanted the students to have a sense of the choices available and to do some prewriting that would lead them to see the different types of writing that could come from their photographs. To quiet the class and get them started, I asked the students to gaze at their photos and write down words that came to mind. Olga, looking at the picture of herself as the Virgin Mary in her church pageant, wrote:

> Anxiety
> baby crying
> smiles
> eyes staring
> nervousness
> I had to sing by myself

After making the lists, some students were ready to write, but others were not. To continue the prewriting, I asked for volunteers to show their pictures and discuss what they were thinking of writing. Lorenzo showed a framed photo he had removed from his living room wall. There are three people in it. Santa Claus, his eyes twinkling above a lush, white beard, is seated on a department store throne. On his left stands Lorenzo's brother, biting his lower lip, looking very serious. On his right knee is Lorenzo, age three or four, crying bitterly.

Standing in line in front of Santa, little Lorenzo noticed that Santa was not the jolly old man he'd anticipated, but a young white man with a false beard, a strange-looking Santa suit, and funny rubber rainboots. When Lorenzo was put on Santa's lap, he tried to pull off the beard, and Santa pinched him hard in the leg, making Lorenzo cry. Since it is not exactly a flattering picture, the class wondered why it was not only saved but framed. They suspected that Lorenzo liked it because it portrayed him as we (and probably his family) knew him to be—curious, a bit of a troublemaker, the center of attention.

"How many of you have department store pictures with Santa?" I asked. Many did—it's a standard American photo. Since Santa Claus is an important American folk character, and since Lorenzo had brought in this photo, we stopped a moment to talk about Santa folklore. "Why," I asked, "do American children meet Santa Claus in a department store?" This provoked a heated discussion about Christmas and commercialism. Americans could have put Santa anywhere. It is not chance but our capitalist, commercial worldview that caused him to end up in a store.[2] Lorenzo could use his photo and his anecdote as the beginning of a piece on Christmas folklore.

Next, Martin volunteered a photo of his sister and himself dressed for their first communion (see Figure 7–1). "I have one like it," Lupe said. We all laughed and knew right away there would be folklore surrounding this photograph. Olga, who didn't have a communion picture, asked Martin, "You posed for it?" Not only had Martin posed; he had taken a bus to the city and gone to a professional photographer.

"What sort of ideas does a picture like this bring to mind?" I asked the class. "What could Martin write about?" No one answered, so I changed my question and tried again. "What do you think about when you look at a picture of yourself as a child?"

"What you were like then," Rosie suggested.

"Sometimes when they were going to take a picture I used to freeze, I didn't want to move," Olga added.

"Where were you?" Arturo asked.

"In Mexico," Martin answered.

"Do you remember getting ready for it?" another student queried. This last question hit home. Martin not only remembered but as he told the class the story, he found his topic.

There was no photographer in the small town where Martin lived as a child. He traveled with his sister and his mother to Guadalajara, the nearest city, to have the photograph taken. Later he wrote about waiting for the bus:

> My sister was throwing fresh chewed gum up and down. I was busy looking at people who were looking at us as if we were fools wearing those clothes. Then suddenly I felt something land on my head. It was my sister's gum.

Listening to Martin, the students were learning two aspects of the folklore of family photographs: that photos are catalysts for storytelling, and that the story often cannot be predicted from the picture.

When the time came to start writing, Alba complained, "I still don't know what to say. My picture isn't telling me anything!" Other

Figure 7-1
Martin's Photograph

students also wanted more prewriting. They asked to go to their response groups to talk more about their photos.

One response group pored over Rosie's second-grade class picture. They were guessing which one was Rosie. Some of the students in the group had been in her second grade class and were also in the photo. "Remember Nigel Gilbert?" she asked them, pointing to his picture. "And Martha Garcia, remember we used to call her Martha Regatha?" Then Rosie studied her own second-grade self. "I look so dorky," she complained, "My mom made me wear some funky old things. . . . My dress looks like a salad!" For homework, students read the chapter "Family Photography" in *A Celebration of American Family Folklore* (Zeitlin, Kotkin, and Baker 1982).

Day Two: The Folklore of Family Photography

Family photographs themselves are commercial items, but they are embedded in folklore. The folklore includes the rituals surrounding the taking of the photographs: when and why they are taken; where they are stored and displayed; on what occasions they are taken out; and how they are discussed and used. The taking and use of the family photographs has become an integral part of the folklore of families. It is these aspects of family photography that are discussed in the chapters "Family Photography" and "Family Albums" in *A Celebration of American Family Folklore*. (Reading this chapter also gives students a sense of how folklorists do research.)

Zeitlin, Kotkin, and Baker did their fieldwork in the Washington, DC area. From 1974–1977, as part of the Smithsonian's Festival of American Folklife, they interviewed over two thousand American families about their family folklore. For their chapter on "Family Photography" they collected six thousand photographs from the "albums, trunks, and shoeboxes . . . from more than two hundred families" (182).

This is what they found. First, "while we are free to photograph anything we want, we don't." Instead, "just as certain categories of stories recur from family to family, similar kinds of photos are enshrined in the home archives" (182). The recurring motifs are of such events as birthdays, holidays, picnics, and vacations. The photos show families seated "around the hearth, on the front porch, or even around the family car" (182). They document the growing up of their children, starting with infancy and stopping at high school graduation. In short, the occasions for the taking of photos are traditional and thus folklore.

Second, the authors noticed that families use photographs to document their histories. Families generally don't, however, attempt to create an accurate history. The authors write, "We're rarely trying, in our photos and albums, to offer a balanced view of family life (199). . . . we tend to take photos according to the way we want to preserve, remember, and be remembered" (183).

The authors quote Susan Sontag from *On Photography* (1977). She writes that the camera has the unique ability to "freeze moments in a life or a society" so that they are salvaged from "the relentless melt of time." But families are highly selective about what they want to present to posterity. The facts are edited, and the result is consciously created folk family history. The authors observe that:

> In depicting certain kinds of events in certain ways, family photos, like other genres of folklore, are a creative transformation of selected experience into fixed images that can be shared in the years to come. They are a stylized reality; an expression of our values and ideals (183).

The students understood this concept well. In the many snapshots they take of each other, they continually edit, discarding photographs, cutting people out, carefully preserving themselves as they want to be remembered and as they believe they are. When they go through a fresh packet of photographs, they despair "that doesn't look anything like me" or "that's a terrible picture of Arturo."

In her monograph *So We Can Remember: Showing Family Photographs*, Pauline Greenhill (1981) makes another important point: the family history represented in photographs is open to continual reinterpretation. Photos are ambiguous. Therefore, when necessary, families can change the stories that accompany them.

In a chapter on family photography in *Images of Information: Still Photography in the Social Sciences*, Christopher Musello (1979) suggests four functions that family photographs serve for family members. His is a slightly different perspective, although it overlaps the interpretations of Greenhill and Zeitlin and his colleagues. The four functions are: communion, interaction, presentation-of-self, and documentation. As communion, the photographs document, reinforce, and reify relationships, beliefs, and shared values, as in photos of major family events such as births and weddings. Picture-taking and sharing are also occasions for special kinds of family interaction. For example, the picture-taking event itself is often a form of entertainment (and can be annoying, as in Miguel's memories of the ritual Christmas morning snapshot). Musello observes, as did others, that picture-sharing occasions are accompanied by storytelling, another type of interaction. The students were, in fact, storytelling on that first day as they shared their photos. Although the others focused on the process of families editing their photographs to present an idealized family record, Musello sees more variation in what he terms presentation-of-self. First, he does mention idealization—one's best picture. But he notes that there are other presentations, among them what he calls "natural portrayal." These are candid shots in which the event is more important than a subject's best image. Finally, there is "demystification." This is represented by the silly or embarrassing photos we often include in albums. Musello's documentation function of photography is the same as that discussed by the others—a way we preserve our past and record change over time in our families. He adds that when we mail photographs to far-away family, it helps to keep the family close.

In class, the students compared their pictures with those in *A Celebration of American Family Folklore*. Many showed the same events: births, picnics, weddings, Christmases, family outings, vacations, and birthdays. But they also had photographs not mentioned in the book: pictures of themselves on Santa's lap (like Lorenzo's), communion pictures (like Martin's), quinceañeras, photographs of themselves playing sports. There was also teenage photography, pictures young people take of one another for various reasons. Students make their own albums, and some of their photographs enter family collections. In general, they felt that although the authors had a good starting list of typical family photographs, the list was incomplete; the folklore of family photography is richer than the book suggests.

Flipping through *A Celebration of American Family Folklore*, some in the class noticed that there were no pictures of Mexican-Americans. Thus, they decided to produce their own book based on photographs from their lives. Students would write from their photos, detailing or narrating whatever the picture brought to mind. Later, they would reflect on its context, why and how it was preserved, when it was discussed, and what value or ideal it embodied.

Days Three and Four: First Drafts and Response

On the third day, the students drafted the first part of their papers. They began in class and finished up for homework. The fourth day was devoted to response. Response groups in this class had been working well, but they were pretty much limited to reactions to written drafts. Students were not seeking each other's help with shaping writing.

To teach them how to start asking for more conceptual help, I read a draft I was having trouble concluding. My photograph showed my brother and me sitting on my back porch with my grandmother, whom I called Bubby.

Bubby and Me

Wrinkled and battered as it is, I love this photo. You can't really see my brother Arthur's face because one of the crease marks runs through it, and my chin is lost in a wrinkle. But Bubby, my wonderful Bubby, who thought the sun rose and set on me, is smiling at me. And I sit there basking in the specialness of her love. Although she has her hands around Arthur, her right hand patting his right hand, her left hand on his small arm, he seems unimportant in the picture. This picture is about me and Bubby.

When I was little, age 4 or 5 as I was in the photo, while I loved my Bubby, there were some mysteries about her. For instance she never ate anything when she came to visit us. She never complained about the food my mother cooked but she never ate it either. No matter what the dinner was, all she ever had on her plate was a few slices of raw onion, total. It wasn't that she didn't eat. In her home in Brooklyn she cooked and ate voluminously. A favorite memory of mine was her chicken soup with noodles served in a low, wide, white soup bowl eaten with an oversized silver European spoon, part of her dowry from Bialystok in Poland. It is this soup that I still crave when I want to feel loved and comforted.

No one messed with Bubby's religion. But my mother, her daughter, raising her children, 35 miles away, slipped once. After Arthur and I begged, pleaded and cajoled for two years, my mother collapsed under our onslaught and allowed us to have a Christmas tree. I was in first grade. I was instructed to call it a Hannukah bush and never under pain of death to tell Bubby that we had it.

A few days after Christmas word came over the phone that Bubby was on her way from Brooklyn for a visit. I watched my mother hang up the phone, walk over to the tree, pick it up and unceremoniously toss it out the window, decorations and all, into the snowy backyard. An hour later when Bubby walked through the front door, there was no trace of Christianity in our house, the tree heaved out, the presents hidden.

After I read, the students talked first about the parts they liked. "No one messes with Bubby's religion," Lorenzo said, "I liked that."

"I liked how you started by saying this picture is about Bubby and me," Lupe said.

"The opening—'Wrinkled and battered,' " Norma added.

"I like how you describe the bowl of soup," Julietta said, and Martin added, "I like the part where you said that you eat the soup when you want to feel comfortable."

I underlined the parts they liked and that I would probably keep in the revision. Then I asked for their questions.

"Why didn't she eat?" Lupe asked. Everyone wanted to know that. And Miguel added, "Why didn't your grandmother like the tree?"

I explained to them that she was Jewish and kosher. She ate only kosher foods, and our house wasn't kosher. Being Jewish, she also didn't like Christmas trees. "I'll explain that in my revision," I told them.

Family is important to these students. They had a lot of questions about mine: "Is your Bubby still alive?" "Is your brother older or younger?" "Where does he live?"

"New York," I told them. "In fact, all my family is in the East." Lorenzo laughed. "I know that telephone bill be mighty high."

We had been working on positive response and questions all term, and it showed in the discussion. Now, however, I had asked for help with the ending for a piece of writing. At first, they found this a difficult matter. Miguel was speaking for the whole class when he responded, "It's kind of hard, man."

But Martin had an idea. "How did you feel when the tree went out of the window?" he asked. And Araceli asked, "What would have happened if she did see it?"

Most of the students wanted an upbeat ending. Luz thought I might write that we were all happy even without the tree. And Rosie said I should say that even though sometimes I didn't like what Bubby did, I still loved her. Their questions and suggestions had been not only very interesting to me but helpful as well.

The second part of the paper was to be a reflection on the photograph or on the writing that accompanied it. As a prewriting activity, we talked about several approaches I could take with my project. For example, I could write about why I retell it, to whom, and ask my listeners (my children), what it means to them. But I settle for a more historical analysis. The story, although inspired by the photo, is unrelated to it. I told the class that I think it's about assimilation, the conflict between my Russian-born grandmother's religion and values and those of my mother, her daughter, who was becoming American-ized—who was no longer kosher and even allowed a Christian icon into her house. I didn't understand any of this when I was five. What I knew than was only that there was something causing tension between my mother and my grandmother. Now I had two parts to add to my writing—an ending and a reflection on the story.

The students next read their first drafts in response groups. Araceli's photo showed several young children playing on a street corner. Here is what she wrote:

It was about 2:00 pm in the afternoon when the rays of the sun were hitting us like balls of fire. My brother Saul, who loves to fight with me, and my little sister Yolanda, who always poses as if she was a model, were at the corner of our house along with three other friends, Jackie, Pebbles and Nickie. As we all played around the stop sign, we decided to take a picture. As usual my brother wanted to put his fingers on Yolie's hair, and as always I tried to stop him.

For about three years we were friends and we all got in trouble expecialy one summer day when we decided to play house. We went to an abandoned house that was inbetween my grandfather's house and my friends house. We decided to play in the backyard where the dried grass was high enough for us to hide. We brought bricks and pots and we made a stove in which we would cook our food. While we had the fire started, we put some water to boil. It didn't take long for us to notice that the dried grass was catching on fire. As my brother ran to get water, I poured water from the jar into the fire. I ran to get more water but when I was gone, Jackie started the fire again. For about ten minutes I went back and forth but the fire was stronger and stronger. And it was going towards my grandpa's garage. I grabbed the water hose and started to water everything I could, while the rest of the kids ran like wild horses trapped in a fire unable to figure out what to do next.

Minutes later we saw people everywhere and we hear a loud siren coming toward us. The fire was put out and all of us were happy, but we knew the worst was yet to come. As we saw the fireman coming, we began to cry. We did not get in trouble but everyone was laughing because we all had dirty faces from the smoke. This time we all looked alike.

Araceli's group liked her writing and was amused because the picture that inspired the story conveys such innocence. It shows a small group of children, Mexican-Americans and Blacks, swinging around a stop sign on a street corner. Araceli's story thus takes the reader by surprise. Her group had some questions too, among them where she got the jar of water. And in the last line, what did she mean by "we all looked alike"? Because of the smoke everyone had a black face, she explained, so we all looked Black. They thought this had to be made clearer. And they discussed ideas for her reflection. Why was this picture saved? Why was the story remembered and retold?

Day Five: Reflections and Analysis

Before the students wrote reflections and revisions, I read changes I had made on the basis of their suggestions, including a new third paragraph to explain being kosher:

Bubby was Jewish and kosher, strict kosher, and only ate kosher food. When I was little, I didn't know about Jewish dietary laws, I didn't understand Bubby's eating habits, and no one thought to explain them to me. Besides I must have relished the mystery in some way because I never asked for an explanation.

I had also added a final paragraph incorporating one of their suggestions for an ending plus some reflection on the meaning of the incident.

> At first I was so shocked at the sight of the departing tree, I didn't feel anything except maybe relief that Bubby would never know. But I also learned something, that Bubby did not approve of Christmas and that in some way, unclear to me, it was wrong to have a Hannukah bush. After that, although we always had a Christmas tree (excuse me—a Hannukah bush) and even though my father explained to me that it was a pagan German custom, not Christian, so it was all right for us to have one, I always felt a little guilty. Bubby would not have approved.

Over the next few days students wrote analytical reflections of their own and revised their writing to ready it for publication.

Several Days Later: Publishing "*Nuestro Pasado* (Our Past)"

Our earlier publications had been run off on purple dittoes. But the students wanted their photographs reproduced with the writing, so this publication was going to be a fancier, photocopied book. The students planned their own pages, deciding where to place the photographs. The cover, designed by Miguel, is a charming sketch of an early formal photographer—perhaps reminiscent of the photographer in Mexico who took Martin's picture (see figure 7–2). After extended debate, a title, *Nuestro Pasado: Our Past*, was chosen. The title reflected the students' dual heritage. It was a book to complement the chapter entitled "Family Photography" in *A Celebration of American Family Folklore*, adding the Mexican-American experience.

Our final activity, a reading of the book, took two full class periods. The class looked forward to making the book—collating and stapling it—and to the reading session, but this hadn't been true of similar experiences earlier in the year. Twice before, we had collected final revised writing into booklets and read them aloud. The first time I announced that we were going to make a book, there wasn't much interest. In the beginning of the year, the students didn't know the pleasures of reading something aloud to the class. To get the first book done, I had to push them to write and struggle to make them revise and edit. When it was finally assembled, I had to coax

Figure 7-2
Cover for *Nuestro Pasado* by Miguel

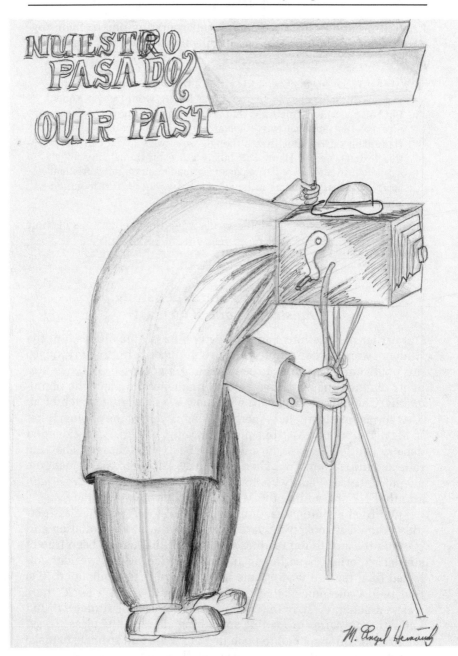

them into a circle. Then they balked at reading aloud. A few students were so fearful that they had friends read their writing for them. After the first few had read and received positive feedback, the class began to relax—a little. When I announced the second publication, students were more interested. And by the time we started studying family photography, Lorenzo came in the first day and asked, "Are we gonna make one of them books?"

Ending the unit with a book and a class reading dramatically makes the point that writing is foremost a form of communication— that audience can make the writing process complete. While reading the book, we discussed the traditions represented in the photographs. Three heritages were represented: Mexican, Mexican-American, and American.

Evaluation: Student Reflections on This Unit

When the unit was over, students wrote in their learning logs on the value of a unit like this and added suggestions for improvement. Norma wrote, "If we take care of the books, we can look back on them when we are older."

Early in the unit, we had discussed the reasons families keep photos. We had also talked about the historical importance of these photographs beyond the family. Now, we talked about the value of the book the class had just produced. Today, as well as twenty years hence, students studying American history should find such a publication to be a valuable primary source on the family folklore and culture of Mexican-American students in California in the late 1980s. When Norma and the others wrote of preserving these books, they were writing personally and showing an interest and perhaps pride in their individual histories. As important as this is, I also wanted them to begin to appreciate their family folk histories as part of the flow of national history. A suggestion from Raul developed the idea:

"I have pictures of my grandfather when he was in the service, fighting for the Mexican government," Raul said. He suggested a new family folklore project focusing on really old family pictures. These would show how our lives were related to historical events, both Mexican and American. It was a lovely suggestion, either as an excellent activity in its own right or as a follow-up to looking at immediate family folklore.

The class noted strides in their writing too. Rosie wrote in her learning log about *Nuestro Pasado*, "Personally I think that the book really worked because everybody was interested in how it was going to sound after it was revised and rewritten." Rosie and others were beginning to believe that revision improves writing. Also they were sufficiently invested in these stories from their lives and looked forward to perfecting them through revision.

An afternote: several days later, Lorenzo walked into class and told us proudly, "I showed it [the book] to my mother. She liked it."[3]

Unit in Brief

Day One: Getting Started

- Students bring in photos, share them, talk about them, and write lists of words inspired by their photos.
- Homework—read the chapter "Family Photography," from *A Celebration of American Family Folklore.*

Day Two: The Folklore of Family Photography

- Discussion of the homework, or another reading on family photography. (See Musello in Works Cited.)
- Discussion focuses on questions: What is the folklore of family photography? When and why do we take family pictures? How do we choose the photographs we keep? How do we keep and use them?

Days Three and Four: First Drafts and Response

- Day three—drafts of writing inspired by the photographs are begun in class (and finished at home).
- Day four—students respond to each other's drafts.

Day Five: Reflections and Analysis (Oral)

- Teacher and/or student drafts are read and discussed. Students speculate on the meaning and function of their family photographs and the writing they inspire.

Day Six: Reflections and Analysis (Written)

- At home or in class students write drafts of their speculations on the writing about the folklore of the photographs.

Day Seven: Response and Book Planning

- Students get a small-group response to their papers. (Several days later their revisions, ready for publication, are due.)
- Class decides on book title, plans the book, decides who will design the cover and who will run off the pages. (And if it is an expensive production, that is, anything fancier than ditto, how will it be financed? If it is a large class and an expensive publication, financing, in the form of a bake sale, for example, might take place earlier.)

Day Eight and Later: Publishing and Reflections on the Units

- Students collate and staple the book.
- Reading aloud from the publication. This takes from one to several periods, depending on how many students read.
- Students write log entries evaluating the unit and discuss them.

Notes

1. At fifteen many Mexican-American girls have a quinceañera. The first half of this coming-of-age ritual is a church Mass which for Norma included reading a prayer and being crowned by the priest with a diadem, a gift from her godparents. After the Mass there was a party, which lasted all night. See John O. West, "Coming of Age," *Mexican-American Folklore* (Little Rock, Arkansas: August House, 1988), pp. 150–51.

2. See Alan Dundes, "Christmas as a Reflection of American Culture," *California Monthly* 74 (1967), pp. 9–14.

3. With an ethnic class such as this one, the focus on ethnic history and developing pride in one's heritage is an added dividend. But the unit works equally well with any students. It celebrates any heritage, rural or urban, minority or mainstream.

Chapter Eight

"Even Heroes Have Heroes"
Mexican-American Students
Study Their Folk Heroes

Background Note: Folk Heroes and Heroines

A folk hero is a man or woman of the people, a person who embodies and lives in accordance with the values of the folk. A folk hero (the word *hero* is used generically to refer to both male and female) spontaneously inspires folklore, usually through anecdotes or stories about his or her life. A person is only a genuine folk hero when there is folklore about him or her, folklore that one person tells another, that changes in the telling and lasts over time.

There are patterns to the legends told about folk heroes.[1] When Abraham Lincoln, Franklin Delano Roosevelt, and John Kennedy, all American folk heroes, died, legends circulated that they still lived. Immediately after Kennedy's death, it was rumored that he was critically wounded and in intensive care somewhere. The legend continued, gradually changing to a claim that he was alive and well in various places around the world.[2]

There are more regional folk heroes and characters than national ones, however.[3] Although national folk heroes were probably rare at any time in history, they are even rarer today as the media probes every facet of the private lives of public figures. The idea of folk heroes is further clouded by a confusion between celebrities and folk heroes. The former are created by the media and are therefore part of American popular culture. (See chapter 1, pages 20–22 for a discussion of popular and folk culture.) Folk heroes originate with the folk groups; celebrities are creations largely fashioned by and reflective of the values of their makers in television, films, and print media, values quite different from those of people as expressed in their folk heroes.

With the students, a new group of heroes emerges; they come from family and friends. Curiously, these folk heroes and the stories told about them usually represent the values that many educators feel are missing from the school curriculum and, in fact, from the nation's ethos. Immigrant students, for example, write of their admiration for the courage and industry of their parents. Native-born Americans write of relatives as mentors. One boy, a junior who loved sports but was very short, wrote of an uncle, also short, who refused to let his height hold him back, played sports, and is now a successful football coach.

Although heroes change, the primary reasons for studying them do not. For a young person, a hero can be both model and mentor. Such people are useful to any student but critical to those growing up in perilous circumstances where heroes can be successful criminals. A second reason to study folk heroes is to undo the confusion between celebrity and folk hero. Without deriding the former, I do want students to see the difference between a person whose fame is based exclusively in popular culture and a folk hero. Finally, there are some genuine folk heroes around, often in ethnic groups.

This and the next chapter both deal with folk heroes. This one concerns a class of Mexican-American students, with focus on a local Mexican-American folk hero. The unit was taught early in the semester, too early for a research project. Thus, it was short, lasting a little over a week. Chapter 9 describes a unit on folk heroes that took place in a suburban classroom and was the final topic of the semester. The students did a small research project on the topic, many of them focusing on the difference between celebrities and folk heroes. The unit was longer, lasting about two weeks. Either unit can be done with any student population. In both units the central issues are: What are folk heroes? and What are the roles they play in our lives?

Day One: Whom Do You Admire?

Class begins with students making a list of people they admire. Next, each student tells the whole class the name of one person from his or her list. Teresa goes first. Her hero is Caesar Chavez. Next, Luz, who chooses her mother, then Ramiro, who admires his grandmother. Many of the students list family members. Miguel, an artist and aspiring architect, names Diego Rivera. The class doesn't know Diego

Rivera, so Miguel acquaints them. While the majority of the heroes mentioned are Latino, some are Anglo. Boys name sports figures. Martin mentions Babe Ruth; Raul lists Tom Landry, then coach of the Dallas Cowboys. There is a sprinkling of popular stars too: Prince, Apollonia, Madonna. Madonna, Alba tells us with authority, is Puerto Rican, making her one of them. (Madonna is Italian, but thoughts like Alba's illustrate how strong the need to connect to heroes can be, and how folklore helps to strengthen that connection.) The students speculate about Apollonia. Is she really Latino? One student balks at the topic of heroes and names as his hero Mr. T. of the TV program "The A Team."

While students are free to write about anyone they admire, I point out that their lists contain people who are folk heroes, celebrities, and combination folk hero/popular culture hero. Babe Ruth, for example, was both, generating oral tradition as well as media coverage. Others, such as pop singers, are celebrities; what students know about them comes mainly from fan magazines and talk shows. Some celebrities inspire both complimentary and derogatory oral tradition. "The Elevator Incident" legend for example, depicts the Black male celebrity named in it as a bit of a hero (see chapter 1, pages 17–18). But often jokes about celebrities told by teenagers ("Did you hear where they found Michael Jackson's other glove? In Boy George's pants.") are, in fact, folk commentary deflating the celebrity's media image. We will come back to the folk hero/popular culture hero again on the last day, so I don't belabor it now. Here I use it more for purposes of defining a folk hero.

From their lists, students choose one person to write about, someone whom they know well. In their first draft, which they write in class, they are to include three reasons they admire the person. For homework, they will choose one of their three reasons and expand on it, giving examples and supporting evidence.[4]

Ramiro offers to read his draft aloud and agrees to use his draft as a model of how to proceed with the homework assignment. After hearing it, the class will make suggestions about which characteristic or aspect of his hero they would like to know more about.

My grandmother was 72 years old when she died about seven years ago. She was a very happy lady, always singing or whistling. Ever since I was borned she looked over me, feed me, changed my diapers or gave me a bath when my mother couldn't do it. When I was older, I remember her telling me stories about the revolution when Villa was trying to take over Mexico. She told me about the rebels braking into houses and stealing chickens and pigs because they didn't have anything to eat. Every time she went out of town when she came back she broat toys and candy for my brothers and me.

While the class is curious about Ramiro's grandmother and has plenty of questions, what they really want expanded are the legends (folklore) about the rebels. Could he remember these and include them? Were the rebels heroes to his grandmother?

Day Two: Pedro J. Gonzalez— A Mexican-American Folk Hero

We spend the second day studying Pedro J. Gonzalez, a little-known local Mexican-American folk hero. The students learn about him from a local newspaper article, "A Folk Hero in Retirement," which begins:

> The old man, now 90, is affectionately known as "Don Pedro," and as he tells his life story for the umpteenth time—in rapid, rambling Spanish—one falls under the spell of great oral history. He seems almost blithe about it, but Pedro J. Gonzalez has lived, and suffered, and survived so much that he now stands as a symbol of the Mexican-American experience.
>
> A large, ruddy man with an intensity that belies his age, Gonzalez lives quietly with his wife of 68 years, Maria, in nearby San Ysidro. To most Americans, he would not even qualify as a trivia question, but to Mexicans with any sense of their heritage, Gonzalez is a folk hero, a kind of Latino Davy Crockett-cum-Woody Guthrie.[5]

The journalist outlines Don Pedro's life in the article. As a boy, Don Pedro worked as a telegraph operator for Pancho Villa (a folk hero). "I loved him like a father," he is quoted as saying. "I would have died for him." After the revolution, Don Pedro came to the United States, where he pioneered Spanish language radio in Los Angeles. A singer of *corridos* (Mexican folk ballads) he and his group *"Los Madrugadores"* (The Early Risers) sang and spoke out about U.S. discrimination against Mexicans. His following was so strong that the "Anglo establishment" feared his powers and managed to get him accused and convicted of rape. The supposed victim later admitted that the authorities had her lie under oath. Even after this evidence, Don Pedro was kept in jail. It took many protests, including two from Mexican presidents, to get him out. After six years, he was paroled and deported to Mexico. As his train passed through Los Angeles on the day of his release, Union Station was filled with supporters who wanted him to sing, but his guards refused permission. Don Pedro countered, "What can you do, send me back to jail? I just came from prison. Do what you want, but I'm going to sing!"

In class, students gather in groups to read the article. They respond to it as they do to peer writing in their own groups, underlining what they like and asking questions. Teresa, Lupe, Julieta, Maria, and Luz are in a group together. In her soft voice, Julieta tells Teresa, who is taking notes for the group, "Write down that he was strong." Teresa adds, "He was proud of being Mexican, and he was outspoken against the U.S. discrimination of Mexicans." Lupe points to the article, which reads, "Don Pedro himself doesn't lobby for fame."

"He doesn't do it for the fame," Lupe adds. "He does it because he thinks it's the right thing."

"He never gave up to the things he wanted to do," Luz observes.

"I love the ending," Julieta tells her friends, "where they say that we came to the land, but actually it's the other way around." Julieta is referring to a quotation from Don Pedro:

> We were here before they were, and we are not, as they still say, "undesirables" or "wetbacks." They say we come to this land and it's not our home. Actually, it's the other way around.

The five girls have questions about Don Pedro. They want to know why the police didn't let him go after the girl told the truth about the rape. They want to know if any Americans know about him today. (No one in the class has heard of him.) Julieta wonders if he gets any credit for his work today. The article mentions a PBS documentary about Don Pedro called "Ballad of an Unsung Hero." They want to see it.

These five girls are shy and reticent about speaking up or expressing an opinion in class, but in their group they have so much to say that they keep interrupting each other. At the end of the period, they don't notice the bell and continue talking until I remind them it is time to stop.

Students in the other groups offer different reasons for liking Don Pedro and the article about him. "It gives you history that is not in the books," Arturo observes. Others add, "It introduces us to people we never heard of before," and "It's great to know about your own people."

The students get a sense of a real folk hero from reading about Don Pedro. They identify the legends about him, discuss the qualities that make him a folk hero to Mexican-Americans (parents and friends can be interviewed for what they have heard about him), and consider the value of studying folk heroes. Furthermore, they learn that heroes exist today and don't have to be national figures.

In a class of predominantly black students, I've used two people, Muhammad Ali, a national hero, and Fannie Lou Hammer, who is less well known. The students read articles about them from the popular press and interview their parents for oral tradition. Ali was a hero to their parents and grandparents, but not to the students.

When Ali was at the height of his fame in the late 1960s/early 1970s, he made excellent copy, and there was a rich press and a lively folklore about him. He was not only a hero to Black Americans but a folk poet in the Black oral tradition as well.

Day Three: Reading More Articles on Folk Heroes

When I see articles in the popular press on heroes, especially those entitled "folk heroes," I clip them. (For references see the suggested student readings at the end of this book.) Students read photocopies of these articles. They talk over which of the "heroes" really are folk heroes and why they are considered so by the writers.

Some students choose to write about historical folk heroes, so when possible, I direct them to articles. Martin, a baseball fan, wants to write about Babe Ruth, so I give him "Ty Cobb, Babe Ruth and the Changing Image of the Athletic Hero" by Leverett Smith (1972).

Homework for the next class is to write a draft of a paper on a hero. It can be a reworking of the paper done the first day, or students may choose another person to write about.

Day Four: Students Read Their Papers in Small Groups

I was hoping that everyone would have a draft in hand, but some did not. Some students had been absent, others hadn't finished their drafts. To accommodate everyone, the students who are finished make up response groups, read papers to each other, and receive comments. The students who have not finished writing do so in class.

This unit comes in the beginning of the semester, and many students are still uneasy about reading their papers aloud. When it comes time for Raul to read, he calls me over to his group and says, "Mine's not very good, Mrs. Simons." I join the group and tell them again how important it is not to worry about it being good, that any first draft has potential. Raul listens but isn't convinced. "I forgot to put the paragraphs in the right place," he tells us, even though I have said many times not to worry about mechanics in a first draft. He is so uncomfortable that I offer to read the paper for him. It is a perfectly acceptable first draft, and his group mates have plenty of positive reaction and several questions for him, but it will take Raul until the end of the year to muster the courage to read his writing aloud, even to a small group. Raul is a junior and, after eleven years in school, firmly believes that good writing is judged by spelling and paragraphs. My advice about freewriting and first drafts seems very peculiar to him. He doesn't trust it. Even at the end of the term, he prefaces his reading with disavowals.

Day Five: Publishing—Papers Are Read Aloud in Class

[This day didn't come directly after day four. The students had a few days before their final drafts were due.]

The papers of these minority students are moving in their revelations about student aspirations. Julieta has an older sister who came to the United States from Mexico and wanted to become a teacher. She worked hard and became a teacher's aide, but ultimately she returned to Mexico to marry. Julieta admires her for her successes here and writes, "She worked herself up to a better future. Even though she didn't finish her career, I really admire her. Yes, I am going to finish what she didn't." Luz writes of her mother, who had only three years of school and went to work at age seven. She learned many skills working for other people: sewing, knitting, animal husbandry. She is also an excellent mother. "I admire her patience," Luz writes. "She almost never gets angry and always is talking to us loving. My mother gives us good advice. She educated us in a good way."

Ramiro fills in his grandmother's legends of the Mexican Revolution. His favorite is about a revolutionary who evaded the *Federales* through daring escapades, until one sad night while making his getaway on horseback, he rode into the branch of a tree, broke his neck, and died.

Most students write about relatives, but those who write about mainstream heroes admire them for reasons similar to those given for family heroes. Martin, for example, writes about Babe Ruth:

> The Babe, George Herman Ruth, was a man who had self-confidence, was a great athlete . . . and helped popularize the game of baseball. Babe Ruth was an orphan and had nothing but the clothes on his back. He grew up and became *one of the greatest success stories, from Rags to Riches.*

Babe Ruth is a hero to Martin, not only because of his athletic skills but because he overcame poverty.

Day Six: Summary Discussion

After the papers are read, we spend a period reviewing what we've learned about heroes and heroines. I put three categories of heroes on the board: *Public Folk Heroes, Private Folk Heroes,* and *Celebrities.*

We list the heroes and celebrities and their characteristics in each category. We talk about the impact of these people on our lives. Folk heroes are characterized as being "brave," "outspoken," "principled," and "suffering." In discussing their stories about parents and relatives, the class sees recurring themes: the hard times and hard work these people endured in America for the future of their children, and admiration for the accomplishments and wisdom of family members who had little formal schooling. Another theme is the deep respect and feeling for family. That the themes of their narratives have repetitive patterns classifies them as folk stories, for they retell individual and collective histories and speak of the values and hopes of Mexican-American families.

By contrast, celebrities are characterized as "outrageous," "rich," and "talented"—repetitive themes but expressive of vastly different values.

"You're making us feel bad about our celebrities," Miguel complains as he looks at the lists. The class gets into a debate; some denigrate celebrities as silly and transient. But Miguel defends them as a type of hero. How dull life would be without the Madonnas and Princes, he argues. I don't deny their worth as entertainers, but I do point out the difference between a hero, someone whom you admire and perhaps want to emulate, versus a singer, for example, whose fame often rests on mouthing sensational or simplistic notions of popular culture. Miguel perseveres and cites his paper about Prince. Prince, he says, is more than a celebrity; his lyrics spell out a philosophy of life:

> I personally admire Prince because of his attitude toward life, using "1999" [a song written by Prince] as an example. This is his attitude toward the end of the world,
>
> > "So tonight I'm going to party like it's 1999
> > So take advantage children, he'll be here soon."

Miguel explains that the "he" of the lyrics is God. Prince sees life on earth as tenuous, and Miguel agrees. Miguel agrees with Prince that since the end may be near for anyone, we should enjoy ourselves now. It is a good debate, and after it the class remains divided. The unit closes with log entries on heroes. Students write about their concluding thoughts on the question, "What are heroes and do we need them?" Lupe addresses her log to Miguel:

> I think that heroes are not the persons who sing and put on make up and go crazy. I think that the real heroes are the ones who really do something that is supported by other people.

Most of the students write in a similar vein. Their thoughts about heroes are different from those of suburban students. They reflect an awareness of what it means to grow up as a member of a minority. Most of the students are striving for a better life for themselves than their parents have. Teresa's log entry is typical:

> We need heroes to continue in this world, to set ourselves goals, heroes help us to try hard for something we need, and admiring them we have something to live for.

Lorenzo offers a nice insight based on Don Pedro's love of Pancho Villa: "Even heroes have heroes." Norma sums up with a sentence that could be read as support for both the folk heroes and celebrities of this world:

> I think we do need heroes because maybe without them the world would be boring and very silent.

Unit in Brief

Day One: Whom do you admire?

- Students make lists of people they admire, share the lists, and choose one person to write about.
- They write a first draft.
- Homework: Students choose one characteristic of the person they admire and expand on this characteristic, giving supporting anecdotes and details. This draft may or may not become the basis for their paper.

Day Two: Pedro J. Gonzalez: A Mexican-American Folk Hero

- Students read an article about a contemporary folk hero and discuss the article in small groups.
- Whole-class discussion defining the folk hero and his or her symbolism to the community.

Day Three: Reading More Articles on Folk Heroes

- Students read Xeroxed copies of articles from periodicals and magazines on heroes and folk heroes as models for their papers.
- Small-group and/or whole-class discussion of these articles.
- Homework: Draft of paper on folk hero. It can be the draft from the first day, or students may choose someone else to write about.

Day Four: Students Read Their Papers in Small Groups

- Students read their papers to their small groups and get responses.
- Homework: Prepare the final version of the paper. This is not due for a few days.

Day Five (actually several days later): Publishing

- Students read the papers aloud to the class. This may take more than one period.

Day Six: Summary Discussion

- Whole-class discussion comparing the public folk heroes, private folk heroes, and celebrities in student papers.

- Final log evaluating the unit, followed by sharing and discussion of the log entries.

Notes

1. Scholars studying ancient heroes have identified patterns (folklore) in legends about their lives. The hero—Gilgamesh, Moses, Sargon, Oedipus, Romulus and Remus, or Jesus, for example—is often of royal birth, an attempt is made on his life when he is an infant, he is raised by foster parents in a foreign land, etc. See Lord Fitz Roy Richard Somerset Raglan, *The Hero: A Study in Tradition, Myth and Drama* (Westport, CT: Greenwood Press, 1975, c1956) and Otto Rank, *The Myth of the Birth of the Hero* (New York: Knopf, 1959).

2. See Bruce Rosenberg's article, "Kennedy in Camelot: The Arthurian Legend in America," *Western Folklore* 35 (1976), pp. 52–59. Rosenberg reports the legend was also told about Charlemagne, Frederick Barbarosa, Nero, Thomas Paine, Zapata, Alexander the Great, King Arthur, and James Dean, as well the antihero Adolph Hitler. Also from the Berkeley Folklore Archives, Jean Grover Loomis of San Francisco reported in 1967 a belief among Latinos that Che Guevara, just like Pancho Villa, still lives.

3. See Tristram Potter Coffin and Henning Cohen, eds., *The Parade of Heroes: Legendary Figures in American Lore* (Garden City, New York: Doubleday, 1978) and Hector Lee, *Heroes, Villains and Ghosts* (Santa Barbara, California: Capra Press, 1984).

4. This activity—writing about a person you admire, giving reasons and then taking one reason and developing it—I first learned from Patricia McGrath, codirector of the Puente Project, Berkeley, California.

5. From Matt Damsker, "A Folk Hero in Retirement," *San Francisco Chronicle*, Sunday Punch. January 27, 1985, p. 5.

Chapter Nine

"Aren't We a Little Old for This?"
Suburban Students Design a Unit on Folk Heroes

In a suburban classroom, Fatinah, a singer, knows her hero, the soprano, Renata Scotto. But other students are skittish. Wendy admits that she admires people, "But," she explains, "to have a hero is too strong of a word." Some are uneasy about revealing their heroes, especially if they are from popular culture. Trisha confesses in her log, "All I could think of was Christie Brinkley and Duran Duran!" Others consider heroes to be kid stuff. George wrote, "The moment I heard the word 'hero,' I said to myself, 'Aren't we a little old for this?'"

In this unit high school juniors in a predominantly White suburban school explore the concept of folk heroes. They begin by identifying their own heroes, then go on to consider others'. They compare genuine folk heroes and celebrities. Finally, they consider the function of folk heroes and the value of studying them.

Day One: What Are Heroes/Heroines? How Can You Study Them?

The class starts by brainstorming the words *hero* and *heroine*. Nick calls out, "Eddie Murphy," and Jon adds "Gumby"; the boys get a laugh and cover their uneasiness about heroes. Other students offer serious thoughts: a hero is "strong," "gets respect," "has courage." With these contributions to the brainstorming, the class becomes serious. Abruptly, however, the joking begins again; students suggest that heroes "wear masks and tights." I stop long enough to ask why they are joking. Peter explains, "People laugh at other people's heroes. . . . If someone says Michael Jackson, or something like that, everyone will laugh."

Lynn thinks there are no more heroes:

> Like during the sixties they had Kennedy. . . . in the last twenty years, there hasn't really been any heroes. There's been no wars. Well, I mean, there was Vietnam, but there were no heroes in Vietnam. World War I and World War II and stuff like that they had heroes, they had MacArthur and Kennedy. . . .

Others agree, and one student voices the worry, "What if we don't have any heroes?"

Attempting to come to terms with the subject of heroes, students have noted cartoon and comic book figures, popular culture heroes, and historical heroes. They have talked about their anxiety over naming their real heroes aloud and have discussed their lack of heroes. It is a good start.

Next, I ask them to write about their heroes in their logs. If they have none—if "hero" is, as Wendy suggested, "too strong of a word" for them—I tell them to write about someone they admire. Although these students have been uneasy discussing heroes publicly, they have learned to trust their learning logs and have no trouble addressing the subject there.

In their log entries, students include lists of public figures they admire, comedians like Eddie Murphy, for example, or actors such as Clint Eastwood and the Dirty Harry character he has played. They also list music groups and singers from Venom to Elvis Presley, political figures like Lech Walesa, Ronald Reagan, and Margaret Thatcher. Many, especially boys, list athletes. The boys don't mention women, although girls list both males and females. Students from immigrant families–Lebanese, Indian, Korean—write about their parents, whom they admire for having made a life in America. Fatinah writes:

> I really look up to my parents. When they first came to the USA, they only had two suitcases and each other. They found a place to live and jobs. They had no help from their families. They made it on their own.

When the class shares their lists of heroes, no one figure emerges; the students have no heroes in common. One can imagine a time when someone, perhaps John F. Kennedy, would be found on many lists, but this is not such a time.

After the topic of heroes is introduced, the students plan their projects. Jane Juska, my team teacher, and I will act as consultants. As a first step, the students need to work out what questions they want to explore about heroes. They start by brainstorming a few:

- Why are there heroes?
- What gets them respect?
- Why are heroes so important?
- How do heroes influence people?
- How do heroes stir people up?

"Good questions," I tell them. "Now, how can you go about studying them?"

"Could we do anything we want?" Janet wants to know.

"We could leave the classroom!" Ann announces joyfully.

"We could interview people," Janet suggests. They discuss this possibility; who would they interview? Little kids, peers, adults? They begin to address problems they might encounter, such as how to get honest answers. "The best way," Janet comments, "would probably be anonymously because then you get what they're really thinking instead of what they're saying to impress you." Another student who is thinking of interviewing children worries, "A lot of kids might be afraid to answer." But Peter dissents: "Little kids, they don't care what people think. If you're like in third or fourth grade or second, you just ramble on forever."

Next they turn to strategy. Janet wants to know, "Do we go by ourselves?" Ann suggests, "Could you do this in a group?" "Yeah, have us go in our groups," George cajoles. There is still time in the period for the students to gather in their groups and begin to talk about their projects. I ask each group to develop a short list of topics they would like to pursue.

Listening to the audiotape of one of the groups, I notice that they don't follow instructions; they never get around to making their list. But they do something more important for them at the moment; they keep on talking about—really working out—the question of what a hero is.

Lynn speaks first and challenges the others: "So then who is your hero?" A serious discussion ensues. They wonder about James Bond as a modern hero and evaluate the topic of heroes. Three of them like it, one does not. They talk about how difficult it is for them to think of heroes—a loaded word—but they want to talk about people they admire.

For homework, each student will write a short paragraph explaining how he or she would like to study heroes. These ideas will help them focus their thoughts for planning sessions the next day.

Day Two: Planning Projects

When the students arrive in class, they go into their groups. They read their homework paragraphs to one another, agree on a project, and begin to plan how to execute it. Toward the end of the period, the groups report to the class on their progress. Ann's group came up with the hypothesis that young children admire cartoon characters, but as children grow older their heroes become real people. She explains their project: "We want to find out why people have heroes. . . . when they stop liking cartoon heroes and start liking like real people heroes like political heroes." They have an ambitious plan. In one day they will visit an elementary school, a high school (a nearby private institution), and a convalescent home to trace the evolution of heroes through the life cycle. Another group decides to interview family and friends. Kerri wants to interview the adults in the cul-de-sac where she lives. Teresa admires her grandfather. She wants to interview family members and write about him. Jon and his friends decide to look into the idea of the antihero. John, who has no heroes, chooses to look into the popular press for articles on the decline of heroes in modern America.

The students take to these self-designed projects with an enthusiasm they seldom show for assigned topics. Two things impress me about their projects: first, many of them are excellent ideas that I wouldn't have thought of; and second, the projects are more ambitious than ones I would have assigned. For example, had I assigned interviewing elementary school children about their heroes, I don't think I would have kindled any fires. But now it is the students' idea; they are inspired, and they telephone to make arrangements without any prompting.

Day Three: More Planning, Writing a Questionnaire, and Making Final Arrangements for Projects

Students spend the day finishing the plans for their projects. "Let's start figuring out our questions," prompts Ted, a serious member of this group, bringing his groupmates round to the task at hand. When they settle down, however, they first tackle logistics, arranging where and when to meet, stressing they don't want to be late for the interviews because it will make a bad impression. Then they discuss their worries. "What if the kids don't cooperate?" Dan wonders. Melissa, who has worked with children, has an idea. "We can bring candy canes, just little ones. You have to anyway, it's Christmas." She convinces the group. Chris suggests that they start each interview by asking the children their names.

With the planning details settled, they turn to their interview questions. One suggests, "What do you look for in a hero?" Dan starts to laugh. "What kind of a question is that to ask a little kid?" He's right; everyone laughs. After much debate about what questions will work with children, they come up with this list:

- Who is your favorite sports hero?
- Who is your favorite comic book hero?
- Who is your favorite movie hero?
- What is your definition of a hero?
- Whom do you look up to in your family?
- Do you have a hero of the opposite sex?
- Who is your favorite hero?
- Who would you like to grow up to be like?

In their group these five students actively collaborate in the planning and enjoy the process. Occasionally, they call on me or Jane Juska for help, but most of the problems, like how to record their interviews, they resolve themselves. Before they leave class, each group goes over its final plans with either Jane Juska or me. At the end of the period, they are looking forward, a little nervously, to the next day.

Day Four: The Research

The students are in the field doing their research.

Day Five: Informal Reports on Field Work/ Beginning the I-Search Paper

Trisha flies into the classroom and races over to my desk. "It was terrific at the old people's home. There was this old lady who was born in Japan, and her father was an admiral in the Royal British Navy who had asked the Japanese Emperor if they could patrol their seas!. . . She had traveled a lot and had met the Gandhis! She really admired Mrs. Gandhi!" Trisha also tells us how the old folks wouldn't let them leave. When the students had completed their interviews, the elders asked for more; didn't they have more questions to ask?

Walking into the room, Wendy looks at me and laughs. "I didn't even talk to the kids for more than two hours, and I was wiped out. I think every kid my age should get in front of a class and see just how hard it can really be." George interrupts with the surprising results of his interviews at a nearby Catholic high school. "Do you know who their heroes are? Martin Luther King and their parents! No one said groups or singers, no U2's, no Duran Duran!"

Lynn's group had gone to a junior high where the students were tracked according to ability. Their first impression was shock at how small the kids were. Their second shock came when they visited the lower tracks. "The girls sat in the back of the room combing their hair, and the whole class was rowdy and uncontrollable." It was a startling comparison to the gifted class where everyone was helpful and eager to answer their questions.

Each group has piles of data. We will talk about ways of tabulating and making sense of their interviews. But first it is time to describe the I-Search paper they will be writing.

Starting an I-Search

The I-Search is a research paper described in Ken Macrorie's book, *Searching Writing* (1984). An I-Search gives equal weight to the process of the research and the results. The paper is a narrative of the writer's search for information. Jane Juska planned a three-part paper based on Macrorie's model:

Part I: What I knew and didn't know (about heroes before studying them)

Part II: The search (for information)

Part III: What I learned (and what I still have questions about)

To demonstrate the style and tone of the papers, we give the students sample opening paragraphs. Jane Juska and I each wrote one, and we use some from *Searching Writing*. The students notice that they are written in first person, and the authors describe their emotional as well as intellectual reactions to the research. Even though the paragraphs are about research, they sound as though the authors are telling a story.

The students draft some introductory paragraphs of their own. John's begins

When Mrs. Simons proclaimed that we were going to do research on heroes I was quite indifferent. Then she proceded to announce that we would design the unit. My first thought was that the class would become a mad-house. It did. But eventually the battered and bruised teachers fought their way to control. When the absence of heroes came up, I was intrigued and immediately broke out of my death-like trance. I had always thought that the glorious days of the hero were over, but I didn't know why, so I set about the dangerous task of finding out.

John's opening paragraph illustrates some of the benefits of an I-Search. The paragraph chronicles his thoughts and reactions to the study of heroes. At first he is indifferent. Next, when I announce that the students will design their own projects, he senses that things are not as they should be, are perhaps out of control. And, most interesting, he records the point at which he becomes engaged, when he breaks out of his "death-like trance." The journalistic, storytelling style of the paper gives John room to experiment in the writing, to be playful, even flamboyant while, at the same time, to seriously present a question about heroes that intrigues him: why the day of the American hero is over.

For homework, the students start drafting Parts I and II of their papers. The drafts are due in three days, when they will read them in response groups.

Day Six: The Folk Hero and the Celebrity

In their projects students bring up and cover the important aspects of heroes. However, one issue, the difference between heroes and celebrities, is unclear. We take a period to discuss it, during which I present some of Daniel Boorstin's ideas on the differences between heroes and celebrities as a starting point for the discussion.[1]

Daniel Boorstin decries the fate of the concept "hero" in the hands of what he terms the "Graphic Revolution." He explains:

> Shakespeare ... divided men into three classes: those born great, those who achieved greatness, and those who had greatness thrust upon them. It never occurred to him to mention those who hired public relations experts and press secretaries to make themselves look great (45).

Boorstin elaborates, "We can ... make a man or woman well known; but we cannot make him great. We can make a celebrity, but we can never make a hero"(48). We "confuse the Big Name with the Big Man"(47). What we have forgotten, Boorstin contends, is that "all heroes are self-made"(48). Furthermore, through their achieved greatness, they "reveal and elevate us"(50). He continues, *"the celebrity is a person who is known for his well-knownness"*(57), not his achievement. The lives of entertainer-celebrities cannot extend our horizons. As a result, he concludes, "in this world of big names our true heroes tend to be anonymous."

Many students take issue with Boorstin, arguing that he overstates his case and that it is different for adolescents (they assume that he is writing about adults). Boorstin's reasoning polarizes heroes and celebrities. While the media does create celebrities, who are in no way traditional heroes, that is only part of the story. Furthermore, Boorstin overlooks folklore, which mitigates the power of the media. People are not totally manipulated by the media in this matter of folk heroes. First, there are still folk heroes who are created by the folk, not the media. (See chapter 8, pages 139-48, for Mexican–American folk hero, Pedro J. Gonzalez.) Second, the celebrities, who are media creations, are the target of a lively "folk" commentary consisting of legends and jokes. Boorstin does not consider the folk opinion of celebrities. The folk bestow celebrities with lore that can elevate or deflate them, give them accolades and heroic attributes, or reduce them to fools. Jokes about celebrities usually undercut them. Some legends, however, can give celebrities something like heroic stature.

Genuine folk heroes are not common. (Boorstin reaches back to Moses and Lincoln for his examples.) In recent times, however, the Beatles are an example of celebrities who, if not folk heroes, were raised to folk heroic status through folklore about them, folklore which continues today. Their music and their lifestyles were iconoclastic; irreverence characterizes the folklore about them as well. For example, an early Beatles legend goes like this:

> The Beatles were in their first recording session with producer, George Martin (late 1962). Martin explained that if there ever was anything they didn't like, they should say so. George Harrison, one of the Beatles, replied, "Well, for a start, I don't like your tie." (Berkeley Folklore Archives, reported by Gary Rappaport in 1979)

Rappaport analyzes the legend:

> ... the Beatles were very much a part of the sixties counterculture movement. The tie is a symbol of the working establishment, an indicator of the sterile conforming business world. Harrison is saying that he doesn't want any association with that world. ...

Today, twenty years after the height of the Beatles' popularity, admirers from all over the world appear daily in front of the EMI studios on Abbey Road in London where the Beatles recorded. These Beatles fans photograph themselves on the zebra crossing in the front of the studios, imitating the Beatles as they are pictured on the *Abbey Road* album cover. Boorstin would dismiss the Beatles as celebrities. But there was and is a Beatles folklore that transforms them.

To sum up, then, the media creates the celebrity, the contemporary rival of the folk hero. While celebrities, as Boorstin points out, are not exemplary, he overlooks the role of the folk as critics of celebrities. Through their folklore, the folk honor few celebrities as folk heroes while puncturing the media images of many others, often through jokes.

In the third section of their papers, students who were studying celebrities were to consider their status: celebrity, folk hero, or a combination of the two. For all types of heroes, I asked the students to consider Boorstin's idea of the cultural role of a hero to "reveal and elevate us."

Day Seven: Response Groups on Parts I and II of Student Papers

Students respond in groups to one another's papers.

Day Eight: Analysis of Data

Most of the students had conducted interviews. Part III of their papers, "What I Learned and Didn't Learn," would include an analysis of the interview data. Before analyzing their material, the class discussed ways to organize the material and then suggested questions to interpret the data once it was organized. Some of their organization schemes were to

1. Tabulate all the heroes and heroines from the interviews:
   - Are they folk heroes, media heroes, or anonymous family and friend type heroes?
2. Tabulate them by age level:
   - Do kindergartners have different heroes from fourth graders?
3. Tabulate them by sex:
   - Do girls and boys have different heroes?

If their projects were interviews or library research, they explored these questions:

1. What are the qualities of the heroes?
2. Why are they admired?

For the rest of this period, the students worked on organizing their data. For homework, they wrote drafts of Part III.

Day Nine: Responding in Groups to Part III of the Student Papers

The final section of the I-Search is analytical, a report of findings, more difficult to write than the narrative-based Parts I and II. Dan had interviewed elementary school children. After analyzing his ten pages of notes, he wrote a first draft:

First draft: What I Learned

I learned most of the children's heroes were male and most of the boys didn't have any female heroines. I was surprised to find that two girls I interviewed looked up to their younger sisters most in the family. I thought the person you looked up to was usually older or the same age as yourself. There were many answers for someone's favorite hero. I thought there would be similar responses to this question but everyone seemed to have their own favorite hero.

Dan's response group had enjoyed his recollections of childhood heroes in Parts I and II:

I remembered back a few years ago when my heroes were comic book characters such as Superman and Spiderman. A year or two later my hero was the 16th president of the United States, Abraham Lincoln. After that it was my favorite football team, the Oakland Raiders during the days of Dave Caser, Ken Stabler and Fred Bletnikov.

The group was disappointed with Part III. They told him to think more about what he had learned. Dan's findings were interesting but he hadn't speculated about their meaning. Why, for example, are there so few heroines? Is it possible for a hero to be younger than yourself? Why was there such a diversification of heroes? Why weren't any one or two dominant?

Dan's revision is an improvement but still does not do justice to his data:

Final draft: What I Learned

I learned from a little first grader named Zara that heroes can come from families and friends. I also learned most of the boys and girls heroes were male. No one boy I interviewed had a heroine. This showed me they either didn't really have a female hero or they were afraid to admit they did. I also found that most of the children's heroes weren't really important to them because they knew their heroes weren't real.

But the thing that I learned that surprised me most was these children had many different heroes and none was more popular than the other with them. They were Sarah Cribb (a book character), Steve Garvey (a baseball player), Dustin Hoffman (actor), Superman (comic book and movie character), Encyclopedia Brown (a book character), E.T. (a movie character) and Joe Montana (a football player). I expected a similar or popular answer to this question. I was wrong as you can see. The last thing I learned was how difficult it is to write an I-Search paper.

Yet, Dan makes two good changes. He offers a reason the boys didn't have female heroes, and he supports his finding of the multiplicity of heroes with examples. He also observes that the heroes are unimportant because they aren't real. (Obviously some are.) But even now Dan's analysis remains thin. He could have done more, for he had good data. He had done a lot of work interviewing students in first, second, fourth, fifth, and sixth grades, but he didn't look for grade-level or developmental differences. He could have done more thinking about the dominance of male heroes. And if he was surprised by the variety of heroes, why was he? Who did he expect to find as elementary school heroes?

That night, Jane and I read the drafts and made comments and suggestions. When the students got their papers back, they had two sets of comments, one from their peers and one from a teacher. Using this advice, they had until the end of the following week to revise and hand in a final draft.

Day Ten: Reports of Findings and Concluding Thoughts

We had a summing-up period, a day of sharing findings and a time to evaluate the hero/heroine projects. A review of Jennifer's paper dramatizes the value of the study of heroes, of student designed research, and of the I-Search. Jennifer opened her Part I this way:

> On Monday Mrs. Simons asked us who our heroes were, and it only took me a few seconds to figure out that I really didn't have a hero . . . but I remember having heroes when I was little . . . the word hero seems intimidating and a word children would use more than teenagers.

Jennifer took the direction of her research from her opening thoughts. She had positive memories of the heroes of her childhood, and thus she decided to interview elementary school children. Part II of her paper follows her research, which she enlivens with her feelings and impressions. She writes of her day of interviewing in the elementary school:

> All of these children made me feel old, and I started to remember when I was that age and people came to speak to my class. I wasn't nervous, but I did want everything to work out just right.

Everything did work out just right. Jennifer and her partner got rich data. Jennifer, who had interviewed kindergartners and fourth graders, took a developmental view. She found that "mommies and daddies" were the heroes of the kindergartners. Fourth graders tended to choose public figures—athletes, singers, the president. Looking at the reasons the children gave for their choices, Jennifer noticed something interesting: although their heroes were different, they served similar purposes and revealed similar needs.

Jennifer found that both fourth graders and kindergartners value power and strength. She speculated that kindergartners looked to parents as powerful heroes because they needed family security. By fourth grade, the children had turned to public figures and told Jennifer of dreams of fame and wealth. She reasoned that by this age, children have begun to move beyond the immediacy of the family circle and that therefore their heroes may also lie beyond the family.

When the papers had been read, I noticed several patterns, which I discussed with the students. The first had to do with public versus private heroes. The former, in particular musicians, actors, and actresses, were not described as mentors but as projected fantasies. More private heroes, such as family members, are mentors. Furthermore, students' reasons for admiring these mentors are the same from paper to paper: they are formulaic and folkloric. Usually they have triumphed over major problems and grown to be generous human beings.

As I had hoped, students seemed to realize the value of the folk hero over the celebrity. From their initial lists of people they admired, they also realized that celebrities are common and public folk heroes are few, but that on rare occasions celebrities can cross the line and become folk heroes.

Finally, the students' research seemed to confirm the demise of national folk heroes. Heroes and heroines still live and serve as useful and perhaps necessary models for American youth, but they are not public figures; they are found close by, among family and friends.

Unit in Brief

Day One: What Are Heroes/Heroines? How Can You Study Them?

- Students brainstorm characteristics of heroes.
- In their logs they list their heroes.
- Class speculates on ways to study heroes.
- In small groups students begin to plan hero projects.
- Homework: Students write a paragraph outlining a project to study heroes.

Day Two: Planning Projects

- Students work in small groups planning projects.
- Each group gives the whole class a progress report.

Day Three: More Planning, Writing a Questionnaire, and Making Final Arrangements for Projects

- The period is spent on final planning. The majority of the class will do interviews. Students design their questionnaires and make phone calls for final arrangements. Students doing research projects go to the library.

Day Four: The Research

- The students are in the field doing their research.

Day Five: Informal Reports on Field Work/Beginning the I-Search Paper

- The class shares their experiences in the field.
- The I-Search paper is introduced.
- Students draft introductory paragraphs for their papers.
- Homework due in two days is to draft Parts I and II of their papers.

Day Six: The Folk Hero and the Celebrity

- Class discussion on the folk hero and the celebrity, what each is, what each represents. One option is to have the students read the Boorstin article as homework in preparation for this class.

Day Seven: Response Groups on Parts I and II of Student Papers

Day Eight: Analysis of Data

- The students bring the data from their interviews, and the whole class discusses ways to organize and tabulate the information.
- Students work individually or in groups on their own data.
- Homework: Students write up Part III, the findings from their research.

Day Nine: Responding in Groups to Part III of the Student Papers

Day Ten: Reports of Findings and Concluding Thoughts

- Students report on the findings of their research.
- Class discussion on the role and value of heroes at different stages in life with a focus on the usefulness of heroes for middle and high school students.

Note

1. See Chapter 2, "From Hero to Celebrity: The Human Pseudo-Event," in Boorstin's *The Image: A Guide to Pseudo-Events in America.*

Chapter Ten

"All Right! We've Got a Substitute!"
School and Teenage Folklore

Adolescent folklore gets less attention from folklorists than children's folklore probably because children's folklore is more visible, and children are usually willing to be observed and to talk about their folklore. By contrast, much teenage folklore is part of a subculture, purposefully less visible and oppositional in nature.

There is an abundant adolescent folklore that not only entertains teenagers but "works at . . . different levels to question, support, and interpret" the social order (Bronner 1986, 127). Two functions stand out in adolescent folklore. The first is a testing of the social order. Adolescent folklore tests in several ways. It allows forays into the adult world. It tries and challenges legal limits. It speaks to the bravado of youth, pushing some to test their body limits as well, as in adolescent drinking contests and feats of derring-do.

A second key function of adolescent lore is the setting of boundaries. Roger Abrahams writes that some folklore is "a means of articulating boundaries in order to include members and nonmembers; but it also may operate as means of distinguishing separate and even antagonistic segments within the community" (1980, 371). Abrahams is writing about ethnic groups, but his description is apt for adolescents. Teenage slang, hairstyles, dress, and dance styles, for example, set adolescents apart from the worlds of adults and children. They want to be recognized as different and separate. Furthermore, within the generic category of adolescence, there are subtypes. The folklores of "nerds" and "jocks" define them and set these types apart from one another.

163

Since adolescent folklore is a relatively unexplored area, students have an opportunity to do some original research. However, for their work to be successful and because of the private nature of adolescent folklore, the students must trust each other and the teacher. This unit should take place late in the semester after a classroom community has been established.

Day One: Introduction to School and Teenage Folklore

Since school and teenage folklore are less apparent than other types, we don't begin with a brainstorming session. Instead, I start by listing examples of teenage folklore and discussing them as they go up on the board. Gradually, the students begin to add their own examples.

In an inner-city classroom, I start the topic with a question: "How many ways can you pass a note in class?" The students smile knowingly. As I am asking the question, Miguel, who is sitting right in front of me in the first row, casually raises his right hand and slowly lowers it behind his back. I can easily see him from where I am standing, but I think he is stretching. In fact, he has unobtrusively dropped a note on Arturo's desk. It takes me a few seconds to catch on to what is happening because it is a masterful demonstration of note-passing skill. Even in the context of studying note passing, a note can be passed under the teacher's nose! For the next few minutes, students describe and demonstrate note-passing skills.

"How many ways can a student cheat in class?" I ask next. Rosie points to Olga, who is sitting in front of her, and explains, "If she was wearing a shirt with a hood, you could put the answers in there [in the hood]." Julieta adds, "Writing the answers real small in your hands," or, "On a little piece of paper in your hand," a classmate says. Araceli has a variation, "Tape a piece of paper on your arm." Quickly we amass a long list of cheating strategies.

We stop a moment and consider these activities as folklore. The students have learned them from others by watching or word of mouth, and they are dependent on context for meaning.

"What about the folklore of the time-honored pastimes of 'boy watching' and 'girl watching'?" I ask. Olga smiles. She and her friends call their version of boy watching "hunting," a well-chosen word.

"What happens when a teacher is absent and there is a substitute?" Impatient hands thrash the air as students begin to tell favorite substitute stories. "Bring your friends to class," Maria suggests. But another student who considers a period with a sub wasted time tells us, "When I see a substitute, I just leave." Supplying a substitute for an absent teacher is school policy, not folklore. But how students treat the substitute *is* indeed folklore, behavior they learn from one another.

The class continues in this fashion; I list types of teenage folklore, the students give examples, and we discuss how the item is or isn't folklore. Here are some sample items from adolescent folklore:

- Folk Groups:
  Often the groups have folk names: jocks, goobers, stoners, simps, wimps, rah rahs, preppies, punks, cholos, nerds, wanabees, surfers, mods. How can you tell a member of a group?

- Senior Pranks:
  For example, letting 200 "paper eating" crickets loose in the library, or having the senior class check out all the books in the library.

- Slang (Folk Speech):
  How many words do you know for "girl"? Fox, broad, piece, chick, bird, ladies, *señoritas*. How many words do girls have for boys? Jock, stud, hunk, jerk, pig. What words or phrases do you use that sound inappropriate from the mouths of adults? Why?[1] When are the slang terms for boys and girls used? What is their meaning?

- Teenage Graffiti:
  See chapter 11.

- Junior and Senior Prom:
  There is both the official school event, the dance itself, and the student folk rituals surrounding the dance: where to eat before the dance, what to do after the dance, what to wear, what flowers to give, etc.

- Hairstyles:
  While we were discussing adolescent preoccupation with hair, Olga told a joke about a teenager dying of thirst on the desert. He is finally found and in his rasping voice requests, "Water." But before he drinks, he dips his comb in the water and combs his hair.

- Dating Folklore:
  Going steady: Who can ask whom out, where do people go on dates?

- Slumber Parties

- TPing Houses

- Cruising

- Yearbooks:
  The yearbook itself is a commercial product, not folklore. However, much of the form of the books, for example the polls of the best dressed, most likely to succeed, etc., is folklore. The content of many of the inscriptions students and teachers write is also formulaic and folkloric. And the ceremonial signing of yearbooks is a folk ritual.
- Verbal Dueling
  This is the folklorist's term for the wars of words common among teenagers. Originating with Black students and known as "Playing the Dozens," it is now widespread and has many names; "capping," "put-downs," "baking," "charging," "roasting," "ranking," and "busting" are a few.
- "Hanging Out"
- The Folklore of Sports:
  Superstitions for good luck, team nicknames, the coach's rituals for getting a winning team, and individual player's superstitions, like wearing the same shirt, are a few.
- Pep Rallies and Homecoming:
  The idea of pep rallies and homecoming is folklore; the events themselves if orchestrated by the administration are not folklore. However, the folk add touches, such as "tailgating" before football games.
- Cheers and Cheerleading:
  Originally, this was purely folklore. But popular culture has seeped in with books of cheers and cheerleading camps. However, cheerleaders still hand on much of the craft to one another as folklore.
- Chants from the Fans and Supporters in the Stands:
  Sometimes these are benign but in some cases they aren't. In a wealthy area of California the students taunted their poorer opponents by waving and rattling their foreign car keys and shouting:
  "It's okay,
  Beat us today,
  Tomorrow you'll be working for us."[2]
- Slam Books
- Spirit Week
- Legends and Rumors
- Clubs:
  School clubs, such as the Ski Club, are not folklore. But the social clubs the students create and perpetuate on their own are.

- Chain Letters
- Jokes Told by Adolescents
- Graduation Rituals:
    Wearing the class ring upside down until graduation, moving the mortarboard tassel from the left to right after graduation
- Excuses
    Homework excuses (My dog peed on it. I train him to do that") and excuses for being absent, being tardy, and cutting.
- Dance fads like Break Dancing
- Greetings and Leave Taking:
    How friends greet each other, and what they say when departing, for example, "I'm outta here" or "Later."
- Gestures
- Drinking Lore:
    You get drunk faster if you drink through a straw, and drinking games like "Quarters."
- Drug Lore
- Driving Lore:
    "Padiddle" and "mooning" are folklore. And some students believe that if a girl is caught in the back seat of a car with a boy and their shoes are off, it's statutory rape.
- Folklore About Sex:
    "You can't get pregnant the first time."
- Folklore About Teachers

As the list unfolds, students make suggestions. "What about talking on the phone?" Olga asks. It is teenage folklore. Lupe wants to know if her friends, who call themselves "The Three Musketeers," would qualify. They're not "preppies" or "stoners," just a group of three friends. Any group with something in common, I remind her, is a folk group, so yes, they are.

After the list is finished, we take a few minutes to study it. What can we learn about adolescents just from the list? The first observation is that there are different folk groups representing very different types of people in the school, each with different folklore. Next, the students notice that there are official, institutionally sponsored rituals that were probably once folklore, such as pep rallies, spirit week, the prom, and homecoming. By contrast, their folklore is what they learn from one another, such as their groups and slang, and the rituals that they build around school-sponsored events. They also notice that much of their folklore is contentious, testing the social order.

Day Two: Gathering More
Information on Teenage Folklore

In order to feel more comfortable with this topic and to get more details and substance into the discussion of their folklore, students choose three topics from the list and write a brief log entry, spending five to ten minutes on each one. When they finish, they share them. Lorenzo reads his opening dialogue:

> "All right! We've got a substitute."
> "A substitute. Ah man, I'm not going to class."
> "I am. It's going to be fun."

He then asks the class to predict what will happen next.

Rosie reads her log on the folklore of drugs:

> Everybody in school has this thing with drugs this is always on everybody's mind. It's like if you don't do it you're a chicken or your not with it. Actually many of my friends take drugs and it really hurts me to see them like that. It might be because of problems they might have, but if you're cool, you won't tell anyone about that problem. It's also like an image or something to talk about to get attention.

We see two folk messages here: you're chicken if you don't take drugs, and it's not cool to reveal personal problems.

Maria wrote about cruising:

> Cruising is not my idea of having a good time, but my boyfriend's hobby is cruising. I don't mind cruising once in a while, but he likes to cruise too much. I like to go cruising when there is a Main because you see all kinds of nice cars from different cities and you see all kinds of different people.

We talk a little about cruising, clearly a folk event.

Five students wrote about groups. Miguel's crowd, who call themselves "the groupies," is interracial.

> The groupies are a vital part of my life, consisting of a bunch of my buddies, black, white, Mexican, Chinese and everything else you can think of. My best friend is a part of that group and I tell him things that not even my brother knows. I tell him things that I can't tell my girlfriend. We go out sometimes to the movie or have a picnic, all of us, together, and it's fun because they're as special to me as my own family.

The class discusses Miguel's notion of his friends as a second family and why groups become so important in adolescence.

Olga started one paragraph about her version of "boy watching."

> My friends and I, every time we go somewhere, we're always looking around for cute guys. We call it "hunting."

After a classmate reads, Lorenzo sighs and comments, "I should have written that." "Exactly the point," I tell him. "Listening to good writing from your friends is like reading good literature. You learn to appreciate good writing, and it gives you ideas for your own writing."

National Issues in Teenage Folklore

Adolescent folklore can be a bridge from the lives of the students to national issues. When they study teenage folklore, students can look into one or two of the nationwide concerns that come up in their folklore to show them how folklore shapes their opinions and behavior. In this class, I considered three topics that emerged from their logs: cheating, drugs, and racial or ethnic discrimination based on stereotypes. Roberto had written a log endorsing cheating, citing extensive cheating by public officials in support of his position. He concluded with a somewhat proud confession that he had passed English the previous year by cheating. His log prompted a heated argument about national morality. As cited above, Rosie had written a log about drugs and the folklore surrounding them. In drafts about their groups, several students had touched on self-segregation by race. Since folklore creates and feeds stereotypes and because the students were most interested in the issues of stereotypes and segregation, we decided to look at these issues from the perspective of school and teenage folklore.

Many of the same issues recur each year, so I keep a file of articles from newspapers and magazines to use as background. The previous year a local paper had reported on a study of segregation in the schools. Another source for readings on stereotypes is *The Things They Say Behind Your Back* (Helmreich 1982). This is a book about stereotypes, and the stereotypes of the nine American ethnic groups described are based in folklore, jokes, legends, proverbs, beliefs, and the like. For homework, the students read two articles from the *San Francisco Examiner*—Charles C. Hardy, "Segregation Continues in Area Schools" and "Segregation Is Mostly by Student Choice." Both articles appeared January 30, 1983, pages 131 and 134.

Day Three: Segregation and Stereotypes— Exploring an Issue Raised in Student Folklore

Not everyone has done the homework, and some students have not fully understood the articles. So, we start class by working on the articles in small groups, underlining the important parts and writing questions to the researchers who did the survey. I ask the students to look out for references to folklore, although it won't be called folklore, and stereotypes, which are heavily influenced if not determined by folklore, in the articles.

The study is summarized in the opening paragraph of the second article:

> Despite nearly 29 years of institutional attempts to desegregate public schools, the educational system and the students themselves are perpetuating racial separation on campus, according to a six-month study of 1,000 Bay Area high school students.

Before the discussion, I ask that students write down the main finding of the study. Sadly, many wrote versions of this log entry: "White and Asian students are smarter than Black and Hispanic students [who] are dumb." Some students have accepted these stereotypes. It is important to talk about them and how they are perpetuated. Two sources emerge: their folklore and school policy and practices. Their folklore reinforces stereotypes in epithets, graffiti, legends, folk beliefs, and jokes. When the folklore is complimentary of a minority, it is not about academic achievement. For example, in this class one boy asked seriously about this bit of folklore: "Do Black people have a special muscle in their legs that makes them run faster?" There are also folk beliefs about Whites, among them that caucasians are naturally smart and don't have to work hard to get good grades.

Pointing to a quote in the article from a local principal, Martin changes the focus of the discussion. It isn't just student folklore that creates stereotypes; it's school policy too. The principal is quoted as saying, "Isolating students racially in separate classes is a factor which leads to racial tension on campus."

Shifting the focus slightly, I ask, "Who are the immigrants in this school?" "The boat people," they tell me. And when I ask how they are treated here, the students become fidgety. "Are they teased as it says in the article?" I wonder aloud.

"Yes, that's true," one of the boys admits. "That's happened on the soccer team 'cause a lot of the boat people came and they would always pick on them. Some of us couldn't pronounce their names, so we would call them something else in Spanish [and] pick on them." We talk about why each group seems to want another to pick on. The article mentions, for example, a group who calls itself WPOD, "White Punks on Dope," and who looks down on African-Americans and has " ... come to regard black people as someone who should be shipped back to Africa" (*San Francisco Examiner*, January 30, 1983, page 131).

The article suggests that it is the responsibility of the public schools to get rid of this segregation, which they say threatens the area's future stability. Lorenzo challenges this: "How are you going to tell people who they can hang around with? You can't!" But Arturo thinks that schools can do something, especially the counselors, who, he alleges, whenever they see a Spanish name put the student in the lower tracks.

One solution, I suggest, is to allow students to plan their own programs, selecting the classes they want to take. They disagree, claiming that they don't have the ability to choose their course of study. But Olga, who is in advanced classes, agrees: "Yes you could, yes you could, you could when you choose your classes for next year, you'd take your choice and if you want to be in an advanced class. . . . "

Someone breaks in, "But what if you're not able?" Before this issue is resolved, another is raised.

Arturo has a suggestion that would eliminate racism in students' placement, "Why don't they put the students by numbers instead of by names because it's their names that take away their chance of getting. . . . " It is a suggestion worth considering, but Miguel impatiently interrupts. "Listen, this is the deal, they shouldn't be starting this in high school, they should start doing it in elementary school so they will already be used to doing it."

Reviewing the discussion, we identify two results of stereotyping and segregation: the maintenance of low self-images among minority students, and the perpetuation of segregationist thinking and behavior toward new groups like the boat people. We perceive the tracking system to be a major cause of segregation. We then discuss some ways of breaking the segregation cycle.

Roberto questions the information itself, asking, "Who did this survey?" Lorenzo answers, "A White man." The students feel that his bias influenced what he observed and concluded. For example, there was no mention of multiracial groups like Miguel's "groupies." It would be informative to know how Miguel and his friends formed and were able to successfully sustain such a group.

Finally, the study's author says that schools must narrow the gap between ethnic groups, but that they appear to be doing the reverse. In fact, the study found that although students wanted to improve race relations, the issue was rarely discussed in class or addressed by the school. A good way to broach the issues of discrimination and stereotyping would be through folklore. The stereotypes that feed discrimination are taught and learned in folklore. Understanding the content and function of this lore would be a first step toward confronting the problems.

For homework, students choose their paper topics, most selecting one from the three log entries they wrote the previous day. They
also write a draft focusing on setting and performance of the folklore.
This is good practice in descriptive writing and essential information
for understanding how the folklore works. I also ask the students to
look for larger societal concerns reflected in their folklore as we did
in class.

Day Four: "Too Much Fun, No Sleep"—
Class Response to Drafts

Alba asked if she could read her draft to the whole class; she wanted
a response from everyone. "Too much fun, no sleep" is the story of a
slumber party she had hosted the previous weekend. A reader of
teenage literature, Alba is captivated by this unit on teenage folklore.
Her paper was consciously styled in imitation of the adolescent fiction she reads.

"It all started three weeks ago at our main hangout, Pioneer," she
begins, and then tells how she and her friends planned a surprise
birthday party for their friend, Maria. "I offered to have the party at
my house which I regret. You'll see why, just keep on reading, and I
offered to buy the hard liquor." Her house was empty because her
parents were at a convention in Montana.

Alba's girlfriends come early, clean the house, and make pizzas,
although they forget to turn on the oven. "The pizzas were laying in
the oven for the longest time with the oven off!" Although she
promised her boyfriend Pacho there would be no boys, a group of
them shows up at the door, and she lets them in. At 3 A.M. Pacho calls.
Alba is alarmed. "'Hi babe,' I said, you know trying to butter him up."
He wants to come over. "Sure," Alba says. Pacho is more than surprised to find twenty boys, some of them in the den watching an
X-rated movie on the VCR. The party lasted until 7 A.M. when the
boys left and the girls went to sleep.

Confident that her writing has been well received, Alba challenges the class, "Well, what did you like?"

"When you are trying to butter up your boyfriend on the phone."

"The part about the oven not being on."

"When you had to make a decision about whether or not to let the
guys in." The class cuts the praise short; they are impatient to ask
their questions.

"How did the boys know about the party and who were they?"
and "What happened to the pizzas?" Teresa wants to know.

"Did anyone offer to clean up?" Ramiro asks. And Martin wonders, "Did your parents ever find out about the guys coming in?"

Maria (not the Maria at the party) asks Alba, "Did your boyfriend get mad when he saw the boys in the house?"

And Araceli wants to know, "What were you thinking when you opened the door?"

"What if my parents came home?" Alba tells her. All the students are curious about the movie, which it turns out Alba did not see. "Why didn't you watch it?" "My boyfriend didn't want me to," she tells them.

The students really want to know what the movie was about, but they are embarrassed to ask. Instead, they ask questions skirting around it like, "How long was the movie?"

"Did you get drunk?" Rosie wants to know. She stayed sober, Alba explains, because she had to take care of the house.

Alba knew she had a hit, not only in content but in style. Lupe told her she liked the way she talked to the reader.

For homework, the students write an analytical piece on their teenage folklore, keeping in mind the lore and the event, the setting and the performances, and considering the purpose and function of the lore. They are also to point out any connections they see with regional or national issues, such as drugs, alcohol, teenage sex. For a little preliminary in-class practice, everyone writes a few lines about what was happening at Alba's party.

"That's easy," Raul comments. "They were breaking the rules." We list the violated rules: drinking, watching an x-rated movie, letting the boys in. Why were these three rules breached? Giving them a hint, I ask, "Who can do these things without breaking rules?"

"Mom and Dad," Lorenzo replies.

There is a moment of silence, then words of agreement. Alba and her friends, who are neither children nor adults, were, in a sense, playing at being grown-ups, doing things that are normal for adults to do, but taboo for adolescents.

They have other ideas about the party's function. It was entertaining. Furthermore, planning it and surprising Maria made the girls, a group, feel closer together. With a slightly dazed look, Lorenzo closes the discussion with this observation, "I thought a slumber party was when you got into your pajamas and told scary stories.[3] But this sounds like a regular party." The girls laugh knowingly.

For the remainder of the period, students read their drafts to each other in small groups and get feedback from their classmates on the meaning of the events in the folklore they are describing. For homework, the students write drafts analyzing the teenage folklore described in their papers.

Day Five: Small Groups

The student papers have two parts, the narrative or description and the analysis. Both are read in small groups and get positive feedback, questions, and suggestions from other members of the groups. This will take one or two periods, depending on the size of the class and the length of the papers. For the next few nights, the homework is to revise the drafts.

Day Six: Reading Final Papers—A Perspective on Adolescence

As students read and discuss the meaning of their various teenage lores, themes emerge. One is forays into adulthood, such as described in Alba's party. A second theme, in clear contrast to the first, is the folklore that returns them to their childhood. Two students wrote about throwing water balloons and walking in mud puddles, a brief regression to childhood, a respite from growing up. Both nostalgia for childhood and yearning for adulthood are reflected in their lore. A third theme is the celebration of adolescence, especially friendships. Luz explains:

> Lupe, Julieta and I are a united group and we like to give our opinions on what we like. Most of the times I do not like to go out of campus. Lupe and I always think the same. We sit on the grass and talk about boys and nature. We like to read poems. However, Julieta sometimes gets bored with us. She likes to get off campus and go some other places. She likes to write her name and ours on hidden places for rememberness. . . . This is how our group works.

The three girls laugh together, plan their futures, judge boys; they support and sustain each other. Lupe writes of them:

> Julieta, Luz and I plan to finish our education and later when Mr. Right is found get married. Of course, we are going to attend to each other's wedding.

A fourth theme is oppositional behavior, flaunting the adult world. "Dogging" is part of the folklore of Miguel's groupies. When they go out as a crowd to the movies, for example, they're noisy. When a patron disapproves, they all "dog" him, that is, turn and stare him down. "This is very effective," Miguel reports, "especially if the person is smaller." While they enjoy a little disruptive fun, the group-ies are also a serious support group. Miguel explains, "An occasional 'Man, I can't hang with school anymore,' comes out from someone in the group, and everyone helps that person through the day."

A fifth theme is the intrusion into their lives of problematic aspects of the larger culture, such as alcohol, drugs, crime, racism, and segregation. Arturo wrote about a drinking contest he had with a friend:

> We were drinking to see who could drink the most. I decided to play a trick on him. He was drinking so much that he had to use the restroom every now and then. Every time he did, I would open the door [of the car] and spill my beer on the ground. I acted drunk but I wasn't.

After a while, he decided to quit because he had to drive. "I said, 'Well, I guess I won,' and he just said, 'Okay, you did.'"

Arturo had several ideas to explain excessive teenage drinking. First, kids want to act grown up. Second, there is peer pressure. Friends tease each other saying, "Is your mommy going to hit you?" and "Chicken, one beer isn't going to hurt you." They respond to peer pressure by competing and showing off. Finally, Arturo writes, teenagers don't see alcohol as a danger. "They all believe that they can overcome it."

Folklorists agree that "the study of folklore itself inherently con-tains one pair of oppositions, the analysis of which can cast much light on the lore itself and its creation and transmission: the conflict between stability (tradition) and change" (Abrahams 1979, 394). Toelken writes, "Constant change, variation within a tradition, whether intentional or inadvertent, is . . . simply . . . a central fact of life for folklore" (1979, 10).

This dynamic of folklore, the constant change, the pull between tradition and stability is readily apparent in adolescent folklore. In part, their lore teaches the maintenance of the status quo, as in Lupe, Luz, and Julieta's group. But the nature of adolescence to test the rules and limits is another part. A further element in this dynamic is change: adolescent lore dates quickly. The folk name for verbal duel-ing, for example, not only has regional differences, it also changes from year to year. In one school in the early 1980s, students said of the peer who lost a verbal duel that he was "molded," but a few years later this was replaced by "capped."

On this last day of the unit, as papers were read and issues discussed, students began to see their folklore and themselves in historical and cultural perspectives. These can be made even more dramatic if students interview parents about the lore of their adolescent years and compare it to their own.

Unit in Brief

Day One: Introduction to Teenage and School Folklore

- Since teenage folklore is not as obvious as other types, the teacher may begin by giving some examples that students discuss. Then they come up with their own.

- After listing the examples, students generalize. What do they tell you about American teenagers?

Day Two: Gathering More Information on Teenage Folklore

- Students do brief drafts on three items from the class list of adolescent folklore.

- They identify some national issues reflected in teenage folklore. In this class, an important topic was the folklore of stereotypes and its role in discrimination. Therefore homework was a newspaper article on segregation and discrimination in high school.

Day Three: Segregation and Stereotypes—Exploring an Issue Raised in Student Folklore

- The homework article can also be read in the beginning of class.

- Students read and respond to the article. Look at the role of folklore in creating and sustaining stereotypes that feed discrimination.

- Class speculates on how the study of folklore could be used to combat stereotyping.

- Since the reading is journalistic, it is a chance to discuss techniques of successfully reporting information.
  (This activity can be done on many other national issues such as drugs and cheating.)

- For homework, students write a first draft on a topic from teenage folklore. Most write first-person narratives mindful of setting and performance as well as the type of folklore.

Day Four: "Too Much Fun, No Sleep"—Class Response to Drafts

- One or more students read their drafts to the whole class, which responds and offers ideas about what is going on in the event or events described.

The time this and any topic takes will vary. In some classes where students are not proficient writers, I find it useful to have them write often in class, and the unit takes longer. In any class, occasional in-class writing is valuable as a chance to talk and think about one's personal writing process.

- More students can read their papers to the class, or the students can share drafts and get ideas for analysis from their small groups.
- For homework, students write drafts of an analytical section for their papers.

Day Five: Small Groups

- Students read their drafts in small groups and get responses on the style and the development of ideas in their papers. Depending on the length of the papers, this may take more than one period.

Day Six: Reading Final Papers—A Perspective on Adolescence

- Day six is several days later, allowing the student some time to write their papers.
- Students read their papers aloud and look for themes. In this class, the themes were excursions forward into adulthood, backward into childhood, celebrations of adolescence, oppositional behavior, and the intrusion or incorporation of problems of the culture.

Notes

1. Some students are taken by language play and enjoy making a slang dictionary. Aside from the obvious value in the learning of dictionary skills, the slang dictionary, once completed, can be studied. Students can investigate what a study of their slang or folk speech reveals about them. They can look into the function of slang, why it exists. They can also notice the ways in which slang has influenced standard English. Invention and change in language comes primarily from slang and professional jargon.

2. Reported by Kendell Fralick. This happened when she was in high school in 1984. At the University of California, Berkeley, she says students still wave their keys. But now it is to bait students from a school like the University of Southern California, an expensive private school. She says it is like saying you bought your way into school, but we got in because we are smart. Berkeley is public, less expensive, and more competitive.

3. Lorenzo is referring to the more innocent slumber party that was popular as early as the 1940s. See "Teen-Age Girls: They Live in a Wonderful World of Their Own," *Life* 17 (December 1944), p. 91.

Chapter Eleven

Tales of the Shopping Mall
Modern Urban Legends

In a suburban junior class, we began the study of modern urban legends by telling a few. I started with this version of "The Killer in the Back Seat":

> A young woman was driving home, when she realized that a car was following her. Every time she slowed down, it slowed down. When she turned a corner, it turned. The driver was male. She began to speed up to get home fast. She drove into her yard, leaped out of her car, and ran up the stairs. Her husband opened the door. "A man's been following me," she told him.
>
> The man ran up to them. "Lady," he explained, "I was driving behind you, and I saw a man crouching in the back of your car. I was trying to catch up to you to warn you!"

Just as I finished, Wendy burst out, "It happened to my friend's sister's friend in college. I believed it!" Wendy elaborated: "But I heard it this way. A car followed her, but it kept honking, and she kept turning back and looking at who it was. It kept honking and finally she stopped and he [the driver] said, 'There's a guy in your car!'"

Others knew the legend. Ann announced, "I heard it happened in the Sun Valley Shopping Mall." Everyone laughed and started talking, asking questions, and airing opinions about "the killer in the back seat."

Background

Students have been telling each other legends since childhood. Legends are folklore, which as Roger Abrahams explains, refers not only to the content of the lore but equally to "ways of talking, interacting and performing [it]. . . . " (1980, 370). In this unit, students study modern urban legends for lessons hidden in the tales as well as for ways of telling, performing and interacting. The study of legends thus provides a place to practice storytelling skills, both written and oral. Since legends are narratives, students have an opportunity to create their own version of a good story, an exercise in narrative and description. In this class the emphasis was on oral skills and storytelling; students performed the legends in front of the class and then led a discussion about the legend.

Modern urban legends are the most common folk narrative of twentieth-century America. The adjectives, however, need clarification. Some "modern" legends date back to the nineteenth century, and "urban" doesn't refer "to geography, but to the socio-psychological conditions of urbanism (Fine 1980, 223). As folklore, legends are passed around in the telling and vary as they are transmitted. They are also frequently reported in writing in the media as human interest stories. Additionally, such legends are set in the present day and take place in the world of the teller and the listener; frequently told and understood as true events; and migratory, moving from place to place and country to country.[1]

For students, the second point is a stickler. They quite reasonably want to know whether or not the legend actually occurred. This issue can lead to a deeper analysis of legends, where students consider conceptual distinctions in the meaning of the word "true": true as in fact, and true as in believable, if not factual.

Whether or not a legend is based on a real event is of minor interest to folklorists. Most dismiss the question by observing that some happened, most didn't.[2] There is no way of estimating the number of legends (including local ones) in circulation. Furthermore, new ones appear regularly. Establishing the factual basis of any of them is almost impossible. Instead, folklorists focus on the function of legends, assuming that most tellers believe the legends are true (based in fact), whatever their origins.

Students, however, begin with questions about the factual basis of legends. They are curious, because they often believe the legends are true—as in factual—and act accordingly. This is nicely demonstrated in Janet's commentary on a legend she retold:

> Last year, someone told me there was a crazy man at Sun Valley Shopping Mall. See this 27 year old guy was finished shopping and walked to his car. When he got in his car, there was an old lady sitting in the passenger's side. She begged him to take her home because she was too tired to take the bus. The young man said, "OK," and said he would be back in a minute. He said he was going to call his wife to hold dinner for a couple of minutes. Instead he

called a security guard, and they found out the old lady was really
a man dressed up like a lady. He was hiding two axes under him,
ready to get and chop up the young man.

After retelling the story, Janet added:

I don't know if I believe this story, but every time I'm at Sun Valley,
I lock my car door and I find myself always looking over my shoulder.

Whether the legend is real or not, after hearing it Janet changed her
behavior.

The rest of this background section covers questions students ask
that often come up when they first encounter legends.

Why Do People Believe Legends? Context and Content

Context can enhance or contribute to belief in a legend. In many
versions of the legend Janet told, the driver realizes that the old lady
is an impostor when he looks down and notices that "she" has a hairy
male hand. Thus, the legend is referred to as "The Hairy Hand." Janet
had heard it from her mother's friend in the course of normal conversation. The friend had heard the story and was passing it on; in the
context there was no reason to question its veracity. Most legends are
told in similar contexts, as part of ongoing conversation.

Occasionally, the context is a legend-telling session that contributes to the story's credibility. For example, such sessions have
long been the high point of slumber parties, where the setting—
nighttime, lights out, no parents present—contributes to belief. Very
young children tell "scary legends"[3] at their parties, but pre-
adolescents begin to tell the stories that folklorists call "adolescent
legends." A classic example is "The Hook":

A young couple were out in the country parked one night. A special
radio broadcast came on the air to say that an escaped lunatic was
in the area and that he could be dangerous. He could be identified
by a hook on his arm in place of a hand. The girl was very fright-
ened, but the boy said there was nothing to worry about. But the girl
insisted that she wanted to go home, so they left and he drove her
home. When they arrived, the boy got out and walked around the
car to let the girl out and he found the bloody hook hanging from
the door handle of the car.[4]

Talking about these legends in class, many high school students
laugh and confess that a few years ago they were believers. Others
report that they had been skeptical.

At least three aspects of the content of legends contribute to
belief. First, the incident is always credible, never so outrageous that

a listener's first instinct is to scoff. Secondly, the *frame* helps. Legends are often prefaced with "This happened to a friend of a friend," or "This happened to my brother-in-law's sister." To a folklorist, the frame is a tip-off that folklore will follow, but to most people, it gives the tale a note of authenticity; the incident really did happen to someone. Finally, as noted in chapter 1, people often embellish, when telling legends, providing local place names and real people, to make the tales more convincing. The Sun Valley Shopping Mall, for instance, gives reality and substance to the two legends that opened this chapter. In the legend of the "Elevator Incident" discussed in chapter 1, the main character is not an anonymous Black man but a celebrity such as Reggie Jackson. These details coax the listener toward belief.

The "Truth" in Legend Beyond Factual Accuracy

Most legends, whether or not they ever took place, are commentaries on pressing human concerns. (As with any folklore, once they cease being relevant, they will disappear from the folk repertory.) Therefore, factual or not, legends contain truth; they accurately touch the lives of the tellers and their audiences. It is this truth, more than verifiable factual accuracy, that makes legends believable.

Another dimension to the matter of belief is discussed by Linda Dégh and Andrew Vázsonyi, who write, "It is possible both to believe unconditionally and to believe with some second thoughts, with a trace of doubt or with mixed feelings" (1976, 99). This suggestion of degrees of belief illuminates Janet's half believing "The Hairy Hand."

Legend versus Rumor

Students want to know the difference between rumor and legend. Bengt af Klintberg (1985), a Swedish legend scholar, separates rumor from legend on the basis of narrative. He considers the question, "Have you heard about the worms in [a popular fast-food chain's] hamburgers?" a rumor, for it is speculative; it hasn't solidified into a full narrative. Legends are narratives.

Often, however, rumors are parts of narratives. Klintberg, Dégh, and Vázsonyi make the point that a legend may be known by some people in fragmentary or rumor form and by others as legend in narrative form. Dégh and Vázsonyi further show that the fragments can come to life (sometimes developing into a narrative) and become believable when the legends are told communally. Dégh and Vázsonyi (1976, 102–107) describe the process in a peasant community, but the same phenomenon can happen anywhere, for example, in class:

Me: I've heard that [a fast-food chain] puts worms in their hamburgers.

Student: No, I heard it was kangaroo meat. [laughter]

Me: That always amused me. Don't you think people would notice sides of kangaroo being shipped out of Australia and imported here?

Student: It's already ground up, you can't tell.

Student: It happened to my aunty's friend. She got a funny hamburger and complained and they gave her free food.

Student: I thought it happened at [another fast-food chain].

Student: I heard [A] started that rumor about [B], and [B] sued them and won.

In class no single narrative about the rumor developed, but it was filled out with details and two brief narratives were offered: one about the "aunty's friend," the other about food chain B suing food chain A.

Old and New Modern Urban Legends

Some "modern" legends are traceable to the nineteenth century. In *Rumour in Orleans* Edgar Morin (1971) studies a French version of a migratory legend that tells of a young girl's being abducted into the White slave trade. According to Klintberg the legend began "at the end of the nineteenth century, when millions of males emigrated from Europe to North and South America and brothels were organized on a large scale (1985, 274)." The legend survives in varying forms today in France and in the United States (and no doubt other countries as well).

Recently, a friend and his mother were visiting from another state. At dinner, the mother told this story:

> My granddaughter was in a department store in Omaha, with her friend and her friend's mother. The girls went into the ladies' room and the mother was outside waiting. Suddenly, she realized the girls had been in there an awful long time. Then she saw them; they'd been drugged, and they were being led away by two women. The mother ran over and pushed the women away and rescued the girls.

I recognized this tale immediately as the old "White slave trade" legend. I listened attentively as my friend indignantly asked his mother, "Did you call the police?" She explained, "Oh, no, we didn't want any publicity."

Old legends survive in modern dress, and new ones are created as the world changes. Now, for example, there are computer legends:

Someone is hired to write a computer program and promised a permanent job; but he is actually fired after he had finished the first program. Since he anticipated being fired, he wrote into the program that if the computer saw his name missing from the payroll it was to erase all the programs he had written.[5]

Sighting New Legends

Once you develop a feel for legends, you can spot new ones in the making. Often the first sighting is a human interest filler in the media. I've heard this story twice on the news; it has the makings of a new legend.

A middle-aged woman goes into an ice cream store and sees Paul Newman [or Robert Redford] sitting at one of the tables. She wants to appear cool and aloof. So she orders a cone, pays for it, and leaves. When she gets outside, she realizes she doesn't have the cone in her hand. Thoroughly confused, she goes back into the store. "I'm sorry," she says to the counterboy, "I don't seem to have my cone." Paul Newman then tells her, "You put it in your purse."

Another new legend is about AIDS, Acquired Immune Deficiency Syndrome. In less than a year, this legend migrated around the world, evidence of widespread concern about the disease. Here's a newspaper version:

. . . . a Hollywood movie mogul. . . . had an affair while his wife was out of town, but awoke to find the woman gone and a scrawled [message]: "Welcome to the wonderful world of AIDS".

Dundes (1971, 24) has described legend as "true" fantasy, that which takes place in the modern world. This may explain the tenacity and appeal of modern legends.

Day One (and Maybe Two): Introducing Modern Legend

The first day or two is a time to tell and collect legends. No legend is universally known, and there is wide variation in the legends known in any given class. Regionalism, ethnicity, and socio-economic status are a few of the factors that influence the legends we know. It is useful in this opening discussion to touch on as many kinds of legends as possible. Therefore, during this telling/collecting time, whenever the pace slackens, I introduce another type of legend. We name the legends as we share them. I write them on the board, and the students keep a running record of them in their notes. There are examples of many of these legends in Jan Brunvand's four books listed in the Selected Resources for this chapter at the end of this book, but in class we start with the ones we know.

Types of Legends

Food contamination legends. Fast-food chain legends, involving ground rats, worms, and horsemeat served in fast-food chains; local legends about "greasy spoons" or about the school lunchroom (finger bits in hot dogs!) and legends about strange foods (cats and dogs), for example, in foreign (especially Asian) restaurants.

The function of fast-food legends is discussed under Day Three, pages 191–94. The reasons for foreign restaurant legends, however, are different. Klintberg explains, "The common feature. . . . is that they are told about a foreign restaurant with an alien food culture. The legends are ethnocentric; they rely upon the universal idea that people belonging to foreign cultures eat certain animals which are taboo as human food in one's own culture (1981, 185)."

Large corporation legends. Large corporations inspire both malevolent and beneficent legends.

Malevolent legends. Gary Alan Fine (1985) has identified the legends of the large corporations as evil, deceptive, and careless. Evil corporations are those secretly controlled by satanic cults. The deceptive ones put worms in hamburgers, spider eggs in bubble gum, and sell Kool-Aid, rumored to be carcinogenic. Careless corporations let mice and other filth drop into soft drinks.

Beneficent legends. Fine (1986) has labeled these "Redemption Rumors," rumors that start people saving cigarette wrappers or pull-tabs from aluminum cans in order to get, for example, a kidney dialysis machine. Fine hypothesizes that people are not only trying to save the victim but "redeem" themselves from bad habits of smoking, drinking caffeine, alcohol, or eating junk food.

Drug and alcohol legends. Students can collect old classics such as the one about aspirin and Coca-Cola from their parents. They have their own: drinking through a straw will get you drunk faster. Here's a local high school drug "education" legend.

> When I was in high school, a policeman from the narcotics bureau came to our school to tell us of the dangers of drugs. He brought with him a number of samples of different types of drugs including a number of marijuana cigarettes. These were passed around on a tray (since they were fake there was no risk) and when the tray came back there were more marijuana cigarettes on it than when it started.[6]

For historical comparison, see Richard Dorson's *America in Legend* (1973). The chapter "Druglore" is about drug folklore of the 1960s.

Teenage or adolescent (and now preteen) legends. "The Babysitter," a typical adolescent legend, tells of a babysitter who gets menacing phone calls from an anonymous male, who is telling her to "Check the kids, check the kids." When she dials for help, the operator tells her the phone calls are coming from upstairs, where the children are sleeping. Students know this legend from the movies "When a Stranger Calls" and "Friday the 13th," as well as from preteen slumber parties.

Most areas have local teenage legends. In the East Bay of San Francisco, there is a park system where students go at night. The park is "inhabited" by many legendary characters, including a "White Witch," whose daughter, in one version, died in a car accident. At night, she takes her revenge on couples parked in cars.

Students who don't happen to know teenage legends from oral tradition still find them intriguing. They enjoy hearing or reading them and speculating about who tells them, when, where, and why. (See Brunvand [1981], *The Vanishing Hitchhiker: American Urban Legends and Their Meanings*, chapter 3, " 'The Hook' and Other Teenage Horrors.")

Diet legends. Diets start Monday morning. Right before starting a diet, you "pig out." Great claims are made for the dieting value of grapefruit. Certain foods (for example, hard-boiled eggs, apples and celery) are "diet negative." That is, they require more calories to digest than they provide when eaten (great diet food).[7] Much folklore surrounds dieting, often spawning legends of successful diets. Brunvand traces one reporter's attempt to find the elusive "Dolly Parton" diet. There are also mock diets like the "stress diet."

Legends about sports. National sports legends are about coaches like Vince Lombardi and Bear Bryant, who reputedly could walk on water. There are migratory legends about the stupidity of college athletes who are paid to report "to the coach every morning on whether or not the stadium is still standing." And schools have local legends about coaches and local athletes. There is also at least one national migratory legend about a promiscuous cheerleader, who takes on the whole team (Fine and Johnson, 1980).

Camp legends. Most of these are local, but many have a common theme. Told by counselors to campers, they feature odd characters and monsters with names like "Wheelchair Annie," "Old Lady

Combat Boots," and "The MacCombie Dog," who inhabit the perimeter of the camp and frighten or kill stray campers. They are warning tales used by counselors to keep their charges in tow.

UFO legends. Like computer legends, UFO legends are relatively new. "Flying saucers" were first sighted and named in 1947. UFO sightings and experiences interest folklorists because they tend to be formulaic, like folklore. They often tell of the landing of a saucer containing little people of high intelligence (Dégh 1977). UFO legends told by students often sound like science fiction, evidence of the constant interplay between folklore and popular culture. (See this chapter pages 190-91 for similarities of UFO legends to ancient myths.)

Monster legends. Today's monsters may be yesterday's trolls. Fairies and elves (who were both good and evil) seem to have been replaced in national and international legends by Big Foot, the Loch Ness Monster, and the Abominable Snowman. Local forests, woods, and lakes are inhabited too. The "Jersey Devil" (often reported as one-third man, one-third deer or horse, and one-third winged creature) lives in the pine barrens of New Jersey. "Hoop snakes," which loop themselves into hoops and roll away, have been cited in Kentucky, and "Jackelopes," crosses between jack rabbits and antelopes, are seen in Montana.

Legends of wildlife in the cities. These range from alligators in the sewers of big cities to snakes, spiders, and other insects. While the alligators are reputed to have started as "pet" babies from the swamps of Florida, the snakes and insects often arrive in products imported from underdeveloped countries in Asia and Africa. There are reports of women being bitten by snakes and insects concealed in clothing made in the Far East, legends of snakes in bananas. As well as reflecting fears of nature, these are ethnocentric legends about strange countries and foreigners.

"Life after death" legends. Persons who have clinically died often tell "life-after-death" narratives. Marcelle Williams has identified three types of afterlife memorates or legends. "The life review," Williams (in press) writes, "occurs most commonly during sudden crises or unanticipated brushes with death—accidents." They are reported by young narrators, usually male. "Visitation" memorates, when a dangerously ill person sees dead relatives or friends, often occur when death is anticipated, such as during a prolonged illness. In the third type, "the journey," the very ill person has "out-of-body" experiences either in this world or another.

Legends from childhood. Young children have a large corpus of legends. Some, like "The China Doll" (noted in chapter 1, page 22) are serious and frightening. Other children's legends, while initially scary, end as jokes, like "The Stolen Liver," (see chapter 5, pages 99–100), and a legend with the refrain, "Now I've gotcha, now I'm gonna eat ya'," and "The Ghost of the Two Bloody Fingers." (See pages 195–97 for a discussion of "The Rocking Horse," a children's legend known to the students in this class.)

Local legends. Most legends are local. The topics of these legends are limitless. Students often report local legends about schools. Several students wrote of "The Three Sisters" (one identified them as Indians) who haunted their junior high. The "sisters" had lived in bungalows on the site of the school, and when the school was built, they were not compensated, so they moved into a cave under the school and now haunt it. A common legend tells of a student who a few years back drowned in the school pool. Local legends also tell of neighborhood characters, like Boo Radley in Harper Lee's *To Kill a Mockingbird* (1960) or old ladies living with cats. Or they may be local teenage legends like "The White Witch."

Legends about famous people. Students often know some "Einstein" legends; one is that his brain is preserved in New Jersey, and it is twice as large as a normal brain; another is that he flunked eighth grade math. Adults also tell an Einstein legend (a legend told about many male "geniuses"), sometimes called "Einstein and the Showgirl." In it, a famous actress writes to Einstein suggesting they have a child, which would have her beauty and his brains. He replies, "But madame, what if she has your brains and my body?" Winston Churchill and John F. Kennedy generated many legends, although legends cluster around many famous people. One known to this class was about Burt Reynolds (also told about other celebrities). Reynolds is said to have won a one-million-dollar lawsuit against AT&T and invites everyone to benefit by using his telephone credit card number. Word spreads, and college students, among others around the country, make free calls on the number.

Miscellaneous legends. Here are just a few; the Brunvand books hold many more. There is the one about the family who goes on vacation and takes grandmother. She dies, and they put her temporarily in a bag on top of the car. While they are talking to the police about funeral arrangements, either the bag or the car with her on top is stolen. Another concerns the lady whose purse is stolen. She receives a phone call from a good samaritan who has found it and asks her to come and claim it. While she is gone, her house is ransacked. There are legends about the subliminal or hidden messages of the lyrics on record albums, especially when they are played backwards. There are amusement park legends such as the one about the ride with a sign saying "Don't stand up." One kid ignored it and his head was cut off. There are occupational legends galore. Flight attendants (and people in other professions) report that their clients or customers behave strangely when there is a full moon. Also, there is the legend about the pilot who crashed and whose ghost now appears and warns pilots about to crash.

In short, legends abound in America today. Whatever the interests of the student, be it cheerleading, bodybuilding, stamp collecting, or chemistry experiments, there will be legends. To add to the class collection, students interview parents and friends for legends from their childhood and from their work.

Day Two: What Is a Legend?

Folklorists often define legend by comparing it to the two other major folk narrative forms, myth, and folktale. Comparison of these three forms of folk narrative also provides some historical perspective. In this class, I started with a myth from *Africa in Myths and Tales*, edited by Susan Feldman (1963).

Man Chooses Death

One day God asked the first human couple who then lived in heaven what kind of death they wanted, that of the moon or that of the banana. Because the couple wondered in dismay about the implications of the two modes of death, God explained to them: the banana puts forth shoots which take its place and the moon itself comes back to life. The couple considered for a long time before they made their choice. If they elected to be childless, they would avoid death, but they would also be very lonely, would themselves be forced to carry out all the work, and would not have anybody to work and strive for. Therefore they prayed to God for children, well aware of the consequences of their choice. And their prayer was granted. Since that time man's sojourn is short on this earth (114–115). (Madagascar)

Next I read a folktale, "The Girl with the Large Eyes," from Julius Lester's *Black Folktales* (1969). It begins:

Many years ago in a village in Africa, there lived a girl with large eyes. She had the most beautiful eyes of any girl in the village, and whenever one of the young men looked at her as she passed through the marketplace, her gaze was almost more than he could bear (57).

The village suffers a devastating drought. The girl goes out each day to find water, and one day a rainbow-colored fish talks to her and offers to fill her pitcher with water. Each day, she secretly meets the fish. He gives her water, and they fall in love and wed. Her family finds out, is ashamed, and kills the fish. She takes her husband's body to a flowing river and:

> Calling her husband's name, she waded into the water until it flowed above her head. But as she died, she gave birth to many children, and they still float on the rivers to this day as water lilies (61).

After reading some myths and folktales, students compare them. They notice that myths usually take place in the past, in a world hazily different from that which we know. Next, they compare myth and folktale with their own legends, which take place in the present and sound plausible.

In this class, two Asian students remember being told folktales as children. The American-born students also know folktales but, by and large, they know them from books, not from oral tradition. Of the three major folk narrative forms, two, myths and folktales, disappear as societies become more urban and technologically advanced. By comparison, legends thrive; old legends continue to be told, and new ones proliferate. I ask the students to speculate about the disappearance of myth from oral tradition.

We don't tell myths, they conjecture, because we are now more interested in scientific explanations of origins. That's true, I agree, but I point out that folklorists have noticed that at least one type of modern legend, UFO narratives, has similarities to certain myths. Klintberg has suggested that like some myths, UFO legends tell of people in distress and danger, hoping for a savior or a messenger, who often comes with a warning about the fate of humanity.

Next, we read a UFO legend retold by a student. In it, a group of scientists are digging in Indian ruins and discover a buried spaceship. At first, the scientists joke about its looking like something out of Star Wars. When they open it, a voice booms out a warning for earthlings that they will be extinct by the year 2050. "The remaining portions of this tape," the voice continues, "can prepare your people to save themselves. Listen carefully to the tape, for after it is heard once, it will self-destruct. There is no other ho—" At this moment, one of the scientists "goes insane" and smashes the computer, which "gasps, as if being slowly strangled, repeating over and over, 'No hope, no hope, no hope.'" It is interesting to compare the pattern of this legend to a myth such as the Aztec "How We Came to the Fifth World."

In the Aztec myth, the people of earlier times forget the lessons of their gods and turn to lying, stealing, and killing. This happens four times; each time, they are punished by the gods, who transform them first into fish, second into animals, third into birds. Finally, they are devoured by jaguars. Each time, the gods find one good couple who survive and start the next world. In the fifth world, the people live in peace and happiness for many years.

In both the myth and the legend, people are in trouble. In the myth, they have ceased to follow the prescripts of the gods. In the legend, the danger is unspecified but can be inferred: humans are doing something wrong. The people in both narratives do not heed the higher voice (the gods in the myths, the extraterrestrial in the legend). The narratives differ, too. The myth is primarily about the past; four times, the people are warned and destroyed for their transgressions. The legend is more future oriented; it warns of destruction ahead and hints at wrongdoing, unspecified because the tape is silenced. While the myth has an ending, "All the earth was good again and peace and happiness continued for many years," the legend is open-ended; we don't know what will happen. (For an illustrated bilingual children's version of the myth, see *How We Came to the Fifth World*, adapted by Harriet Rohmer and Mary Anchondo [1976]).

This activity can be done as a whole-class lesson or in small groups. In each case, the students read a myth, a folktale, and a legend and try to identify the characteristics of each type of narrative. Then they speculate on the functions of the three forms and why our dominant narrative form today is the legend.

The next class will be on the function of legends. Therefore, a useful reading for homework is a section from any of Brunvand's books that include an analysis of a legend.

Day Three: Making Sense of Legends

Gary Alan Fine's study, "The Kentucky Fried Rat: Legends and Modern Society" (1980), is a good model for legend analysis. In class, knowledge of the supposed incident was pretty much limited to rumors about rats or mice mixed in with chicken. I read this 1971 version from Brunvand's *The Vanishing Hitchhiker*:

> Two couples stopped one night at a notable carry-out for a fried chicken snack. The husband returned to the car with the chicken. While sitting there in the car eating their chicken, the wife said, "My chicken tastes funny." She continued to eat and continued to complain.
>
> After a while the husband said, "Let me see it." The driver of the car decided to cut the light on and then it was discovered that

the woman was eating a rodent, nicely floured and fried crisp. The woman went into shock and was rushed to the hospital. It was reported that the husband was approached by lawyers representing the carry-out and offered the sum of $35,000. The woman remained on the critical list for several days. Spokesmen from the hospital would not divulge the facts about the case and nurses were instructed to keep their mouths shut. And it is also reported that a second offer was made for $75,000, and this too was refused. The woman died and presumably the case will come to court (82).

When a legend is as long-lived and widespread as this one, it reflects national concerns.

One way to analyze a legend is to study the motifs: the characters, the objects, and the actions. "Who are the main characters?" I ask. "The rat!" the class shouts back in unison.

"Good," I encourage them. "Would it be the same if it were a dog?"

"No," Roger replied, "because people like dogs."

"What can a rat symbolize?" The students have many answers: filth, sewers, rabies, fleas, poison. (Fine also notes that the rat is a symbol of urban decay.)

"Who do the couples symbolize?"

"Suckers," says Jon. But another student objects, "They're just typical Americans." Indeed, the story could happen to any of us.

"What's the main action?" I ask. That's easy. "Eating the rat!" "Why does it happen?" This gets a variety of answers.

"Because they were in the dark."

"It's a prank." (In some versions, a worker puts the rat in the frying vat as a joke.)

Another student, remembering a version in which the victim dies because the rat was poisoned, protests. "I don't think it's a prank. . . . it's poisoned—nobody puts poison in as a prank."

"It could have been an accident in a dirty kitchen."

"What's the outcome or result?" I ask. The victim gets sick or dies. "And what can be done about it?" Without a second thought, the class shouts back, "Sue 'em!," which, of course, happens in many versions of food contamination legends.

Next, we discuss the settings. Some versions take place in the restaurant, but often the chicken is taken out and eaten at home or at the movies. We speculate about each setting and what it symbolizes. Kentucky Fried Chicken outlets have multiple symbolic meanings for the class. They represent fast food, junk food, big business. They are also a symbol of the South, especially the character of Colonel Sanders.

While it is possible to do an analysis of one or two versions of a legend (which is what the students will do), more versions make for a better analysis. The students have heard only a few versions of this one, so they don't know that in 80 percent of the legends Fine studied, the victim is a woman. Why?

"Women hate mice." "Women are seen as weak." "Women are supposed to be more evil and stuff." Jon offers this last observation knowing full well that it will start an argument, and it does. His response, however, provokes a useful debate on the folklore about women. Fine theorizes that we feel the woman should be at home cooking. In the legend, it is she who is punished for her transgression.

Food contamination legends aren't new. Earlier ones were about local greasy spoons and foreign restaurants. These still exist, along with those about fast-food operations. The legends all reflect our uneasiness as customers in restaurants; we can't see what is happening in the kitchen. Greasy spoon legends are about fears of dirt. What then is this legend about? It seems to reflect the anxieties Americans feel about changes in the American landscape. First, large corporations are usurping the role of small businesses; for example, fast-food chains are replacing "mom and pop" or family-owned restaurants. Second, Fine writes, this change/usurpation, signals an erosion of traditional institutions.

> The growth of fast food chains represents a change of function to profit-making enterprises, away from home cooking and the community or church supper. By implication this change symbolizes the decline of the family, the church, and community organizations in their most basic function—that of nourishment. Nourishment is now provided by those who strive for economic gain, rather than personal satisfaction (237).

Third, we are accomplices to this change because of our own ambivalent, love/hate relationship to fast food. On the one hand, we are suspicious of both its origins and nutritional value. It comes from outside the community; we have no say about its ingredients. We're also suspicious of its value and label it "junk" food. However, we consume it in great volume.

Finally, as always, some students want to know if the legend is "true." "Why do you care?" I ask.

"Well," one boy explains, "if it's true, then it will affect you more than if it's made up."

"You'll stop eating fast food," his friend agrees. But others debate this.

As further preparation for their small-group sessions analyzing legends, we discuss a few more legends together. (If the class read a short analytical selection from Brunvand for homework, it should be evaluated now.) Since many modern legends are cautionary tales, I

read them the version of "The Hook" (see page 181), and we speculate about context. Who might tell this legend, when and where?
"Mothers," Christopher thinks, might tell it to their daughters, "so
they won't go parking and make out." But in this class, girls remember telling it at slumber parties where it was a warning of the dangers
of parking in deserted places. Others dissent about the legend's
meaning. One student sees it as a generic warning against "crazy or
weird people." Others think it is about strangers. Each student is
challenged to defend his or her speculation.

I read them a version of a local legend and ask them to try a
one-paragraph analysis of it for homework. I'll read these quickly the
next day to get a sense of how the lesson went.

Day Four: Small-Group Preparation for Oral Presentations

In this unit, each group will make an oral presentation rather than
write papers. Students meet in their small groups and choose a legend. Most select one they know from oral tradition, although a few
select legends that are new to them. I have copies of Brunvand on
hand as resources. Their classroom teacher, Jane Juska, and I are also
there as resources.

The instructions to the students are to consider the motifs and
what they symbolize, to think about the context—who tells the legends and how and where they are told. They then consider purpose
or function: Why is the legend told?

They are given one class period to prepare. Their grade, a collective one, will be based on three things:

1. The way the group works. (Jane Juska and I will walk around and
   sit in on the groups to determine this.)

2. An outline of the presentation, which should include the legend's motifs and the group's ideas on the legend's meaning and
   functions.

3. The presentation. One member from the group will do the actual
   oral presentation, but the grade will be collective, based on:
   - poise (making eye contact with the audience)
   - preparedness (knowing the material)
   - the telling of the legend
   - the analysis (motifs and context)
   - the conclusion (what is learned about the world of teller and
     listener from this legend)

After the presentation, we'll have a general discussion of the legend, with all members of the presenting group answering questions.

Day Five (and Maybe Six): Oral Presentations

The presentations are superb. Wendy is the spokeswoman for her group. I had not known their legend, but Jennifer, a member of Wendy's group, learned it as a true story told at slumber parties when she was younger. Wendy begins the presentation by retelling the legend of "The Rocking Horse." Here is a transcription of her recorded presentation:

> There was this little girl and it was her birthday. Her daddy said he would take her to the toy store. . . . She saw this . . . you know, this rocking horse, and she said, "Daddy, daddy, please can I have this rocking horse?" [Wendy perfectly imitated the cajoling whine of a little girl working on her Daddy, to the class's amusement.] And he goes [this time Wendy puts on a gruff, adult male voice], "Okay." So he buys the little rocking horse, and they put it in her room, and all day she's rocking on this rocking horse getting her trips. [Wendy laughs.] She's rocking on it [laughter] and time for bed. And he goes, "Okay, time for bed." And she goes, "No, no, I want to rock. No go to bed!" And he says, "Don't rock on the rocking horse any more." "Okay daddy," and so they go to bed or she does.

Wendy catches her slip of the tongue, "they go to bed," and amends it, laughing a little at herself. It takes a few seconds to register with the class, then they start to laugh, and Wendy has to stop for a moment before continuing.

> The next morning, Ahem! [Wendy is calling the class to order]. . . . the next morning, he opens the door and the child's dead. No she's not dead, she's asleep like a log. And he looks over at the rocking horse, and it's rocking [said ominously]. I mean she had gone against his will and rocked the horse and faked she was asleep. And that day she rocked on the rocking horse all day long again—don't ask me why—and he says, "Okay, time for bed." The same problem, she wants to rock on the horse. So he goes, so this time he puts it in the den, so he makes sure she won't rock on the horse anymore. The next morning he goes in the bedroom and it's there rocking all by itself. And he's getting pretty mad [laughs]. The next night he locks it in the garage to make sure, 'cause how's the little girl going to unlock the door, right? So next morning he's all happy 'cause the horse won't be in there. And he looks in the room, and the child's asleep, and the horse is rocking in there again. [Wendy laughs]. So he says, "No more of this."

So he takes the horse back to the store, and he gives it back, and the next morning the same thing happens and the horse is there by itself. So he decides once and for all to get rid of this stupid horse. So he burns it, and he spreads the ashes all over the countryside and he's all happy. And the next morning he goes to wake up his daughter and he sees this rocking horse rocking in her room. Okay, that's a wonderful story. [Wendy laughs.]

Most students don't know Wendy's story but it intrigues them. She moves on to present the group's analysis:

The characters are number one, the rocking horse, and the father. The rocking horse is a symbol of childhood. When it rocks and it comes back into the room, it's kind of supernatural, and it's a friend for the girl, and the girl uses this horse to get away from the family, maybe family problems. And the father thinks that the daughter will be too attached to this horse, and he's afraid that the horse is possessed. I mean, what would you think if a horse is possessed. I mean, what would you think if a horse is rocking by itself? Ummmm, the father is also a symbol of care and worry and also kind of jealous of the horse. The place is home, which is a symbol to most of us of security, safety, and the horse invades the home and the family and causes problems. Ummm, the action was getting rid of the horse and the horse returns. Ummm, analyzation—the father doesn't want the daughter to [nervous laugh] ... doesn't want the daughter to grow up and get independent; the horse is like a boyfriend who might come and take the daughter away; the horse is taking the daughter away from the family happenings. It's also like The China Doll who kinda breaks up the family.[8]

Although Wendy starts her analysis by saying that the rocking horse is a symbol of childhood and the supernatural, her analysis shows that it is more a force separating the girl from her childhood and competing with her father. When Wendy finishes, a classmate asks, "Who tells it?"

Wendy answered, "Well, when we were at slumber parties you heard it a lot when you talked about the China Doll."

"Why was it told by little girls to other little girls?" Jon wants to know. No one answers for the moment.

One student is dissatisfied with the legend. "I was kind of waiting for a ending like something the rocking horse did."

Wendy agrees and confesses, "I wanted to make up an ending," she laughs. "I have this really grand ending for it."

When she was asked why she didn't, Wendy says, "That's the way it's told." I object: "But the ending is that the horse ... " and before I finish my sentence, several students finish it for me; "Lives." This, I explain, is true of many modern legends. They are open-ended, unresolved. Both the Rocking Horse and the China Doll live on; the man with the hook is still out there.

The discussion returns to Jon's question. Why do girls tell it? In the group they had thought about this.

"'Cause they want to be independent."

"It's got to do with the separating from the family."

We compliment the group on their work and point out an oversight. In their initial listing of the characters, they forgot the girl, although she played a major role in the analysis. Was the story about her or the rocking horse? Jane Juska tells the students about D. H. Lawrence's short story, "The Rocking Horse Winner," a closely similar story, which raises the matter of the interplay of literature and folklore. Had Lawrence heard the legend?

Conclusion

We live in close contact with legends. In the normal course of events, we simply enjoy them uncritically as good stories. But incorporated into the curriculum, modern urban legends serve multiple purposes. First, they are expressions of Americans' anxieties, and anxieties reflect values. The "Kentucky Fried Rats" legend, for example, is an indirect expression of the importance of home, family, and church to Americans who see them being eroded by big business and urbanization. Second, oral presentations are particularly appropriate for the study of legends, a story-telling genre. They are a break from writing papers and a chance to work on oral language skills. (This topic can also be approached through writing, of course.) Another activity can be to create literary versions of the tales, as Lawrence may have done, or to try scripting them for film or live performance. Furthermore, since legends are narratives, students can study them critically, focusing on, for example, character, plot and symbolism.

Unit in Brief

Day One (and Maybe Two): Introducing Modern Legend

- Essentially this is legend-telling session. When the pace slackens, the teacher can bring up new types from the list.

Day Two: What Is a Legend?

- In folklore, there are three major types of narratives: myths, folktales, and legends. Students read examples of all three and speculate on why it is that legend is now the major narrative form. They also work toward a definition of modern urban legends.

- Homework can be any section from Brunvand's book that includes some analysis of the legend described.

Day Three: Making Sense of Legends

- Students read or listen to a version of the legend of the Kentucky Fried Rats and analyze it with hints from the work of Gary Alan Fine.

- Homework is a quick analysis of any legend. Local legends or national legends told of a local place, however, are good.

Day Four (this can take two periods): Small-Group Preparation for Oral Presentations

- Start with a discussion of student findings in homework.

- Small groups select a legend for oral presentation and analysis and begin work on it.

Days Five (and Maybe Six): Oral Presentations and Evaluation

- Each group first performs their legend by telling it. They then offer their interpretation, which is critiqued by the rest of the class.

- Students evaluate the unit in terms of skills and content learned. This can be done orally or in logs or both.

Notes

1. Swedish folklorist, Bengt af Klintberg's *Rattan i pizzan*, (Rats in the Pizza), (Stockholm, 1986), for example, has many of the same legends that appear in Jan Brunvand's books of American legends.

2. As mentioned in Note 9, chapter 1, Gary Alan Fine researched the legends about mice and other foreign matter in soft drinks and found many legal cases concerning food contamination. Any one incident could have been the start of a legend, but it is probably impossible to prove.

3. Alvin Schwartz has collected these in *Scary Stories to Tell in the Dark* (New York: Harper Row Junior Books, 1981) and *More Scary Stories to Tell in the Dark* (New York: Harper Row Junior Books, 1984).

4. Retold in 1969 by Mark H. Shenfield who learned it circa 1963 in high school in Tucson, Arizona. Berkeley Folklore Archives.

5. Told by Richard Harris, 1974, who says stories such as these are often told among computer students and workers. Berkeley Folklore Archives.

6. From Blair Carroll, a student at the University of California, Berkeley, 1974. Berkeley Folklore Archives.

7. F. McConnel, a compulsive dieter, reported these "diet negative" foods. Berkeley Folklore Archives, 1986.

8. Students do not usually offer psychoanalytic interpretations of their legends. Therefore, it seems appropriate not to raise them, although to anyone of a psychoanalytic bent, some legends seem to cry out for such interpretation. Readers interested in psychoanalytic interpretations of folklore should look to the works of Alan Dundes. For a psychoanalytic discussion of the teenage legend of "The Hook," see his "On the Psychology of Legend," in *American Folk Legend: A Symposium*, Wayland Hand, ed. (Berkeley: University of California Press, 1971, and *Analytic Essays in Folklore* (The Hague: Mouton, 1975).

Chapter Twelve

"Nuke the Raiders!"
The Folklore of Graffiti

Elliott Oring (1986), a folklorist who feels that a hard-and-fast definition of folklore is illusive, instead prefers to approach the subject in
terms of the qualities or means by which it is perceived. He writes:

> ... folklorists seem to pursue reflections of the *communal* (a group
> or collective), the *common* (the everyday rather than extraordinary),
> the *informal* (in relation to the formal and institutional), the *mar-
> ginal* (in relation to the centers of power and privilege), the *personal*
> (communication face-to-face), the *traditional* (stable over time), the
> *aesthetic* (artistic expressions), and the *ideological* (expressions of
> belief and systems of knowledge) (17–18).

"... Folklorists," Oring continues, "approach the study of forms,
behaviors, and events with two or more of these concepts in mind."
   Some graffiti meets all of Oring's description. Graffiti is common,
informal, and marginal. It has an obvious communal dimension, and
it can be personal (although not face-to-face), as well as traditional,
aesthetic, and ideological. Both the form and the behavior of graffiti
writing and drawing are folkloric. Writing where it is inappropriate
or unlawful is a folk behavior. In settings such as the New York City
subway system, graffiti is actually taught by some graffiti artists. But
generally, transmission happens not by observation of the act, which
is covert, but by observation of the product. Often, the form and

content of graffiti are patently folklore; e.g., the drawing of a heart with lovers' initials is a very old folk symbol. Others—Kilroy Was Here (see page 212) for example—are transitory. A relatively new figure is the little man with a screw through his middle[1] who adorns much office xerography, papers from the office workers' subculture that are reproduced and circulated via photocopying.

Throughout the 1970s and into the 1980s, the top of any hierarchy was announced in graffiti with the verb *rule*. Teenagers announced their support of a music group with such graffiti as "The Rolling Stones Rule, O.K." The folk created endless variations, e.g., "Amnesia Rules." "Rules" folklore has faded by now, but a new verb, *nuke* as a synonym for *kill*, has appeared and is widely used in the graffiti of one of the classes described in this chapter.

Graffiti is more than simply marginal; it can be downright illegal. Thus, the first question to ask is: Why study it? Alan Dundes and Carl Pagter give this reason:

> Almost every major problem of urban America is touched upon in these marvelously expressive materials: racism, sex, politics, automation, alienation, women's liberation, student riots, welfare excesses, military mentality, office bureaucracy, ad infinitum. It would take an encyclopaedic sociological study to analyze exhaustively all the issues raised by the traditional materials we have assembled (1978, xviii).

Equally important, student graffiti reveals the major interests and preoccupations of junior and senior high school students. And although it is written individually, gathered into a collection, it draws a communal picture of the students or folk who write and draw it.

Day One: Introducing Graffiti

In a city classroom, I announce the next topic, graffiti. "All right!" the students respond. "When you hear the word *graffiti*," I ask, "what comes to mind?" Everyone starts to talk at once. I hear Keith's voice above the others suggesting, "Trash!" I write it on the board. Then I call on Robert. "Words," he says.

"American," Louis shouts out. "American?" I question. "Are we the only ones with graffiti?" "No, the movie, I mean the movie *American Graffiti*.

"Paint," Phymensky offers. But Robert disagrees. "Not necessarily."

"It's what comes to *my* mind," Phymensky informs him.

Rhonda interrupts, "Buildings."

"Oh, buildings," Robert repeats and then says, "Walls."

"Houses."

"Bathroom stalls," Robert blurts out, playing for a laugh, which he gets.

"Buses." Rhonda is serious again.

"Subways," Phymensky remembers. Robert corrects him impatiently: "We don't have no subways."

"We can read about them," I tell the class. "There is a book I think you'd enjoy—*Getting Up: Subway Graffiti in New York.*" It was written by Craig Castleman (1982), a professor at Baruch College in New York City. While researching his book, Castleman spent time with graffiti writers, interviewing them as well as the transit police. The graffiti writers he describes are a folk group with their own slang (folk language) and behavior codes.

This is a volatile, noisy class, but it falls silent as I describe Castleman's book. Yvette speaks for everyone when she says, "I didn't know they had a book on graffiti." Her comment is followed by murmurs of agreement. It startles these students that university professors study graffiti.

"Clothes?" Pam wants to know if the words and letters kids get put on sweatshirts and T-shirts are graffiti.

"Misspelled words," Keith suggests, and everyone laughs. In this city, it's common to see graffiti with misspelled words.

"The Rock, you know where that is." Keith addresses the class. "It's in the hills." Two girls squeal with recognition and describe a graffiti-covered rock in a local park.

Louis, with his sense of comic timing, casually looks down at his desk and says, "Desks." Everyone starts reading from the desks.

"Billboards, you know the stuff written on billboards?"

"Gangs leaving their motto," says Keith, who is less familiar with gangs than are some of his classmates. The others start to laugh; "motto" isn't a word they associate with gangs.

"Motto?" James says, teasing Keith. Others join in.

I try to help Keith out. "Gangs sometimes mark the boundaries of their territory—" I too am interrupted with laughter. Robert patiently corrects me: "It's 'turf.'"

Rhonda, as she often does, interjects a serious note by suggesting, "Vandalism." Several boys greet her comment with negative murmurs, yet she is right. Phymensky is quick to defend his pro-graffiti position: "Art," he says, "Some people think it's art."

Robert is anxious to share a new insight. "They write graffiti on dirty cars and stuff, like 'Please wash me!'"

"I remember as a kid," I tell the class, "writing in the condensation on the inside of the car windows. Maybe that was childhood graffiti."

Yvette is puzzling over a new problem. "What kind of graffiti is that when a man just paints a wall?"

"Murals," Phymensky explains and elaborates. "That's a legal form of graffiti."

When this opening session is over, the chalkboard is covered with the brainstormed class knowledge of graffiti.

In a suburban freshman class, the study of graffiti began with a similar brainstorming session. The result on the chalkboard can be seen in Figure 12–1. The information gathered in urban and suburban classes is remarkably similar. In both, a discussion/brainstorming session is a natural introduction to the study of graffiti. Students are experts on the topic and will spontaneously raise questions worthy of study such as: Who writes graffiti and why? What are the materials of the graffiti writer? Where does he or she write? Is it trash, vandalism and/or art? Is it legal? What is the meaning of graffiti?

Controversial aspects of graffiti, such as vandalism, need to be addressed early in the unit. When vandalism is mentioned, I explain the role of a folklorist as a student of culture and make it clear that this is our role and that in it we encourage nothing, least of all vandalism: we simply study what is. In any high school, even those with graffiti-free walls, there is no shortage of graffiti. In the schools reported in this chapter, for example, the walls were pristine. But students still wrote on desk tops, on the covers of their notebooks and inside them, on their book covers and inside their textbooks, on their hands, on their shoes, on notes passed in class, on the chalkboards and in the lavatories. There was plenty of graffiti to study.

Erotic and scatological graffiti is also controversial. While this graffiti is off-limits for discussion in most schools, we can talk about why it exists and why it cannot be studied in class. The issue of censorship of erotic content from the classroom is not new to students, but they like to speculate about the reasons for its absence. What does this censorship say about our culture? Why will we get into trouble if we talk about sex, even though violence, common in teenage graffiti, is acceptable? Through these discussions, illicit graffiti is not overlooked or denied, and real issues of censorship and the reasons for it are discussed.

After talking in general about graffiti, students write a learning log entry giving their opinions and thoughts about it. In the urban class, many students are torn between attraction and disgust, as Rhonda is.

Figure 12-1
Graffiti Brainstorm

I think some graffiti is wrong especially when people write dirty words about other people's family. . . . [but] In some graffiti it's kind of nice when people write in assigned places, they tend to write kind things such as poems. I'd rather see people write in assigned places than to vandalize a car or something.

Rhonda has an example of "nice" graffiti: "Sex without love is like food without flavor—not as good as it could be but better than none at all!" Most students share Rhonda's ambivalence about graffiti, but some argue forcefully for or against it. For example, an ex-gang member writes:

I like graffiti because when I used to hang out with gangs, we used to get on to the bus and write all over the seats, walls, everything. It kind of makes you happy when you get on a bus and see your name or most likely your nicknames on the bus.

For some students, graffiti is a way of speaking to adults:

Graffiti is a type of art in which teenage kids show their opinions of certain things since older generations won't listen.

At the other end of the spectrum are students who flat-out hate graffiti, as in, "I don't like graffiti because it makes our city look bad."

In the suburban class, opinions were also divided. Nick writes: "I enjoy graffiti. I couldn't live without it." To make his point, Nick includes two of his current favorites:

Clearasil people
of the world
UNITE

and

Oxy-10
Rules

(Clearasil and Oxy-10 are commercial preparations for getting rid of adolescent acne.) There is ambivalence among suburban students too, an attraction to the content of graffiti but a wariness of vandalism. Brian writes:

Not all graffiti is bad because you might agree with it, like "Assassinate Reagan" (only kidding) but I do agree with the nuclear freeze and when I see that on a wall it doesn't make me mad even though it is vandalism. . . . I would not write graffiti on a wall but I might agree with it.

They too have a sense of where graffiti is appropriate:

I love graffiti but don't think it should be vandalistic. It is ok to write on your personal property but to ruin others with spray paint is definitely not cool.

In both classes, students enjoy hearing and discussing one another's logs. While there were similarities across the two classes, there were differences also. More city students talk of graffiti as a way to get recognition and fame. More suburban students express anger about graffiti, connecting it to poverty and crime.

For homework, students write a definition of graffiti in their own words. They may use a dictionary and class discussion as resources.

Day Two: Defining Graffiti and Drafting Memories of Writing (or Not Writing) Graffiti

After the introductory class on graffiti, students find dictionary definitions narrow. Typically, they read like this: "Crude drawing or inscription scratched on stone, plaster, or some other hard surface," or "Any scrawling written or drawn so as to be seen in public, as on a wall or lavatory door."[2] In class, the students read their homework definitions and together develop a common working definition: "Writing done in places where writing is not intended, usually meant to be read by others."

As a way of collecting graffiti, we cover one wall of the classroom with butcher paper. I supply markers and allow some time in class to start the writing on the wall. The graffiti wall is an ongoing project—a source of constant comment and discussion covering a wide range of topics. For instance, sports fans defend their teams:

> Cowboys Stink
> Seahawks are Cool
> But the Pittsburgh Steelers
> Will Always Rule

and

> LA Raiders will kick tush

After a poorly officiated football game, fans strike back in graffiti:

> Washington Referees 24
> SF 49ers   21

Political opinions are aired:

> Join the army,
> Visit strange new places,
> Meet new people,
> And Kill Them!

Arguments for drugs surface:

> Reality is for people who can't handle drugs.

As do comments on users:

> COCAINE,
> RICH MAN'S
> ASPIRIN

Some of the graffiti is racist:

Surfers rule the beach and sands
Cholos rule the taco stands.

and

Kill the white people, Eddie M [Murphy]

Names, nicknames, and declarations of relationships, as in "Christine loves Keith," are the most common graffiti. The graffiti sheet, as it evolves over a week's time, is a good read, witty and controversial.

Students now write a learning log on "memories of writing graffiti." In a suburban freshman class, Demetria writes:

> I remember writing lots of graffiti. But the only one I have a reason for is this one. When I was in 6th grade, I remember at the end of the year when we were just about to move from San Francisco to Walnut Creek. On the last day of school I wrote "Demetria was here 80-81" on the school desk. And then when I got home there was wet cement and I wrote my name on that with a stick. And then in the house in my room right by my door I put a little line of how tall I was and my name and age. I guess I put all that there because I wanted people to know that a girl 12 years old lived there for 10 years.

This entry gets a warm response. Her peers understand her feelings. Her motive for writing is one of the most common—a fear of being forgotten and the need to make one's mark. A male classmate writes:

> The first time I really wrote graffiti not just pencil and pen writing on a bathroom was just a little while ago on a wall at a school. I got the two best colors I knew, red and black, and wrote Raven, which is my favorite group. It only stayed up for a little while and then it was erased. But every time me and my friends went by it they would say, "That's a killer!" And I would say, "Yaaaa, I did that!"

In class we compare the two, similar in that both use graffiti for recognition but different in what they want recognized—the former her presence, the latter his favorite group and his artistic skill–different in that one is written for a select few, the other for a general public. Listening to these learning logs, students begin to understand why children and teenagers write graffiti.

As the logs are read aloud in the city class, we notice some trends, among them that graffiti seems to peak at junior high. As Rhonda remembers it:

> The biggest memory I do have of graffiti comes from junior high. I used to write in bathrooms, buildings and desks. Whatever I could reach, I would write on it. I remember doing it out of boredom, for

fun, or because I was mad at someone. . . . Another reason I would write graffiti was because of peer pressure. . . . I knew it was wrong. But then I said, what the heck, you only live once. Plus I wanted to be *popular*, to be *known!* So I did it through graffiti.

Anthony, who never wrote graffiti, also wrote about graffiti in junior high.

Graffiti in junior high seemed to be an epidemic. . . . Day after day maintenance workers must have spent hundreds of dollars trying to erase all the graffiti. . . . I always wondered why the school principal never suspended anyone.

Pam impresses the class with a solution to the junior high graffiti problem:

Junior high was when it all started. We wrote on the walls so much at school and they painted over it so much that the school might just be paint! The students in Mrs. Pines art class (including #1 student, me) had to think of a way to get people to stop writing on walls. The principal signed a statement which said we could draw and paint enlarged graffiti on the walls as long as it was legitimate. On the cafeteria walls we drew hamburgers, hot dogs and sodas. On the boy's side of the gym we drew a tennis shoe and on the girl's side (we voted), a playgirl bunny. . . . It stopped people from writing on walls too. We got a piece of see-through paper and had all ninth graders sign and the names were enlarged on a wall with our names.

Now at age seventeen and eighteen, these students are embarrassed about their graffiti writing days. Many write sentiments like Louis's: "For a while I thought graffiti was something but I soon found out that my foolishness was costing taxpayers lots of money." Nonetheless, the students remember well their reasons for writing graffiti. "I became a little gossip columnist," one writes, "telling everyone's business on walls, paper and anything I could." Another tells of anonymous vengeance. "I'd be afraid of someone, so writing on the walls would help me get back at them, hopefully without them knowing." Other students describe "threat" notes in their graffiti.

Day Three: Lecture—A Brief Look at Graffiti Through History

Students are often unaware that scholars, artists, and the commercial world study and use graffiti. Therefore, we spend a period talking about the history, significance, and influence of graffiti. We begin with cave paintings. Robert Reisner (1971) and Herbert Kohl (1972), date graffiti from the wall paintings of prehistoric man, circa 15,000 B.C.

We look at slides of paintings from Lascaux and Altamira. Students speculate about why they were painted and if they can be considered graffiti.

We skip about 16,000 years to Pompeii in 79 A.D. When Vesuvius erupted, the graffiti of Pompeii was preserved. Helen Tanzer, an archeologist who studied the graffiti as a primary source of information about the daily lives of the common people of Pompeii, writes:

> .... it is extraordinary that these trifling notes should have been preserved for us, and that they should, in connection with other remains, throw so much light on the minds and manners of this people of long ago (1939, 5–6).

Tanzer notes that the discovery of extensive graffiti is evidence of widespread literacy in Pompeii. In fact, she found graffiti that children scrawled while practicing the alphabet. When the students see examples of graffiti from Pompeii, they first notice the similarities between it and their own.[3] "Figulus amat Idaiam," for example, is a revelation. It delights students that the "A loves B" graffiti formula, Figulus loves Ida, has been around for at least 1900 years.

Much of the graffiti from Pompeii is erotic in nature:

> Here I recall I had a girl of late!
> The intimate details I shall not relate.

In the city class, the students think about their own sexual graffiti, much of which comes from song titles and lyrics of their favorite groups and reads like this:

> Do me baby!
> Kinky
> I'll make you wanna scream
> Drive me wild

By comparison, the sexual graffiti of Pompeii appears refined. "They don't have dirty words," one student observes. "Of course they do," I have to confess, "I just haven't included them." But even the postings of prostitutes sound quaint in translation:

> Eutychis a Greek girl 2 coppers
> She is all that could be desired

In their graffiti, Pompeiians expressed opinions about most aspects of life. They supported political candidates:

> Statia and Petronia urge you to vote for Casellius and Albucius

They inveighed against the abuses of the establishment:

> Amnaeus Seneca is the only Roman writer to condemn the bloody games

and offered advice on how to distribute wealth:

> Here's my advice. Share out the Common Chest
> For in our Coffers piles of money rest.

Pompeiians enjoyed gladiatorial spectacles and advertised them in graffiti:

> The troupe of gladiators owned by Aulu Suettius Certus will give a performance at Pompeii on May 31; there will be an animal show; the awnings will be used. [A. Suetti Certi aedilis familia gladiatoria pugnabit Pompeis Pridie Kal. Iunias. Venatio et vela erunt.]

As I mention each type of graffiti, I urge students to give contemporary examples.

For Medieval graffiti, the students look at a scholarly study, *English Medieval Graffiti* by Viola Pritchard (1967). They see graffiti drawings of knights off on crusades to the Holy Land. I tell them that scholars have studied the graffiti on everything from the cave paintings to the pyramids to Norwegian stave churches of the Middle Ages.

In the late nineteenth century, the English were debating the Education Act, which was passed in 1870. Some argued against it, because they feared general education would result in more graffiti. In Thomas Hardy's *The Return of the Native*, written in 1878, is this complaint:

> Ah, there's too much of that sending to school in these days! It only does harm. Every gatepost and barn's door you come to is sure to have some bad word or other chalked upon it by the young rascals— a woman can hardly pass for shame sometimes. If they'd never been taught how to write they wouldn't have been able to scribble such villainy. Their fathers couldn't do it, and the country was all the better for it (113).

An example of nineteenth-century American teenage folklore is found in Robert Woodward's article "Marginalia in Old Textbooks" (1962) in the *New York Folklore Quarterly*. In the 1890s, Christa Valentine, a teenager in the small town of Pendleton, Indiana, wrote in the margins of her textbook, *The Leading Facts of American History*. Some of her graffiti is wonderfully dated:

> Mary had a little lamb
> With which she used to tussel
> She hulled the wool from off its back
> And stuffed it in her bussel.

But some of it is familiar:

> Love many, trust few,
> And, do good unto them, which hate you.

and

> Love many, trust few,
> And, always paddle your own canoe.

In the city class, students pick up on Christa's sense of word play. One student chants back, "Do unto others as they do unto you." Another adds, "Do unto others, before they do unto you!"

During the Depression in the 1930s large numbers of unemployed roamed the country in search of food and work. To help each other out, these hoboes developed a graffiti, an elaborate set of chalk marks such as squares, circles, and parallel lines that indicated to hoboes what kind of treatment to expect in the places marked. As they got out of boxcars in freight yards, they would look for graffiti left by other hoboes to see if the place was hospitable to hoboes. Dawn, of Studs Terkel's *Hard Times* remembers that her apartment had a mark, and from it the hoboes knew her mother would give them food but not money.

> I remember that our apartment was marked. They [the beggars or hoboes] had a mark, an actual chalk mark or something. You could see these marks on the bricks near the back porch. . . . They'd come out from Chicago and they'd hit our apartment, and they knew they'd get something. Whatever the mark meant, some of them were like a X. They'd say, "You can't get money out of this place, but there's food here anyway" (1978, 56).

During World War II, the graffiti drawing of Kilroy was ubiquitous (see Figure 12–2). In the United States and wherever American troops were stationed and/or fighting overseas, Kilroy appeared on bombs, walls, doors, latrines, even carved into cliffs. Kilroy was a symbol of the American G.I., of his ingenuity and wit. When Americans liberated cities, they would find that Kilroy had preceded them. No one knew if the graffiti had been drawn by the people being liberated or by G.I.'s who had penetrated in advance and left their mark.

However, the classic response to American intervention abroad remains, "Yankee, go home." During the Vietnam war, cynicism at home about the conflict was expressed in graffiti. Students wrote:

War is good business
Invest your sons

Figure 12-2
Kilroy Was Here

The feminist movement encouraged more women to write graffiti:

> When God made man, he was just practicing.
> When God made woman, he got it right.

New York City's subway graffiti has been a matter of public controversy since the 1960s. While Mayor John Lindsay urged a ban on spray paint back then, artist Claes Oldenberg spoke in support of the medium:

> You're standing there in the station, everything is gray and gloomy and all of a sudden one of those graffiti trains slides in and brightens the place like a big bouquet from Latin America (Kurlansky, Naar, Mailer 1974, unpaged).

Since the 1970s, graffiti has made an impression in elite and popular culture. Several graffiti artists began to paint canvases that were sold in New York galleries. Twyla Tharp, the choreographer, commissioned a group of such specialists to paint a backdrop for her dance, "Deuce Coupe." Graffiti designs have appeared on Swatch watch faces, and often fabrics copy graffiti designs.

At the end of the period, I sum up. First, graffiti is old; throughout recorded history, it has been written primarily by common people or those who lack the power to be heard through other channels. On occasion, graffiti has become a national symbol, as with Kilroy, or an international symbol, as with the peace/antinuclear symbol. By itself, graffiti can't tell us much, but as an adjunct to other information, it is a valuable primary source for the concerns of the people writing it.

Day Four: Choosing Topics and Analyzing the Graffiti Wall

By the fourth day, students have quite a few options for projects and paper topics. They spend some time reviewing possibilities. Many will make a collection of graffiti and analyze it. In preparation, we spend some time deciphering the class graffiti wall. One way to approach this is to categorize the content. In an inner-city junior high classroom, the students found these categories: names and nicknames, relationships (as in "JK loves JM"), music, school and rival schools, politics, heroes (since these were sports heroes, the category could as easily have been sports), and signs of the zodiac, as in the graffiti:

> Sabrina
> B/K/A [better known as]
> Lady Cancer

Is this information useful in understanding junior high interests? Can we reasonably generalize about students from the graffiti board? Students argue. Some feel that the categories are an accurate reflection of their major concerns (excepting sex, which wasn't included); others are skeptical. But one thing is clear—the data alone is limited; to fully interpret and understand it, the writer needs to know what the students know: the context in which this graffiti exists.

Another approach to the graffiti board could be to study one aspect, such as the use of the verb "nuke," which was prominent in the suburban class graffiti. There were "Nuke the Smurfs!" "Nuke Southern Cal!" "Nuke Religion!" "Nuke The Plastic People of L.A." We discuss the prevalence of this verb in their graffiti. They have good explanations. We joke about "nuking," they explain, because the real thing, a nuclear holocaust, is too terrifying to talk about.

Students now have several days to do their research and write a draft of their paper.

Days Five and Six: Doing the Research

Once the students have chosen their projects, they need time for research and for collecting graffiti. We begin a new activity and each day set aside some class time for the graffiti project, time for answering questions, and time for small group response to drafts.

Sample Graffiti Paper Topics

In the suburban class, several students got their topics from the lecture on the history of graffiti. Steve, for example, focused on "tourist graffiti," which I had mentioned in the lecture. In the library, he found an inscription made by a Greek tourist who carved his name on the pyramid at Giza and some nineteenth-century religious graffiti in Rome.

Wendy and Jennifer studied contemporary teenage graffiti and collected male and female graffiti from the bathrooms in their high school. They did their research together but wrote separate papers. Jennifer's paper, "Boys' and Girls' Graffiti—Differences That Make a Difference" began with her hypothesis that boys and girls write about the same topics, but their different approaches document and reflect important differences between the sexes. "Nuke Grenada," "For a good time call 939–4630," and "Satanic music rules" are graffiti typical of the boys' lavatories, whereas "I love Rob," and "John Cougar is fine" are written on the girls' lavatory walls. Male political graffiti ran to "nuke" the culprit, whereas that of girls was more along the lines of "Save the whales." Sex is the most commonly written about subject. But boys write "For a good time (or fuck) call 939–4630," whereas girls write "Rape counseling 932–6903."

Jennifer and Wendy pinpointed four major focuses of high school graffiti: music, politics, sex, and relationships and gave copious examples of male and female approaches to the content. Among their conclusions are that boys' sexual graffiti is more explicit and cruder than girls', involving "dirty pictures and crude writing." Second, boys are more interested in competing and coming out best, whereas girls often want to communicate and even ask for advice:

> Dear Abby,
> I like this boy but he doesn't even know I exist, what should I do?

While the writer risks flip comebacks like "Get a face lift!" the question form of graffiti isn't used by boys.

Jennifer and Wendy go on to identify male and female problem-solving styles and attitudes toward violence as expressed in the graffiti from their school lavatories. In short, the girls had done a sophisticated and useful bit of original research.

In the same class, Nick focused on sports, a major category of male graffiti that Wendy and Jennifer had overlooked. Nick had an eye for good examples:

> Cowboys are to football
> What Etch-a-sketch is to art.

and

> If you gave me a dime everytime the Oilers won
> I could at least phone home.

A few days earlier, these students had written learning logs on their opinions of graffiti. Several found their topics in these entries and wrote argumentative papers on topics like "Graffiti: Is It Good or Bad?" and "Graffiti: Art or Vandalism?" Dan did a survey of school graffiti and concluded that the major type was about music. He decided that the importance of music in the lives of high school students is dramatized in their graffiti and generally overlooked and misunderstood by adults. Fatinah took the issue of who writes graffiti and why they write it. Ron tackled humor in graffiti.

In the city classroom, the topics were just as varied. Thomas, who had never written any graffiti, took a developmental view of graffiti writing, drawing on his personal history. "At Brookfield Elementary School," he wrote, "writing graffiti was considered a social crime." By comparison, "In junior high school, graffiti seemed to be an epidemic." And finally, "But here at —— High School, you can

hardly see graffiti because the students tend to be more mature."
Using documentation from his life, Thomas arrived at the same conclusion as folklorists and sociologists studying graffiti: it peaks in
junior high.

Some students, like Pam, elaborated on log entries. After describing the murals she and her friends painted in junior high, she talked
about the institutionalization of graffiti at her school, how it reduced
the practice and, sadly, how transient the victory over graffiti had
been. The next year, a new principal got rid of Pam's revered art
teacher and had the murals eradicated. She concluded:

> The walls were painted over and the school is the plain color it
> always was, but I do remember the good times we had painting the
> walls.

Rhonda addressed the question of why people advertise their
relationships in graffiti, an adolescent posting of bands. Some students wanted to study their own personal graffiti. I supplied them
with blank ditto sheets to fill. Others made collections of desktop
graffiti. Monica was friendly with graffiti artist and local celebrity
"Little Kool Star." She interviewed him and wrote about his development as an artist.

Day Seven: Response Groups

Students read drafts of their papers in response groups.

Day Eight: Reading Papers, Summing Up, and Evaluating

It was the last class of the semester in an inner-city classroom. We
were reading through a book rich with graffiti graphics that the class
had written. Two female students who had jointly written a paper
comparing male and female graffiti were the last to read. They concluded:

> ... guys write about themselves, for example, they write their nick-
> names and clubs that they belong to. .... The graffiti that girls write
> is very different from guys. Girls write their name and their boy
> friend's name. They write hearts by it.

This finding touched a nerve. The boys agreed that they didn't write
the "John loves Mary" type graffiti. But, Juan explained, "The reason
a girl writes that is because they are dependent on their boyfriend to
beat someone up or if something happens. ... "

An irate chorus of girls protested, "Nooo, nooo, I'm sorry. . . . " Juan, however, would not yield the floor and continued: "Hey, don't tell me they [the boyfriends] aren't some kind of Teddy Bear, a security blanket for you girls."

A girl shot back, "No, you think you guys are so cool not to be writing 'Luis loves this other girl' because you're scared that your friend will tell you, 'Oh, man, you're in love.'" A female classmate agreed: "They have to keep up this image." But the boys were relentless: "Men, as they are themselves today, do not commit themselves to women, women choose to commit themselves to men."

The period was coming to an end. I had been a guest teacher in this classroom for about a month and a half and this was the last day of the semester. I tried to sum up, pointing out that the girls' analysis of the graffiti had brought into focus an interesting difference in how the boys and girls in this school viewed commitment in relationships. I then made a few hasty closing remarks about how much I had enjoyed working with them. But they were impatient to get back to their argument.

As they were walking out of the classroom, Juan began to change his argument to placate the girls. He turned to a girl who had been vociferously arguing the female position and confessed, "Guys write that too [John loves Mary] but they write it only on the inside of their folder." Far from pacified, the girl returned a parting blow: "You're afraid to publicly state commitment."

If there had been more time, I would have liked them to write logs on this issue and continue their debate. But the event nicely makes the point that studying and writing about their graffiti is one way into the real concerns of students.

Coda

For evaluation at the end of several units or a semester, I ask students what they think is the most important thing they have learned. There is diversity in their answers, as well as three clear themes. For many students the most important discovery is the field of folklore. For others it is specific units, folk heroes, children's folklore, or family stories. For Rosie the funny stories they told about themselves as children doing "weird and crazy things such as stealing cats, eating canaries, digging holes, and the beating the bully of the block (which some of us still do)" was a chance to see how they had both changed and stayed the same as when they were children. Other students focus on the writing. Arturo wrote, "I liked best the way our papers turned out after we had written them over."

For many students it is the experience of working in groups. "I thought that everything we did was important but getting into groups really helped us, not only in our oral reading but getting together and working as a team, correcting each others papers." And, "I liked how we got in groups and listened to different ideas and thoughts that other people had."

Some students take a more global view. Robert, a Black student, wrote that he learned, "My background is exciting." Miguel wrote, "This class has taught me and my peers to learn from ourselves." Norma said, "The most important things I think were communicating with each other, getting along, getting the chance to write about our past and our families."

In each class the same points are made: folklore is an interesting subject, it lends itself to writing and to group work. As one student said, "Everyone likes to write about himself and that made us write good papers. Folklore is a good way to start learning to write because most of it is just telling [a story]." The content and structure of the class, especially the extensive use of groups, helps students learn from each other. And students, both majority and minority, perceive that their personal backgrounds are interesting to others and even exciting.

Unit in Brief

Day One: Introducing Graffiti

- Students brainstorm the word *graffiti*.
- They write a learning log on their thoughts and opinions about graffiti. These are shared in class, some with the whole class, the rest in groups.
- Homework is to look up a definition of graffiti in the dictionary (they are usually inadequate) and write one in light of class discussion.

Day Two: Defining Graffiti and Drafting Memories of Writing (or Not Writing) Graffiti

- Whole class drafts a working definition of graffiti.
- One wall of the classroom is covered with paper and students write graffiti on it.
- Students write learning logs on their memories of writing graffiti, which are shared in class.

Day Three: Lecture—A Brief Look at Graffiti Through History

- Students are usually unaware of the history of graffiti and its uses to historians, sociologists, anthropologists, etc. The lecture briefly touches on graffiti from the caveman to Pompeii to the New York City subways.

Day Four: Choosing Topics and Analyzing the Graffiti Wall

- Students review all the possibilities for their paper topics from the brainstorming, their two learning logs, the lecture, and the graffiti wall.
- Together we analyze the graffiti wall as a model of how to go about studying a graffiti collection.

Days Five and Six: Doing the Research

- This can be done several ways. In some classes, students do their research on their own time while we begin something different in class. In others, they are given class time to do the research, collecting data and/or library research.
- Homework is a draft of their paper.

Day Seven: Response Groups

- Students read drafts of their papers in response groups.

Day Eight: Reading Papers, Summing Up, and Evaluating

- Class reads papers and evaluates topics.

Notes

1. A version is on the cover of Alan Dundes and Carl R. Pagter, *Work Hard and You Shall Be Rewarded: Urban Folklore from the Paperwork Empire* (Bloomington, Indiana: Indiana University Press, 1978).

2. Taken from *The American Heritage Dictionary of the English Language*, ed. William Morris (Boston: Houghton Mifflin, 1970).

3. The graffiti from Pompeii cited here comes from three sources: Helen Tanzer, *The Common People of Pompeii*; Jack Lindsay, *The Writing on the Wall* (London: F. Muller, 1960) and Richard Freeman, *Graffiti* (London: Hutchinson, 1966).

Selected Resources for Teachers and Students

The resources given here are useful in teaching folklore. Some sources provide background for teachers, others are for student use. The references come from both academe and popular culture and include pamphlets and books as well as articles from newspapers, magazines, and journals. They are separated first by chapter, then by audience, indicating if they are primarily for teachers or for students and teachers. Some newspaper and magazine references are included as a guide to the types of articles to look for when developing files of media coverage of folklore. The sources in this section are in addition to those found in the Notes and Works Cited.

Chapter 1
An Introduction to Modern Folklore

Resources for Teachers

Brunvand, Jan Harold. 1978. *The Study of American Folklore: An Introduction*. 2d ed. New York: Norton.

———. ed. 1979. *Readings in American Folklore*. New York: Norton.

Dorson, Richard M. ed. 1983. *Handbook of American Folklore*. Bloomington: Indiana University Press.

Dundes, Alan. 1980. *Interpreting Folklore*. Bloomington: Indiana University Press.

———. 1987. *Parsing through Customs: Essays by a Freudian Folklorist*. Madison: University of Wisconsin Press.

Folklore/Folklife. 1984. Washington, DC: The American Folklore Society. This is an introductory pamphlet available from The American Folklore Society, 1703 New Hampshire Avenue, NW, Washington, DC 20009.

Odean, Kathleen. 1988. *High Steppers, Fallen Angels: Wall Street Slang*. New York: Dodd Mead. (An example of a study of the folklore of the stock market.)

Oring, Elliott. ed. 1986. *Folk Groups and Folklore Genres: An Introduction*. Logan, UT: Utah State University Press.

———. 1988. *Folk Groups and Folklore Genres: A Reader*. Logan, UT: Utah State University Press.

Chapter 2
Teaching Writing While Teaching Folklore

Resources for Teachers

Atwell, Nancie. 1987. *In the Middle: Writing, Reading, and Learning with Adolescents.* Portsmouth, NH: Boynton/Cook.

Buckley, Marilyn Hanf, and Owen Boyle. 1981. *Mapping the Writing Journey.* Berkeley, CA: Bay Area Writing Project.

Fulwiler, Toby, ed. 1987. *The Journal Book.* Portsmouth, NH: Boynton/Cook.

Healy, Mary K. 1980. *Using Student Writing Response Groups in the Classroom.* Curriculum Publication No. 12. Berkeley, CA: Bay Area Writing Project.

Kirby, Dan, and Tom Liner. 1981. *Inside Out: Developmental Strategies for Teaching Writing.* Portsmouth, NH: Boynton/Cook.

Macrorie, Ken. 1970. *Telling Writing.* 3d ed. Portsmouth, NH: Boynton/Cook.

Mohr, Marion. 1984. *Revision: The Rhythm of Meaning.* Portsmouth, NH: Boynton/Cook.

Rico, Gabriele L. 1983. *Writing the Natural Way.* Los Angeles: Tarcher. Distributed by St. Martin's Press.

Romano, Tom. 1987. *Clearing the Way: Working with Teenage Writers.* Portsmouth, NH: Heinemann.

Chapter 3
"Bloody Mary"
Introducing Students to Folklore

Resources for Teachers

Gillespie, Angus K. 1970. Comments on Teaching and Collecting Folklore. *Keystone Folklore Quarterly* 15: 59–73. (Describes college-bound, prep-school boys studying folklore. Gillespie's article is followed by four papers written by the boys in the class on topics such as faculty imitations, college interviews as a folklore genre, and dirty jokes told at the school.)

McCann, Bob. 1982. Before Suburbia Collapses: Teaching and Collecting Folklore among Adolescents. *Keystone Folklore Quarterly.* New Series 1: 34–50.

Chapter 4
"My Name Was Carlos"
The Folklore of Naming

Resources for Students and Teachers

Newspapers and Magazines

Good sources for readings are newspapers and magazines that frequently carry articles on all aspects of names, from columns in Ann Landers to sports columns on the nicknames of athletes (George Vecsey, "What's in a

Name?" The New York Times, July 2, 1984, Section C, 3), to articles on how people react when you change your name. I keep a file of such articles. Here are some examples:

Alexander, Ron. 1983. How Famous Nicknames Were Born. *The New York Times*, 6 Jul., III, 10.

Baker, Russell. 1984. A Name for All Seasons. *The New York Times Magazine*, 21 Oct., 24.

Carroll, Jane. 1983. The Name Game. *California Living Magazine, San Francisco Examiner*, 9 Oct., 9.

Friedrich, Otto. 1986. What's in a Name? *Time*, 18 Aug., 76.

Harre, Rom. 1980. What's in a Nickname? *Psychology Today*, Jan., 78–84.

Hoffman, Roger. 1985. Nicknames. *The New York Times Magazine*, 12 May, VI, 58.

Kalb, Bernard. 1984. Naming Names. *Esquire*, Sept., 90–92, 94.

Suarez, Rafael A., Jr., 1986. Being a Jr. *The New York Times Magazine*, 6 Apr., 42.

Taylor, Jared. 1987. I Mourn the Loss of My Surname. *San Francisco Chronicle*, 29 Dec., A.15. (Articles such as this one appear often; the author was offended because a stranger addressed him by his first name. It's an interesting issue: What is the folklore of who can use one's first name? What does it mean when the social code is broken?)

Books

Angelou, Maya. 1971. *I Know Why the Caged Bird Sings*. New York: Bantam. (Pages 90–93 are about the emotions of a Black being called a name other than her own. Angelou writes, "Every person I knew had a hellish horror of being 'called out of his name'" [91]).

McCarthy, Mary. 1957. *Memories of a Catholic Girlhood*. New York: Harcourt Brace. (This book contains a chapter on McCarthy's thoughts about names when she was in junior and senior high school.)

Dictionaries

Resources that students enjoy are name dictionaries and books on what to name babies, which list names and give their histories. There are many of these, such as Leslie Dunkling and William Gosling's (1983) Everyman's Dictionary of First Names. London: J. M. Dent & Sons.

Resources for Teachers

Books

Dundes, Alan. 1983. Defining Identity through Folklore. In *Identity: Personal and Socio-cultural.* ed. Anita Jacobson-Widding, 235–61. Atlantic Highlands, NJ: Humanities Press.

Morgan, Jane, Christopher O'Neill, and Rom Harre. 1979. *Nicknames: Their Origins and Social Consequences*. London: Routledge and Kegan Paul.

Journals

Names is an academic journal that has many articles on place naming and personal naming in folklore and literature.

Chapter Five
"When I Was a Little Girl . . . "
The Folklore of Childhood

Resources for Students and Teachers

Bronner, Simon. 1988. *American Children's Folklore.* Little Rock, AR: August House.

Jones, Bessie, and Bess Lomax Hawes. 1972. *Step It Down: Games, Plays, Songs, and Stories from the Afro-American Heritage.* New York: Harper & Row. (Reprinted 1989 by University of Georgia Press, Athens.)

Juska, Jane. 1985. Levitation, Jokes, and Spin the Bottle: Contemporary Folklore in the Classroom—A Teacher's View. *English Journal* 74: 37–38.

Samuelson, Sue. 1980. The Cooties Complex. *Western Folklore* 39: 193–210.

Simons, Elizabeth Radin. 1985. Levitation, Jokes, and Spin the Bottle: Contemporary Folklore in the Classroom—A Folklorist's View. *English Journal* 74: 32–36.

Chapter 6
The Cat Burglar
Family Folklore I—Stories Our Families Tell About Us

Resources for Students

Newspapers

Collins, Glenn. 1983. Telling a Story About Family Lore. *The New York Times,* 12 Sept., 19.

Rose, Phyllis. 1984. Hers. *The New York Times,* 3 May.

Books

Stone, Elizabeth. 1988. *Black Sheep and Kissing Cousins: How Our Family Stories Shape Us.* New York: Times Books.

Weitzman, David. 1975. *My Backyard History Book.* Boston: Little, Brown.

Wigginton, Eliot. ed. The *Foxfire* Series. Garden City, NY: Anchor Press/ Doubleday.

Resources for Teachers

Baker, Holly Cutting, Amy J. Kotkin, and Margaret Yocom. 1979. Family Folklore: Interviewing Guide and Questionnaire. Superintendent of Documents, U. S. Government Printing Office, Washington, DC 20402. (This is an earlier version of "How to Collect Your Own Family Folklore," which appears in *A Celebration of American Family Folklore.*)

Family Folklore: A 4-H Folk Patterns Project. Available from 4-H Youth Programs, Cooperative Extension Service, Folk Arts Division, The Museum, Michigan State University, East Lansing, MI 48824. (This is a booklet and a packet of activities. It's designed for younger children but has useful suggestions for all ages.)

Chapter 7
Nuestro Pasado (Our Past)
Family Folklore II—Family Photography

Resources for Students and Teachers

Greenberg, Harry. 1983. Writing with Family Album Photos. *Teachers & Writers* 14: 1–4.

Noren, Catherine. 1976. *The Camera of My Family.* New York: Knopf.

Chapter 8
"Even Heroes Have Heroes"
Mexican-American Students Study Their Folk Heroes

Resources for Students and Teachers

Newspapers and Periodicals

Heroes, especially "folk" heroes, are of continuing interest in the press. If you keep an eye out for articles on the subject, you'll soon have a bulging file. In each, the students look for the themes that make the writers consider people folk heroes. Some of the articles I've used follow:

Clark, Kenneth E. 1982. America Needs Heroes to 'Pull the Country Together.' *U.S. News and World Report,* 7 June, 68.

Gaines-Carter, Patrice. 1985. Martin Luther King, Jr. Didn't Die for Us to Sleep In on His Birthday. *The Washington Post National Weekly Edition,* 11 Mar., 23.

Gottlieb, Martin. 1986. An 80's Folk Hero: Lee A. Iacocca. *The New York Times,* 3 Jul., II, 4.

Wycliff, Don. 1985. Where Have All the Heroes Gone? *The New York Times,* 31 Jul., 15–16.

Books

Although some books on heroes are dated, they are useful for students who want articles on historical and early twentieth century folk heroes such as Charles Lindbergh, Babe Ruth, etc., folk heroes of the past.

Boorstin, Daniel J. 1980. From Hero to Celebrity: The Human Pseudo-Event. In *The Image, A Guide to Pseudo-Events in America,* 45–76. New York: Atheneum.

Browne, Ray B., Marshall W. Fishwick, and Michael T. Marsden. 1972. *Heroes of Popular Culture.* Bowling Green, OH: Bowling Green University Popular Press.

Browne, Ray B., and Marshall W. Fishwick. eds. 1983. *The Hero in Transition*. Bowling Green, OH: Bowling Green University Popular Press.

Fishwick, Marshall W. 1969. *The Hero, American Style*. New York: David McKay.

Lubin, Harold. ed. 1968. *Heroes and Anti-Heroes: A Reader in Depth*. San Francisco: Chandler.

West, John O. 1988. *Mexican-American Folklore*. Little Rock, AR: August House. (This book includes songs and narratives about Mexican-American heroes such as saints and revolutionaries.)

Chapter 11
**Tales of the Shopping Mall
Modern Urban Legends**

Resources for Students and Teachers

Newspapers and Magazines

Newspapers and magazines often cover legends, although they seldom identify or understand them as folklore. For instance, as I was writing this chapter, there was an article, "Don't Think of Stealing This Radio" by Sarah Lyall, in The New York Times *(October 10, 1988, p. A12), on the theft of car radios in New York City. It concluded this way:*

> In a city where nearly everyone with a car seems to have his own tale of burglary or break-in, there is a story making the rounds *that may or may not be true* [emphasis added]. It is the story of the car owner who parked and left a "No Radio" sign in the windshield.
>
> When he came back, he found that all his windows had been smashed. His "No Radio" sign had been turned over, and on the other side, someone had written "Get One."

Belkin, Lisa, 1985. Procter & Gamble Fights Satan Story. *The New York Times*, 18 Apr., III, B3.

di Salvatore, Brian. 1988. A Reporter at Large (Truck Driver—Part I). *The New Yorker*, 12 Sept., 39. (This article on truck drivers begins with two truck driver legends.)

Flanagan, Mike. 1986. The Things We Have Believed. *San Francisco Chronicle*, Sunday Punch Section, 31 Aug., 4. (This article has brief versions of legends from the 1930s–1980s.)

Parent, Gail. 1976. Folklore from the Fifties. *Esquire*, Mar., 76–77.

Sharpe, Ivan. 1982. Why Those Wicked P & G Rumors: Maybe the Devil Made 'Em Do It? *San Francisco Examiner*, 23 Jan.

Another excellent sources of legends is in cartoons.

Books

Brunvand, Jan Harold. 1981. *The Vanishing Hitchhiker: American Legends and Their Meanings*. New York: Norton.

———. 1984. *The Choking Doberman and Other "New" Urban Legends and Some Old Favorites*. New York: Norton.

———. 1986. *The Mexican Pet: More "New" Urban Legends and Some Old Favorites*. New York: Norton.

———. 1989. *Curses! Broiled Again: The Hottest Urban Legends Going*. New York: Norton.

Dickson, Paul, and Joseph C. Goulden. 1983. *There Are Alligators in Our Sewers and Other American Credos*. New York: Delacorte Press. (This is a potpourri of folklore, proverbs, jokes, superstitions, and the like. It includes short versions of legends. There is no analysis.)

Wachs, Eleanor. 1988. *Crime Victim Stories: New York City's Urban Folklore*. Bloomington: Indiana University Press.

Chapter 12
Nuke the Raiders!
The Folklore of Graffiti

Resources for Students and Teachers

Newspapers and Magazines

As with the other topics, articles on graffiti are common in the press. I keep a file on these and use them for reading in class. Also, any collection of graffiti is useful, and there are many.

Books

Cooper, Martha, and Henry Chalfant. 1984. *Subway Art*. New York: Holt, Rinehart and Winston.

Freeman, Richard. 1966. *Graffiti*. London: Hutchinson.

Hager, Steven. 1984. *Hip Hop: The Illustrated History of Break Dancing, Rap Music, and Graffiti*. New York: St. Martin's Press. (Break dancing, rap music, and graffiti are all forms of folklore.)

Lindsay, Jack. 1960. *The Writing on the Wall: An Account of Pompeii in Its Last Days*. London: F. Muller.

Reisner, Robert, and Lorraine Wechsler. 1980. *Encyclopedia of Graffiti*. New York: Galahad Books.

Santiago, Danny. 1971. The Somebody. In *The Best American Short Stories 1971*, ed. Martha Foley and David Burnett, 291–97. Boston: Houghton Mifflin.

———. 1984. *Famous all Over Town*. New York: New American Library.

Works Cited

Aarne, Antti, and Stith Thompson. 1961. The Types of the Folk-tale: A Classification and Bibliography. *Folklore Fellows Communication*, 184. Helsinki: Suomalainen Tiedeakatemia.

Abrahams, Roger D. 1979. Folklore in Culture: Notes Toward an Analytic Method. In *Readings in American Folklore*, ed. Jan Brunvand, 390–403. New York: Norton.

———. 1980. Folklore. In *Harvard Encyclopedia of American Ethnic Groups*, ed. Stephan Thernstrom, 370–79. Cambridge: The Belknap Press.

———. 1983. Interpreting Folklore Ethnographically and Sociologically. In *Handbook of American Folklore*, ed. Richard M. Dorson, 345–58. Bloomington: Indiana University Press.

Bascom, William. 1954. Four Functions of Folklore. *Journal of American Folklore* 67: 333–49. Reprinted in *The Study of Folklore*, ed. Alan Dundes, 1965. Englewood Cliffs, NJ: Prentice-Hall.

Ben-Amos, Dan. 1971. Toward a Definition of Folklore in Context. *Journal of American Folklore* 84: 3–15.

———. 1984. The Seven Strands of Tradition: Varieties in Its Meaning in American Folklore Studies. *Journal of Folklore Research* 21: 97–131.

Boorstin, Daniel. 1980. *The Image: A Guide to Pseudo-Events in America*. New York: Atheneum.

Britton, James, Tony Burgess, Nancy Martin, Alex McLeod, and Harold Rosen. 1975. *The Development of Writing Abilities (11–18)*. London: Macmillan Education Ltd.

Bronner, Simon J. 1986. *American Folklore Studies: An Intellectual History*. Lawrence, KS: University Press of Kansas.

Brunvand, Jan Harold. 1981. *The Vanishing Hitchhiker: American Urban Legends and Their Meanings*. New York: Norton.

———. 1984. *The Choking Doberman and Other "New" Urban Legends*. New York: Norton.

Castleman, Craig. 1982. *Getting Up: Subway Graffiti in New York*. Cambridge: MIT Press.

Dégh, Linda. 1977. UFO's and How Folklorists Should Look at Them. *Fabula* 18: 242–48.

Dégh, Linda, and Andrew Vázsonyi. 1976. Legend and Belief. In *Folklore Genres,* ed. Dan Ben-Amos, 93–123. Austin: University of Texas Press.

Dorson, Richard M. 1959. *American Folklore.* Chicago: University of Chicago Press.

———. 1968. "What Is Folklore?" *Folklore Forum* 1: 37.

———. 1973. *America in Legend: Folklore from the Colonial Period to the Present.* New York: Pantheon.

Dorson, Richard M., and Inta Gale Carpenter. 1978. Can Folklorists and Educators Work Together? *North Carolina Folklore Journal* 26: 3–13.

Dresser, Norine. 1973. Telephone Pranks. *New York Folklore Quarterly* 29: 121–30.

Dundes, Alan. 1965. *The Study of Folklore.* Englewood Cliffs, NJ: Prentice-Hall.

———. 1971. On the Psychology of Legend. In *American Folk Legend: A Symposium,* ed. Wayland D. Hand, 21–36. Berkeley: University of California Press.

———. 1973. Folk & Lore. In *Mother Wit from the Laughing Barrel,* ed. Alan Dundes. Englewood Cliffs, NJ: Prentice-Hall.

———. 1975. Slurs International: Folk Comparisons of Ethnicity and National Character. *Southern Folklore Quarterly* 39: 15–38.

———. 1985. The American Game of "Smear the Queer" and the Homosexual Component of Male Competitive Sport and Warfare. *The Journal of Psychoanalytic Anthropology* 8: 115–29.

Dundes, Alan, and Carl R. Pagter. 1978. *Work Hard and You Shall Be Rewarded: Urban Folklore from the Paperwork Empire.* Bloomington: Indiana University Press.

Edmunds, Lowell, and Alan Dundes, eds. 1984. *Oedipus: A Folklore Casebook.* New York: Garland Publishing.

Feldman, Susan. 1963. *African Myths and Tales.* New York: Dell.

Fine, Gary Alan. 1980. The Kentucky Fried Rat: Legends and Modern Society. *Journal of the Folklore Institute* 17: 222–43.

———. 1985. The Goliath Effect: Corporate Dominance and Mercantile Legends. *Journal of American Folklore* 98: 63–84.

———. 1986. Redemption Rumors: Mercantile Legends and Corporate Beneficence. *Journal of American Folklore* 99: 208–22.

Fine, Gary Alan, and Bruce N. Johnson. 1980. The Promiscuous Cheerleader. *Western Folklore* 39: 120–29.

Folklife and Fieldwork. Pamphlet. The Library of Congress, American Folklife Center, Washington, DC, 20540.

Goldstein, Kenneth. 1971. Strategy in Counting Out: An Ethnographic Folklore Field Study. In *The Study of Games,* ed. E. Avedon and Brian Sutton-Smith, 167–78. New York: John Wiley.

Granger, Byrd Howell. 1961. Naming: In Customs, Beliefs, and Folk Tales. *Western Folklore* 20: 27–37.

Greenhill, Pauline. 1981. *So We Can Remember: Showing Family Photographs*. Ottawa: National Museums of Canada.

Grider, Sylvia. 1980. Gotcha! In *Children's Folklore*. Issue of *Center for Southern Folklore* 3: 12.

Haley, Alex. 1977. *Roots*. New York: Dell.

Hardy, Thomas. [1878] 1987. *The Return of the Native*. New York: Signet Classic, New American Library Penguin.

Harris, Trudier. 1978. Telephone Pranks: A Thriving Pastime. *Journal of Popular Culture* 12: 138–45.

Helmreich, William. 1982. *The Things They Say Behind Your Back*. Garden City, NY: Doubleday.

Homer. 1932. *The Odyssey of Homer*. Trans. T. E. Shaw. New York: Oxford University Press.

Jorgensen, Marilyn. 1984. A Social-Interactional Analysis of Phone Pranks. *Western Folklore* 43: 104–16.

Klintberg, Bengt af. 1981. Modern Migratory Legends in Oral Tradition and Daily Papers. *Arv* 37: 153–60.

———. 1985. Legends and Rumours About Spiders and Snakes. *Fabula* 26: 274–87.

Knapp, Mary and Herbert. 1976. *One Potato, Two Potato . . . The Folklore of American Children*. New York: W. W. Norton.

Kohl, Herbert. 1972. *Golden Boy as Anthony Cool: A Photo Essay on Naming and Graffiti*. New York: Dial.

Kurlansky, Mervyn, John Naar, and Norman Mailer. 1974. *The Faith of Graffiti*. New York: Praeger.

Lawrence, D. H. 1977. The Rocking Horse Winner. In *The Portable D. H. Lawrence*, ed. Diana Trilling. London: Penguin.

Lee, Harper. 1960. *To Kill a Mockingbird*. Philadelphia: Lippincott.

Lester, Julius. 1969. *Black Folktales*. New York: Grove.

Macrorie, Ken. 1970. *Telling Writing*. Portsmouth, NH: Boynton/Cook.

———. 1984. *Searching Writing*. Portsmouth, NH: Boynton/Cook.

Mechling, Jay. 1986. Children's Folklore. In *Folk Groups and Folk Genres*, ed. Elliott Oring, 91–120. Logan, UT: Utah State University Press.

Moffett, James, and Betty Jane Wagner. 1983. *Student-Centered Language Arts and Reading, K–13: A Handbook for Teachers*. 3d ed. Boston: Houghton Mifflin.

Mohr, Marian M. 1984. *Revision*. Portsmouth, NH: Boynton/Cook.

Morgan, Kathryn L. 1980. *Children of Strangers: The Stories of a Black Family*. Philadelphia: Temple University Press.

Morin, Edgar. 1971. *Rumour in Orleans*. New York: Pantheon.

Musello, Christopher. 1979. Family Photography. In *Images of Information: Still Photography in the Social Sciences*, ed. Jon Wagner. Beverly Hills: Sage.

Newell, William Wells. [1883] 1963. *Games and Songs of American Children*. New York: Dover.

Opie, Iona and Peter. [1959] 1967. *The Lore and Language of Schoolchildren*. New York: Oxford University Press.

———. 1969. *Children's Games in Street and Playground*. Oxford: Clarendon.

———, eds. 1973. *The Oxford Dictionary of Nursery Rhymes*. Oxford: Clarendon.

Oring, Elliott. 1986. On the Concepts of Folklore. In *Folk Groups and Folklore Genres: An Introduction*, ed. Elliott Oring, 1–22. Logan, UT: Utah State University Press.

Peters, Thomas J., and Robert H. Waterman, Jr. 1982. *In Search of Excellence: Lessons from America's Best-Run Companies*. New York: Harper & Row.

Pritchard, Violet. 1967. *English Medieval Graffiti*. London: Cambridge University Press.

Reisner, Robert. 1971. *Graffiti: Two Thousand Years of Wall Writing*. New York: Cowles.

Rohmer, Harriet, and Mary Anchondo. 1976. *How We Came to the Fifth World*. San Francisco: Children's Book Press.

Smith, Leverett. 1972. Ty Cobb, Babe Ruth, and the Changing Image of the Athletic Hero. In *Heroes of Popular Culture*, ed. Ray Browne, Marshall Fishwick, and Michael Marsden. Bowling Green, OH: Bowling Green University Press.

Sontag, Susan. 1977. *On Photography*. New York: Farrar, Straus & Giroux.

Sutton-Smith, Brian. 1968. The Folk Games of Children. In *Our Living Traditions*, ed. Tristram Coffin. New York: Basic Books.

Tanzer, Helen H. 1939. *The Common People of Pompeii: A Study of the Graffiti*. Baltimore: Johns Hopkins Press.

Terkel, Studs. 1978. *Hard Times: An Oral History of the Great Depression*. New York: Pocket Books.

Thompson, Stith. 1932–36. *The Motif-Index of Folk Literature*. 6 vols. Bloomington: Indiana University Press.

——— 1951. Folklore at Midcentury. *Midwest Folklore* 1: 5–12.

Toelken, Barre. 1979. *The Dynamics of Folklore*. Boston: Houghton Mifflin.

Williams, Marcelle. In Press. Near Death Narratives as Folklore. *Omega Journal of Death and Dying*.

Woodward, Robert H. 1962. Folklore Marginalia in Old Textbooks. *New York Folklore Quarterly* 18: 24–27.

Zeitlin, Steven J., Amy J. Kotkin, and Holly Cutting Baker. 1982. *A Celebration of American Family Folklore: Tales and Traditions from the Smithsonian Collection*. New York: Pantheon.